PENGUIN BOOKS

THE RAILWAY NAVVIES

Terry Coleman went to fourteen schools, read Law at London University and was for many years chief feature writer and roving correspondent for the *Guardian*. For that paper he interviewed the last seven British prime ministers, from Lord Avon to Mrs Thatcher. *The Railway Navvies* won the *Yorkshire Post* prize for the best book of 1965, and was first published in Penguin in 1968. His other books include *Passage to America*, a history of emigration to north America in the mid-nineteenth century and *The Liners*, a history of the north Atlantic crossing. He was co-author of *Providence and Mr Hardy*, a biographical study of Thomas Hardy, and also edited the first edition in England of Hardy's previously unpublished first novel. He is the author of two books of collected journalism, *The Only True History* and *The Scented Brawl*. His most recent book is *Southern Cross*, a historical novel set in Australia, which was an international best seller and was called by American critics 'an Australian *Gone With The Wind*'.

TERRY COLEMAN

THE RAILWAY NAVVIES

A history of the men who made the railways

PENGUIN BOOKS

by arrangement with Hutchinson of London

Penguin Books Ltd, Harmondsworth, Middlesex, England
Penguin Books, 625 Madison Avenue, New York, New York 10022, U.S.A.
Penguin Books Australia Ltd, Ringwood, Victoria, Australia
Penguin Books Canada Ltd, 2801 John Street, Markham, Ontario, Canada L3R 1B4
Penguin Books (N.Z.) Ltd, 182–190 Wairau Road, Auckland 10, New Zealand

—

First published by Hutchinson 1965
Published with revisions in Pelican Books 1968
Reprinted 1969, 1970, 1972, 1976
Reprinted in Penguin Books 1981

—

—

Made and printed in Great Britain
by Richard Clay (The Chaucer Press) Ltd,
Bungay, Suffolk
Set in Monotype Garamond

TO MY FATHER, AN ENGINEER

There comes a crowd of burly navvies, with pick-axes and barrows, and while hardly a wrinkle is made in the fading mother's face, or a new curve of health in the blooming girl's, the hills are cut through, or the breaches between them spanned, we choose our level, and the white steam-pennon flies along.

GEORGE ELIOT

Acknowledgements

I SHOULD like to thank many people for their help, particularly the staff of the British Museum newspaper library at Colindale and of the Reading Room at Bloomsbury, the librarians of the *Guardian* in Manchester and London, the archivist of the British Railways Board, and the staff of Manchester Central Library, Liverpool reference libraries, Poole Library, Leicester Museums, and the Science Museum, Kensington. Also Miss Ruth Peto for lending me the privately published memoir of her grandfather; the Rev. R. S. Roch for showing me the Woodhead registers; Mr L. T. C. Rolt for correcting some errors; Mr R. K. Middlemass for his advice; Mr Donall MacAmhlaigh for introducing me to Patrick MacGill; and the reporters, long dead, of the *Manchester Guardian*, the *Railway Times*, the *Poole and Dorsetshire Herald*, and many other newspapers, whose reports have given me much of my best material. The quotations from Sir Henry Clifford's *Letters from the Crimea* are made by kind permission of Michael Joseph Ltd, that from *Grace Before Ploughing* by permission of the Society of Authors and the late John Masefield, O.M., and those from *Edwin Chadwick and the Railway* by R. A. Lewis by permission of the editors of the *Economic Labourers History Review*. Illustrations 20 and 21 are reproduced by permission of the *Illustrated London News*, 22 and 23 by permission of *Punch*, 25 by permission of the Industrial Christian Fellowship. Last (and most) I thank my wife Lesley for careful reading and tactful editing, and for making the index.

Sources

LITTLE has been written directly about navvies. Much of the material for this book comes therefore from incidental references scattered about in early railway literature and, most of all, from contemporary magazines and newspapers. To avoid footnotes these sources are set out, chapter by chapter, in a list on pages 238–43. Some sources are clearly named in the text (as, at the beginning of Chapter 6, the report of Hobday's trial is attributed to the *Carlisle Patriot* of 27 February 1846) and such information is not repeated in the main list.

Contents

List of Plates

LIST OF FIGURES

A to F are from *Our Iron Roads* by F. S. Williams, 1852.
G is from *Ensamples of Railway Making* by John Weale, 1843.

A map showing the Woodhead Tunnel is on page 134.

I

The Navvy Age

THOMAS EATON was one of the 1,100 navvies who made a railway tunnel three miles long through the Pennines. It took six years, from 1839 to 1845. No one kept an exact count of how many men died blasting through the millstone, or how many were buried by sudden falls of sandstone, or tipped out of a swaying bucket half-way up a 600-foot air shaft. But Eaton knew for sure that at least thirty-two men had died in one way or another, and the surgeon, whom he had got to know well, seeing so much of him, said another 140 had been badly hurt. In the end things got so rough at the tunnel that Eaton could stand it no longer, and he left in the early winter of 1845, just before it was finished. The year after, he was one of the navvies who went to Westminster to give evidence before the Commons committee which was inquiring into the evils of the railway works.

When he said he had worked on the railway for twenty-seven years they asked him, 'You have had some ups and downs?'

'Yes, many up; not very far up, but many down.'

Then they asked, 'How did most of the accidents happen; were they from carelessness on the part of the men themselves?'

It was a difficult thing, he replied, for anyone who had not been there to understand how accidents happened in the tunnels. But he went on to tell them about a man who lit a fuse to blast rock at the bottom of a tunnel, and then, as he was being pulled up in a bucket, got stuck part way up the shaft.

'There was one man, the engine was stopped, and he lighted the match, then the engine could not draw him up, and he was there, and stopped there while the shot went off, and he did not get hurt in the least. Several were killed, though; sometimes when the engine was drawing them up, sometimes

striking at the side, it threw them out and killed them. . . .
These two men, thrown out of number four shaft, the pricker
catched in the shaft and turned the bucket over; and the men
fell out.'

In 1845 there were 200,000 men like Eaton working on
about 3,000 miles of new line. In the eighty years from 1822
onwards, millions of navvies made 20,000 miles of railways in
Britain, and thousands of miles more in Europe and the rest
of the world.

The nineteenth century is not only the railway age but also
the age of the navvy. The railway brought cheap, fast travel,
encouraged commerce and ideas, and did a lot to create
Britain's national prosperity and international ascendancy.
But the railway was made by navvies, not by machines. A
piece of engineering like the Great Western Railway from
London to Bristol – known as Brunel's billiard table because
the mean gradient is 1 in 1,380 – was built with picks, shovels,
and gunpowder.

Much of the glory went to the engineers, and much of the
profit to the entrepreneurs. Thomas Brassey, probably the
most successful of the contractors, was called a European
power, through whose accounts more flowed in a year than
through the treasuries of a dozen duchies and principalities,
but he was such a power only with his navvies.

The railway age began in Stockton on 23 May 1822, a
Thursday afternoon, when a crowd of 300 shouting, singing
navvies dragged a local dignitary in his carriage into Stockton,
where, at St John's Well, he laid the first rail of the Stockton
and Darlington Railway. Then they all sang 'God Save the
King', the dignitaries went off to the mayor's reception, and
the navvies feasted on bread, cheese, and ale at the Black Lion
Inn. Some say the Stockton and Darlington was not the first
true railway but more like the apotheosis of the colliery
tramroad, and that the first railway, designed as a public line
to carry both goods and passengers, was the Liverpool and
Manchester, which was not opened until 1830. It is true that,
for years, passengers on the Stockton line rode in carriages
hauled by horses, and as the descents were so great that the

loaded wagons would run down by themselves for ten miles
out of the twenty-five, it was usual at first to take off the horse
and hang him by a halter to trot after the wagons. This
trotting so shook up the poor animal that in 1828 an improvement was devised. A little light truck on two wheels was
fastened behind the ordinary wagons, so that the horse could
ride in it down the runs and eat his provender from a manger
attached. The horse, said the *Liverpool Mercury*, seemed greatly
pleased with his conveyance, and to be aware how much
labour he was spared.

He gallops up, and jumps into it at full speed, and can be got out
and attached again without stopping . . . should the dreadful accidents, which have recently occurred from explosions, lead to the
abandonment of the locomotive engine, the saving to the Stockton
and Darlington Railway from this contrivance cannot be estimated
at less than a thousand a year.

This does not sound like a modern railway. But locomotives
or no locomotives, it was the first public railway of any size,
and the first where great earthworks were created by an army
of navvies got together for that purpose. It was the beginning
of the railway revolution that was to transform the country.
Those who built the first railways knew quite well what they
were doing. Henry Booth, treasurer of the Liverpool and
Manchester Railway, said in 1830:

We must determine . . . whether it be desirable that a nation
should continue in the quiet enjoyment of pastoral or agricultural
life, or that it should be launched into the bustle and excitement of
commerce and manufacture. [But] it must be admitted that the
golden age is past, and it is to be feared the iron age has succeeded.
The locomotive engine and railway were reserved for the present
day. From west to east, and from north to south, the mechanical
principle, the philosophy of the nineteenth century, will spread and
extend itself. The world has received a new impulse. The genius of
the age, like a mighty river of the new world, flows onward, full,
rapid, and irresistible.

This glorious philosophy described by Mr Booth needed
spades to spread it. An anarchic élite of labourers grew up

who worked in constant danger, miles from civilization, and lived according to their own laws. At Woodhead in 1845, where 1,100 men were camped in shanty huts, they even had their own marriage ceremony: the couple jumped over a broomstick, in the presence of a roomful of men assembled to drink upon the occasion, and were put to bed at once, in the same room. They were heathens in a Christian country, they drank, had many women but few wives, broke open prisons, and were not received in good society. It was fashionable to laud the ideal of labour, but the men themselves could go hang, as some of them did. They were compared to an invading army. They came, made their earthworks and their depredations, and went, taking a few of the local women and leaving the ruin of a shanty town. Of the arrival of the navvies, the report of the House of Commons Select Committee on Railway Labourers said in 1846:

... its suddenness, and its temporary location at particular localities, often spots before but thinly populated, have created or developed evils (touching both the welfare of the labourers employed and the interests of society), the taint of which seems not unlikely to survive their original cause. They are brought hastily together in large bodies; no time is given for that gradual growth of accommodation which would naturally accompany the gradual growth of numbers; they are therefore crowded into unwholesome dwellings, while scarcely any provision is made for their comfort or decency of living; they are released from the useful influences of domestic ties, and the habits of their former routine of life (influences and habits the more important, in proportion to their want of education); they are hard worked; they are exposed to great risk of life and limb; they are too often hardly treated; and many inducements are presented to them to be thoughtless, thriftless, and improvident.

Lieutenant Peter Lecount, one of Robert Stephenson's twenty-five assistant engineers on the London and Birmingham Railway, completed in 1838, did not think much of navvies either. 'These banditti,' he said,

known in some parts of England by the name of 'Navies' or 'Navigators', and in others by that of 'Bankers', are generally the terror

of the surrounding country; they are as completely a class by themselves as the Gipsies. Possessed of all the daring recklessness of the
Smuggler, without any of his redeeming qualities, their ferocious
behaviour can only be equalled by the brutality of their language. It
may be truly said, their hand is against every man, and before they
have been long located, every man's hand is against them: and woe
befall any woman, with the slightest share of modesty, whose ears
they can assail. From being long known to each other, they in
general act in concert, and put at defiance any local constabulary
force; consequently crimes of the most atrocious character are
common, and robbery, without an attempt at concealment, has
been an everyday occurrence, wherever they have been congregated
in large numbers.

All this, as a celebrated woman missionary was later to
exclaim, all this in Christian England. But the history of the
first fifty years of the century is one of violence. The Stockton
and Darlington Railway was begun only seven years after
Waterloo, and only three years after the cavalry charged into
the Manchester crowd at Peterloo. Slavery was not abolished
in the British Empire until 1833. It was only in 1822 that
more than 200 offences ceased to be capital, and executions
were held in public until 1868. Two navvies were hanged
beside the line during the construction of the Edinburgh and
Glasgow Railway for killing a ganger.

The first railways were built in a time of political unrest.
Before the Reform Act of 1832 the composition of the Commons had been substantially unchanged for 150 years, and
when the Liverpool and Manchester Railway was opened on
15 September 1830 the passengers on their way to Manchester,
which had no Members of Parliament, passed through the
insignificant village of Newton, which had two.

The solid, secure image of Victorian England is really only
that of the second half of the century, when Britain was for a
few decades, until about 1890, at the height of her mercantile
and naval power. But this ascendancy had been achieved only
by the frantic expansion of industry after 1815. The first railway boom of the 1830s was half over before Victoria became
Queen in 1837: the London and Birmingham Railway and a
good part of the Great Western were built before she was

twenty. By 1840 there were 1,497 miles of railway, compared
with 97 in 1830. The second railway mania was in the mid
forties. In 1845 no fewer than 4,800 miles of railway were
authorized by Parliament, and 4,540 in 1846. By 1860 nearly
all the main lines were built.

The years of the second boom, in the mid and late forties,
were years of revolution in Europe and near-insurrection in
Britain. In the autumn of 1846, while English and Irish
navvies were scrapping it out on the new Bury line with
'spades, clubs, and other deadly weapons', 12,000 men
attended a Chartist meeting near Rochdale and heard Ernest
Jones, from London, demand why £70,000 a year was allowed for Prince Albert's horses, and why Albert, as well as
the rest of the Royal Family, was living in luxury while the
working class were toiling away their days in slavery. They
must, he said, never relax in their efforts to obtain the people's
charter, and possession of the land. After this, Feargus
O'Connor, the most militant of the Chartists, tossed in the
remark that Prince Albert and the bishops were a pest on the
community. 'Several of the county police,' says the *Manchester
Guardian* report, 'attended in plain clothes.' Several is probably all there were. The first organized police force was Sir
Robert Peel's London force, formed in 1829, and provincial
police in any numbers came much later. At Penmaenmawr, in
May 1846, 300 Welshmen drove away the Irish navvies on the
line. Some of the ringleaders were captured by the police. One
in particular, whom the police had great difficulty in capturing,
they placed in prison. 'Immediately afterwards,' wrote a
resident of Penmaenmawr, in a letter,

the conflict became so violent that it was deemed necessary for the
magistrates to read the Riot Act, which was done. During these
proceedings, a party of the Welsh went behind the prison and
threw a rope over the wall, by means of which the prisoner managed
to effect his escape. Most of the railway contractors along the line
were sworn as special constables, and were on duty in this capacity
on Saturday. A body of soldiers was expected to arrive on Monday,
and then the police would apprehend a number of the rioters whom
they knew, but dare not take until backed by a strong force.

Again and again the only resource of the local police against the navvies seems to be to get the magistrates to read the Riot Act and call out the military.

*

What sort of men became navvies, and where did they come from? First, they must never be confused with the rabble of steady, common labourers, whom they out-worked, out-drank, out-rioted, and despised. A navvy was not a mere labourer, though a labourer might become a navvy. The first navvies came from the bankers, the fenmen of Lincolnshire who had built the sea walls, and from the gangs who had built roads and canals. Many came from Scotland and Ireland, and from the dales of Yorkshire and Lancashire. The Irish were not nearly so wild as their reputation. In 1846 Thomas Carlyle wrote:

The country is greatly in a state of derangement, the harvest, with its black potato fields, no great things, and all roads and lanes overrun with drunken navvies; for our great Caledonian Railway passes in this direction and all the world here, as elsewhere, calculates on getting to heaven by steam. I have not in my travels seen anything uglier than that disorganic mass of labourers, sunk three-fold deeper in brutality by the three-fold wages they are getting. The Yorkshire and Lancashire men, I hear, are reckoned the worst; and not without glad surprise I find the Irish are the best in point of behaviour. The postman tells me that several of the poor Irish do regularly apply to him for money drafts, and send their earnings home. The English, who eat twice as much beef, consume the residue in whisky, and do not trouble the postman.

The railway was also the refuge of a few criminals. They tramped to a place where they were not known, gave a false name, and got work with no question asked, as long as they looked strong enough. Navvies did the hardest and most hazardous work, the blasting and cutting, and left truck-filling and menial jobs to the boys and locally recruited casual labourers. They followed the rail, and travelled with one contractor until he had no more work to offer or until they heard of higher wages elsewhere.

The men who gathered at Stockton in 1822 were true

navvies, who had probably been working on canals. They came together, as a body, to do the work, and lived on the line. Up to the middle of the century such men were always sharply distinguished, in newspaper reports, from local labourers who were taken on for the moment. Lecount, who described navvies as banditti, also claimed that the London and Birmingham had been constructed not by such men but by what he calls the 'surrounding agricultural population'. For three years, he said, 15,000 to 20,000 men, taken almost invariably from the nearby towns and villages, had been employed. But Lecount had an interest in saying this. The ravages of the workmen on the line, navvies or not, had been much condemned and he was no doubt concerned to defend his company. He went on to say, to the greater credit of the railway, that nearly £4,000,000 had been paid in wages to the local labourers, some of whom would otherwise have been out of work and a burden on the poor rates.

It is strange also that Lecount should be able to assert so firmly that few navvies were employed, because the men would have been taken on not by the railway company, nor by the company's engineers, nor even by the contractors themselves, but by the sub-contractors and gangers on the works. At any rate, even if the contractors did employ local labourers, 15,000 of them, it is very likely they ended up by creating 15,000 navvies. It took a year's solid work to turn an agricultural labourer into a navvy. When a man first came to the railway he was likely to be an indifferent specimen of a labourer. At about three in the afternoon he would down tools and be too exhausted to go on, and would not be worth more than two shillings a day. But he gradually got better, his wages rose, he could buy better food, and in twelve months he was about as strong as he ever would be.

The word navvy itself comes from navigator. This was the name given to the canal-builders of the eighteenth century, and was inherited by the railway men. The Rev. D. W. Barrett, a railway chaplain in Northamptonshire in the 1880s who frequently softened his hellfire with whimsy, adds his gloss to this:

The term navvy is simply an abridgement of the longer and less poetical word navigator, which savours too much of the sound of alligator to be pleasant. And in fact some people have a rough idea that the navvy is a sort of human alligator who feeds on helpless women and timid men, and frightens children into fits.

The word was in any case interchangeable with several others. The men who worked at Woodhead during the years 1839–52 were most certainly navvies, but those who were killed were written down in burial registers not only as navigators but as miners, bricklayers, railway labourers, tunnellers, masons. The word was sometimes used more particularly to mean a man with pick and shovel, an excavator, as opposed to, say, a mason or bricklayer, but navvy almost always meant any man who regularly worked on railway building. The spelling varied too. Before 1850 the word was generally written as navey, with the plural naveys. Later it became navvie, plural navvies, and the modern spelling, navvy, did not become regular until the 1870s. Early on, the word was usually put in quotation marks, and was plainly regarded as slang: the polite term was railway labourer. 'Navvy', however spelled, was generally used either as a term of condemnation, or, later, in an attempt to be friendly, as in the *Quarterly Letter to Navvies* (published by the Navvy Mission Society) in which the men were addressed as 'Dear Mates'. But after the great railway works were finished the word went out of fashion again. In 1893, for instance, the Society changed the name of its pamphlet, apparently without explanation, to *Quarterly Letter to Men on Public Works*.

What, then, are the tests of a navvy?

First, the nature and severity of the work, which must be excavating, or tunnelling, or blasting, or bridge-building, on public works. Not necessarily railway construction, although most navvies, in the railway age, did work on the railways. They also worked, often between railway jobs, on docks, reservoirs, and roads, and a celebrated gang erected the Crystal Palace.

Second, the working together, the living together in encampments by the line, and the inclination to move with the railway to new works.

Third, the ability to drink, and eat, like a navvy. Two pounds of beef and a gallon of beer a day, and a man was accepted.

The dress, too, was distinctive. They wore moleskin trousers, double-canvas shirts, velveteen square-tailed coats, hobnail boots, gaudy handkerchiefs, and white felt hats with the brims turned up. They would pay fifteen shillings, a great price, for a sealskin cap, and their distinct badge was the rainbow waistcoat. They were often known to the contractor, and to everyone else, only by their nicknames – Gipsy Joe, Bellerophon, Fisherman, Fighting Jack.

The railways came suddenly. After the surveyors, the navvies; perhaps, as at Blisworth in the late thirties, 3,000 of them on a five-mile stretch of line. They lodged, when they could, in the villages, and when there were no villages they herded into turf shanties thrown up by the men themselves or by the contractors. A few brought their wives. Most had women not their wives. The navvies were paid once a month, sometimes not so frequently, and usually in a public house, and then for days afterwards they drank their pay, sold their shovels for beer, rioted, and went on a randy.

'They appeared to me,' said an engineer, 'when they got half drunk, the same as a dog that has been tied for a week. They ran about and did not know what to do with themselves.'

The Irish marched to fight the Scots, the English fought among themselves, and no work was done until all the money was gone. Then for the next month, until the next pay, the navvies lived on truck, taking tickets from the contractor to tommy shops, owned by the contractor, to buy high meat at high prices. A sovereign was worth at most fifteen shillings at a tommy.

Often they worked drunk. On many contracts a man would not be given work unless he took part of his pay in beer. Publicans toured the line, and where whisky was forbidden, as it sometimes was by the magistrates, it was brought up in kegs marked paraffin. The brewers allowed gangers five shillings for every barrel of beer they sold to their men. Even where a contractor like Peto put a stop to the sale of beer on the works, he did not attempt to prevent drinking altogether. 'A man,' he said, 'has a right to bring a gallon with him if he likes in the morning.'

The navvies were careless, and lived up to their reckless reputation with bravado. In the Kilsby Tunnel, on the London and Birmingham Railway, three men were killed as they tried to jump, one after the other, over the mouth of a shaft in a game of follow my leader. One navvy on the Great Western line at Whiteball was twice reproved by his ganger for earthing under too great a fall of dirt, undercutting into the face of the soil. He carried on: it was quicker that way. A quarter of an hour later the overlap fell in and killed him. 'He was a good workman,' said the ganger, 'and a nice sort of chap.'

They had a tradition of tramping from job to job, leaving one place on the slightest pretext or none at all. Some deserted their families: others took wives and children with them on treks across England. A woman missionary found one such man destitute on Clifton Downs. He had been on the tramp for three months, his wife and children were starving, and he was in despair. She gave him his fare to Newbury where there was thought to be work; he spent the money on food for his family instead, and then tramped to Newbury to find there was no work after all. He returned to Bristol, where he had left his family, and ended up selling fish in the streets. Others did worse. Warwick Jack (real name supposed to be John Morgan) died on the tramp at Eccup at six o'clock in the evening of Christmas Day, 1880. He got to the works at three that afternoon, and dropped dead three hours later while he was sitting on a chair and talking. Perhaps he was one of the loafers that Thomas A. Walker, a missionary for thirty-seven years, so much disliked. 'I can't understand,' he told the men,

why chaps like you should support in idleness a lot of cadging loafers, who go about from one job to another, never doing a stroke of work themselves. I have seen a fellow come to a cutting, no kit on his back, or a very small one you may be sure. He never asks the ganger if there is any chance, he sits down and begins to talk; his business is to tramp about from one job to another; and tell the news, and a precious pack of lies no doubt he often tells. Well, he tells you in his own way, and to suit his own ends, what works he has been to, what new works are starting, what wages are being paid. In return you make a collection, a penny apiece or more, and he goes away to the pub with more money in his pocket than you can earn by your day's labour. I saw a fellow of this stamp on the Severn Tunnel [this was in 1884], a week or two ago, who has been there six times, and never asked for a day's work. Why do you do it?

They did it because it was also the tradition that a navvy on tramp who came to a contract where there was no work for him should be given what was called the tramping bob to help him on his way. Or if a destitute navvy passed others who had money he could ask for this shilling and they were expected to give it.

Brunel found his navvies 'very manageable'. Other engineers did not find things so easy, but a show of moral fibre was felt to be all that was necessary to quell the rabble. Frederick Williams, in an early history of the railway published in 1852, tells a story in which 300 navvies, 'manifesting their rage by the most terrible oaths and threats', were confronted by an engineer. 'You know, my men, that I am always your friend if you are in the right; but you are not now, so go back and mind your work.' The workmen, says Williams, knew their man and went back like a flock of sheep. He goes on, however, to commend prudence.

But when [they were] once excited by liquor it was useless to restrain them, for this would only increase their violence; the engineers never stopped then to parley, but as they passed along on horseback, where the men might be standing in the way, an authoritative, 'Whar off' was the only remark made as the horseman rode past.

But the men were not all devoid of the Victorian virtues. They could be grateful to a competent master. On the G.W.R., when some navvies unearthed a Roman urn, one of them seized a handful of some sixty coins, for which the men were scrabbling, saying, 'These are for Mr Shedlock.' John Shedlock was the engineer on that part of the line. Nor were they beyond self-help. John Francis wrote in his *History of the English Railway* in 1851:

. . . there are many men who, twenty years since, delved and dug, and gained their bread by the sweat of their brow, who are now in possession of most valuable estates.

But most drank their pay.

For their riots and their drunkenness, and for more than that, the navvies were feared. Francis wrote of them:

At war with all civilized society, the great mass glorying in Chartism, they are to be dreaded, for their thews and sinews would form no trifling element of success.

This was nonsense. The great mass of them were no more Chartists than they were Christians, and it was really their impiety that so concerned Francis and many others. The navvies were infidels, and as such should be condemned. And condemned they were.

The clergy did most of the damning. The Rev. William St George Sargent, one of two chaplains to the Lancaster and Carlisle line (stipend £150 a year and appointed by a bene- volent family, 'pitying the moral destitution of these men'), was one such clergyman. To the Select Committee on Railway Labourers he said:

I should think, comparing them with others of the lower class of society, and I have had much experience with the lowest, having been chaplain to a Mendicity Institution for common beggars (before the Poor Law was introduced into Dublin they had a Mendicity Institution), I think that they are the most neglected and spiritually destitute people I ever met. Yes, most vile and im- moral characters . . . they are ignorant of Bible religion and gospel truth, and are infected with infidelity, and very often with revolu- tionary principles.

At this, Viscount Ebrington, a member of the Committee,

asked: 'You spoke of infidel opinions. Do you believe that many of them are Socialists?'*

Mr Sargent replied: 'Most of them in practice; though they appear to have wives, very few of them are married. Their infidel opinions lead them to doubt the authority of the word of God, and very often to deny the existence of a First Cause.'

Mr Sargent also complained that the men seemed ignorant of the use of money. One navvy had told him he would not know what to do with his money if it was not for the beer shop, and that he would rather spend it himself than put it by for others to spend after he was dead.

They were not Christians and they did not know the use of money: therefore they were revolutionaries. But Mr Sargent did his best. He sold the navvies 350 bibles (costing sixpence to one-and-six each, according to size), 200 prayer books, and 200 hymn books.

Thomas Jenour, formerly a soldier but in 1845 employed by the Pastoral Aid Society as a reader on the Croydon and Epsom Railway, also tried to 'impress upon men's minds that they are reasonable creatures and not merely machines of flesh and blood'. He succeeded, up to a point.

'They certainly wonder,' he said,

and have expressed astonishment that God should have made some rich, and some so dreadfully poor; but after, if you tell them the value of the soul, that the whole world is of no value in comparison to the soul, it has made them pay great attention to my observations: in fact, I am convinced they would be a very different class of people if you could convince them of the value of the soul.

The railway companies were convinced, at any rate, of the

* Lord Ebrington might have been interested to know that though the navvies were hardly Socialists, the son of one was to become a Minister in a Labour government. Mr Tom Fraser, when he was Minister of Transport in 1965, presented a copy of the first edition of this book to the Cabinet library at 10 Downing Street. He said the first job his father had at the turn of the century was carting material for the embankments of the new line between Larkhall and Coalburn, and that his grandfather, who was born in Inverness, came to Glasgow when he was sixteen and worked all his life on the railways.

value of the railway, but hardly of the value of their men's lives. Railway engineers rarely kept any count of the men killed. Even Robert Rawlinson of the London and Birmingham, one of the most humane of engineers, said he did not. In Scotland there was not even a formal coroner's inquest held on the victims. It was customary to ignore the navvies, as if railways built themselves. In his history Francis mentioned them, but excused himself for it.

A chapter devoted to the railway labourer may be regarded as intrusive by some, and as gossipy by others: by a third class it may be considered as repulsive. But the 'navigator' is necessary to the rail.

The intrusive, repulsive life of a navvy was not commonly a long one. An old navvy was rare. When James (Daddy) Hayes died on the works at Eccup on 23 January 1882, at the age of eighty-six, his age and his funeral were remarkable. His mates, who buried him, said he was one of the first navvies in England. Many navvies died as boys, run over by the wagons they were leading to the tip-head. The few who survived until they were sixty looked seventy, and most died at forty – a good age for a navvy.

While they lived they lived riotously. They poached the women along the line, and they poached the game, though not the Earl of Harewood's, because Lady Harewood was known and beloved by the men for her many kindnesses. They contaminated the population by easy vice and easy money. As Williams wrote in 1852:

Painful is it to find that the triumphs which the human intellect has achieved should be so intimately associated with the moral degradation of so large a section of the community.

Many histories of the railways have been written. Their heroes are the Stephensons, Brunel, Locke, Vignoles – engineers; Brassey, Peto, Firbank – contractors; Hudson – organizing genius and talented fraud. But there are others who also had a hand in making the railways. William Birchenough, who survived the collapse of a viaduct he was building, and

William Hardwick (Trump), who did not; George Hatley, learning to read in a shanty camp, and Redhead, eating nothing but potatoes; Denis Salmon, Irishman, beaten up with a pick shaft, and John Hobday, Englishman, transported for fifteen years for doing it; Mary Warburton, who ran off with a navvy, and Rachel Foulkes, navvy nurse, who died of cholera; Thick-lipped Blondin the thief, Ene-Eyed Conro the forger, Devil-driving George the seducer; Bible John who was gored to death by a cow, Alexander Anderson who wrote bad verse, William Lee who died slowly of a broken back, and Happy Peter the navvy preacher who dropped dead one hot day as he said amen.

2

The Works

THE engineering of the early railways was like nothing before. Only the cathedrals were so audacious in concept and so exalted in their architecture, but they were few and the building of one, in God's good time, could take a hundred years: the railways were many, and made in the contractor's good time, which was money. True, there were roads in Britain before the railways came, but since the Romans they were only little roads, and few. Even the turnpikes were made in bits and pieces from here to there, with no sense of a system. The Liverpool and Manchester Railway was built before there was any decent road between the two cities. Only the canals of the eighteenth century can compare in any way with the railways that so soon killed them. Only the cathedrals before were so vast in idea: nothing before was so vast in scale.

It is easy to forget this vastness, or never to see it at all. The same visitor to Bristol who sees Brunel's suspension bridge at Clifton, and will not forget it, may quite possibly, on the way down in the train from London, have remained unaware of the same engineer's gigantic railway tunnel at Box, near Bath. Passengers to Bournemouth do not see Locke's great cuttings between Basingstoke and Winchester; the traveller through Stockport does not notice that the broad viaduct on which his train stands, ninety feet high, cuts the town in two and dominates everything for miles; the passenger from Manchester to Liverpool never even glances up at the sheer rock walls of George Stephenson's cutting at Olive Mount. Nowadays a motorway may be admired, but the railways have been there too long to be considered, though as a feat of engineering the M.1 is nothing to the London and Birmingham Railway, completed 120 years before. There is hardly a branch line in Britain whose earthworks would not be marvelled at if they were those of a new road or an ancient fort. John Ruskin called them, 'Your railway mounds, vaster than the walls of Babylon.'

These earthworks are so much greater than those of roads because a railroad is more than a simple road with rails on it. A road, even a good road, can curve, and climb hills. A railway, by its nature, cannot do this. There are two things to consider. First, the lack of friction between metal wheel and metal rail, and second, the result of the first, the much heavier loads which can be hauled on a railway than on an ordinary road surface. On the level this is fine, but when a railway comes to any slope at all there is trouble. The very lack of friction between wheel and rail which enabled bigger loads to be pulled now becomes a lack of traction. The wheels cannot get a grip to haul the big load up a slope against the pull of gravity. In 1833 experiments showed that if a locomotive would draw sixty-seven tons on the level, it could draw only fifteen tons on an incline of 1 in 100, and could not move at all on 1 in 12. In the early days it was estimated that to overcome a gradient of 1 in 300 required a tractive power nearly twice as great as was needed to move the same load at the same speed on a level, and that to ascend an elevation of thirty feet required as much power as would move the same load along a mile of level line.

So a railway must be level and also, because a train cannot safely take curves at any speed, as near straight as the engineer can devise. Across the plains of Canada a railway was easy to lay, and gangs could put down an average of two miles a day and sometimes much more, but over even the easiest of country in Britain a railway was difficult. A line from London to Southampton or Birmingham was an immense undertaking. Lecount, who made many ingenious calculations, reckoned that the London and Birmingham was unquestionably the greatest public work executed in ancient or modern times. If its importance was estimated by labour alone, perhaps the Great Chinese Wall might compete with it, but if the immense outlay of capital, the great and varied talents of the men who worked on it (Lecount meant the engineers, himself among them), and the unprecedented engineering difficulties were taken into account, then, he said, the gigantic work of the Chinese sank totally into the shade. Perhaps hoping to impress by sheer weight of numbers, he went on to compare the railway with the Great Pyramid of Egypt – 'that stupendous monument which seems likely to exist to the end of all time'. The labour expended on the pyramid was equivalent to lifting 15,733,000,000 cubic feet of stone one foot high. This was performed, according to Diodorus Siculus, by 300,000 or, according to Herodotus, 100,000 men, and took twenty years. To build the railway 25,000,000,000 cubic feet of material was lifted one foot high, or 9,267,000,000 cubic feet more than for the pyramid. Yet this had been done by 20,000 men in less than five years. Mr Lecount did not want to dispraise the pyramid; he made generous allowances.

'From the above calculations,' he said,

has been omitted all the tunnelling, culverts, drains, ballasting and fencing, and all the heavy work at the various stations, and also the labour expended on engines, carriages, wagons, etc.; these are set off against the labour of drawing the materials of the pyramid from the quarries to the spot where they were to be used – a much larger allowance than is necessary.

Not content with having vanquished the Chinese Wall and the pyramid, he then remarked that if the circumference of the earth were taken in round figures to be 130,000,000 feet, then the 400,000,000 cubic feet of earth moved in building the railway would, if spread in a band one foot high and one foot broad, go round the equator more than three times.

This was the way an engineer saw the London and Birmingham. Charles Dickens also saw part of the line while it was still being built, and in *Dombey and Son* he wrote this description of the cutting at Camden Hill, in North London:

The first shock of a great earthquake had, just at that period, rent the whole neighbourhood to its centre. Traces of its course were visible on every side. Houses were knocked down; streets broken through and stopped; deep pits and trenches dug in the ground; enormous heaps of earth and clay thrown up; buildings that were undermined and shaking, propped by great beams of wood. Here, a chaos of carts, overthrown and jumbled together, lay topsy-turvy at the bottom of a steep, unnatural hill; there, confused treasures of iron soaked and rusted in something that had accidentally become a pond. Everywhere were bridges that led nowhere; thoroughfares that were wholly impassable; Babel towers of chimneys, wanting half their height; temporary wooden houses and enclosures, in the most unlikely situations; carcasses of ragged tenements, and fragments of unfinished walls and arches, and piles of scaffolding, and wildernesses of bricks, and giant forms of cranes, and tripods straddling above nothing. There were a hundred thousand shapes and substances of incompleteness, wildly mingled out of their places, upside down, burrowing in the earth, aspiring in the air, mouldering in the water, and unintelligible as any dream. Hot springs and fiery eruptions, the usual attendants upon earthquakes, lent their contributions of confusion to the scene. Boiling water hissed and heaved within dilapidated walls, whence, also, the glare and roar of flames came issuing forth; and mounds of ashes blocked up rights of way, and wholly changed the law and custom of the neighbourhood. In short, the yet unfinished and un-opened Railroad was in progress; and, from the very core of all this dire disorder, tailed smoothly away, upon its mighty course of civilization and improvement. But as yet, the neighbourhood was shy to own the Railroad. One or two bold speculators had projected streets; and one had built a little, but had stopped among the mud and ashes to consider further of it. A bran-new Tavern, redolent of fresh mortar and size, and fronting nothing at all, had taken for its sign The Railway Arms; but that might be rash enterprise – and then it hoped to sell drink to the workmen. So, the Excavators' House of Call had sprung up from a beer shop; and the old-established Ham and Beef Shop had become the Railway Eating House, with a roast leg of pork daily, through interested motives of a similar immediate and popular description. Lodging-house keepers were favourable in like manner; and for the like reasons were not to be trusted. The general belief was very slow. There were frowsy fields, and cow-houses, and dunghills, and dust-heaps, and ditches, and gardens, and summer-houses, and carpet-beating grounds, at the very door of the Railway. Little tumuli of oyster shells in the oyster season, and of lobster shells in the lobster season, and of broken crockery and faded cabbage leaves in all seasons, encroached upon its high places. Posts, and rails, and old cautions to trespassers, and backs of mean houses, and patches of wretched vegetation, stared it out of countenance. Nothing was the better for it, or thought of being so. If the miserable waste ground lying near it could have laughed, it would have laughed it to scorn, like many of the miserable neighbours.

But before a railway could get that far, before it even started, the surveyors came to decide the route. Even here the navvies had their part. Many proprietors opposed the railway, because it ran through their orchards, or would dry up their cows, or set their ricks on fire, or scare away the foxes and ruin the hunt, or because railways were the devil's device anyway. Many owners hoped, by their reluctance to sell their land, to increase the compensation they would get. For many reasons the railway surveyors were unwelcome, and navvies were sometimes used to persuade landowners of the value of the projected lines. As one Victorian commentator said:

In some cases large bodies of navvies were collected for the defence of the surveyors; and being liberally provided with liquor, and paid well for the task, they intimidated the rightful owners. The navvies were the more willing to engage in such operations because the project, if carried out, afforded them the prospect of increased labour.

Having completed his survey, and collected the information of his assistants, the engineer then decided the line the route

A. A levelling party

should take. Rivers and streams were crossed as near their source as possible, hills, valleys, and undulating ground were passed or only touched, towns and places where the land was expensive approached with caution, pleasure grounds and gentlemen's seats avoided.

The engineer and his surveyors chose the easiest route, but still there were hollows to fill in with embankments or span by viaducts, rising ground to penetrate by cuttings, hills to tunnel through. Such railway engineering would not have been easy at any time, but it was made specially difficult in the early days by the limited performance of the first steam locomotives. On the Liverpool and Manchester Railway George Stephenson included gradients of 1 in 96 and 1 in 89 near Rainhill, but these proved so awkward that lightly loaded trains could at first only crawl up the incline. In the years immediately after this, in the late 1830s, the railway-makers were more cautious. Robert Stephenson included no gradient more severe than 1 in 330 on the London and Birmingham Railway, except for the initial climb out of Euston station as far as Camden, where the trains were at first not drawn by locomotives at all but hauled up on the end of ropes which were wound in by stationary engines. And on the Great Western to Bristol, Brunel laid the line nearly dead level for the first eighty-five miles out of London. Only a few years later, in the 1850s and 1860s, locomotives had improved so greatly that lines could be much more severely graded. The classic contrast between an early line and one constructed only a little later is that between the original London and South Western line from London to Southampton, and the later London to Portsmouth line. On the first line, built by Joseph Locke and completed in 1840, the easy gradients were achieved only by some stupendous cuttings between Basingstoke and Winchester. (Even this line itself was, when it was proposed, regarded as severe compared with the G.W.R. to Bristol. On the Southampton line, Litchfield is nearly 400 feet above the termini at London and Southampton, and one gradient of 1 in 250 runs for a distance of seventeen miles.) Twenty years later, when the Portsmouth line was completed, through Woking, Guildford, and Petersfield, the engineer permitted gradients of 1 in 80 and thus carried the line, with few earthworks of any size, uphill and downhill over the South Downs.

But the main lines were almost all built early, and so were almost all massively engineered. After that the improved performance of locomotives made things easier, but even with the steeper gradients then permissible some lines of the 1870s, like the celebrated Settle and Carlisle, passed over country whose severity demanded huge tunnels and viaducts. So it happens that British railways, with few exceptions, are carried over and through great earthworks.

Robert Stephenson put it this way at a dinner in Newcastle upon Tyne in August 1850. It was, he said, but yesterday that he had been engaged as an assistant in tracing the line of the Stockton and Darlington Railway. Since that period the Liverpool and Manchester, the London and Birmingham, and a hundred other great works, had sprung into vigorous existence. So suddenly, so promptly, had they been accomplished, that it appeared to him like the realization of fabled powers, as by a magician's wand. Hills had been cut down, and valleys filled up; high and magnificent viaducts had been erected. Where mountains intervened tunnels of unexampled magnitude had been unhesitatingly undertaken. Works had been scattered over the face of the country, bearing testimony to the indomitable enterprise of the nation.

All this was done with navvies and horses. Brassey said that a full day's work for a man was fourteen sets. A set was a number of wagons, a train. These wagons were drawn by horses up to the works, the cutting or embankment, on a temporary line of rails which was extended as the earthworks grew. Each wagon in this train was filled by two men working together. If the train was filled and carted away fourteen times in a day then each pair of men would have filled fourteen wagons, and each individual navvy seven. A wagon was reckoned to hold two and a quarter cubic yards of muck, which was the navvy name for all kinds of earth and rock, so each man would lift nearly twenty tons of earth a day on a shovel over his own head into a wagon. This was the fourteen-set day. Some men did sixteen.

But before the men could come to the more conspicuous earthworks the level ground had to be prepared to take the permanent way, which was not always easy: the ground might not be firm enough to take the weight of a loaded train. This was the trouble at Chat Moss, on the Liverpool and Manchester line. Chat Moss is a bog six miles out of Manchester, and it was said, when the Bill for the railway first came before a parliamentary committee in 1825, that no carriage could stand on the Moss short of the bottom. After the Act was obtained, and when George Stephenson started work on Chat Moss in June 1826, he found that the pessimists were very nearly right. The surface was coarse, ridgy grass, tough enough to walk upon about half-leg deep. In places the soggy soil went down thirty-four feet and then rested on layers of clay and quicksand until it reached solid bottom more than forty feet below the surface. Local farmers, who feared their cattle might stray there, shod them with wooden pattens. Stephenson said he would float the road across the Moss, and he did. At some points embankment after embankment disappeared gradually and silently into the Moss. His men shod themselves with planks, like skis, to sustain their weight by spreading its pressure. Sometimes they made little or no progress with the work and had to report that the Moss had swallowed down the results of their labour. Yet at last Stephenson conquered the Moss by the Moss. On overlapping hurdles made of branches and of the heather and brushwood that grew there, he laid sand, earth, and gravel, thickly coated with cinders, until at last he got a firm but elastic road to carry the railway.

Even where the land was not bog, rain could turn the churned-up soil into liquid mud. In February 1847, after heavy and lasting rains, the soil at Brockenhurst, in Hampshire, became dangerous to men and horses. The *Poole and Dorsetshire Herald* reported that in one week, 'two horses, celebrated for their sagacity in carrying out the intentions of their owners, were killed through being unable to extract themselves from the soil'. Altogether eleven horses were similarly destroyed on the line between Brockenhurst and Osmansley Ford that season.

But the principal works of the navvies were banking, cutting, and tunnelling. In embanking the aim was always to extract the necessary soil from the nearest possible place, and the engineers would have allowed for this when they first surveyed the way. One method was to take the earth from a side cutting, so that the finished work would consist of a raised embankment with a ditch running on one or both sides. This was done where there was no other feasible way of getting the soil wanted, but the more frequent method was to cart the soil to an embankment from a cutting a little farther back. This was done by tipping. A light tram road was made from the cutting to the edge of the embankment, and at the extreme verge a stout piece of timber was fastened to prevent the wagons toppling over the edge when they discharged their contents. A train of loaded trucks was then brought up to

B. Making an embankment

within fifty yards of the edge, and the first truck was detached from the train and a horse hitched to it. The horse that drew the wagon walked not directly in front of it between the tram lines, but to the side of the track, as if it were a canal horse on a towpath drawing a barge behind and to its side. The horse was made to walk, then trot, then gallop. When the truck got near the embankment edge the man running with

C. The tip

the horse detached its halter, gave it a signal it had been taught to obey, and horse and man leaped aside. But the truck continued until it struck the baulk of wood laid across the end of the track, when it tipped forward, ejecting its contents over the edge of the bank. The horse was immediately brought up again and hooked on, and the truck was righted and drawn away to join an empty train waiting to be taken back to the cutting. In large works two lines of rails and two teams of horses and wagons would work together. If the soil did not fall just where it was wanted the spades of the navvies did the rest. As a boy, John Masefield, who was to become the Poet Laureate, saw a new branch line made from Gloucester to Ledbury, and watched the navvies tipping. Much later he wrote:

The earthwork was manned by gangs of Public Works men who soon could be seen high up on the embankment top with trucks and horses working all day long at a game delightful to us to watch. They were employed in building the embankment by trolley loads of earth. The loaded trolleys were drawn along the top of the work by clever horses which knew exactly, or were made exactly to stop and turn aside at the proper instant. The horse went aside, but the truck went on and at the critical moment at the right spot was checked and tipped with its tons of material. We could never see the device at work, but they delighted by their precision and skill. . . . Now and then to this day, I wonder where the Public Works men found all the earth that they tipped to make that strong embankment, shall we say half a mile long, thirty feet high, at least twenty feet broad at the top and three times that breadth at the base. We could never

D. Making a cutting

see them loading the trucks, and never could find any big gap in any known landscape. No one was able to inform us. The earth was found I know not where, and used with great skill, leaving no great pit to show whence it had come.

Making a cutting was heavier work. On the face of the hill through which the cutting was to pass, bodies of men started work between the posts and rails which marked the intended line of the railway. The upper surface of the earth was carted away, and soon hill was laid open and a gullet excavated.

This was a little cutting just large enough to take a row of
wagons which were used to take the earth away. In this gullet
the wagons could be brought alongside the navvies who were
working on the banks just above the temporary line. Meanwhile, as the muck was removed by the navvies on both sides,
the gullet was continued into the hill by those ahead. This was
the method used when the soil from the cutting was needed
for an embankment farther along the line, to which the stuff
was carted off in horse-drawn trains of wagons.

E. Making the running

Sometimes, when there was no use for the soil, it had to be
lifted up the sloping walls of the cutting and dumped at the
sides. This was done by barrow runs, and this 'making the
running' was the most spectacular part of navvy work, and
one of the most dangerous. The runs were made by laying
planks up the side of the cutting, up which barrows were
wheeled. The running was performed by the strongest of the
men. A rope, attached to the barrow and also to each man's
belt, ran up the side of the cutting, and then round a pulley at
the top, where it was attached to a horse. When the barrow
was loaded, a signal was given to the horse-driver at the top,

and the man was drawn up the side of the cutting, balancing the barrow in front of him. If the horse pulled steadily and the man kept his balance everything went well. The man tipped his barrow-load on to the top of the cutting, turned round, and went down the side of the cutting again, this time drawing his barrow after him and with his back to it, while the horse all the time kept the rope taut and took most of the weight of the empty barrow.

But if, on the upward climb, the horse slipped or faltered, or if the man lost his balance on the muddy plank, then he had to do his best to save himself by throwing the loaded barrow to one side of the plank, and himself to the other. If both toppled over on the same side the barrow and its contents might fall on the man. In the Tring Cutting, on the London and Birmingham Railway, which runs through chalk at a depth of forty feet for two and a half miles, there were thirty to forty horse-runs, and nearly all the navvies were thrown down the slope several times, but they got so used to it, and became so sure-footed, that only one man was killed. One engineer invented a moving platform to take the stuff up the side of the cutting without a navvy having to go with it, but the men thought it was a machine designed to cut their wages, and broke it.

Excavating was done almost entirely by hand, by pick and shovel, by row on row of navvies. One of Brassey's time-keepers said:

I think as fine a spectacle as any man could witness, who is accustomed to look at work, is to see a cutting in full operation, with about twenty wagons being filled, every man at his post, and every man with his shirt open, working in the heat of the day, the gangers looking about, and everything going like clockwork. Another thing that called forth remarks was the complete silence that prevailed among the men.

But things were different when the line ran through hard rock, and the engineers blasted their way through. Bugles were blown to give warning of the blasts, and the twanging of horns, the grating noise of the iron borers, and the heavy incessant explosions on all sides might have induced a traveller, said one engineer, to believe he was in the neighbourhood of a sharp engagement.

The engineers could blast their way through nearly everything. Round Down Cliff, on the South-Eastern Railway, between Folkestone and Dover, was 375 feet high, and it was in the way of the railway. To tunnel through would have been difficult, to dig it down would have taken a year and cost £10,000, to go round it was impossible because this would have meant carrying the line into the sea, so the only way was to blast the cliff away. This the engineer, William Cubitt, decided to do. What he had to move was a mass of chalk 300 feet wide and about seventy feet deep, and to do the job he planted in the cliff 19,000 lb. of gunpowder. At the time appointed for the blasting the railway directors and their guests assembled at a marquee on the top of another cliff about a quarter of a mile from the point of explosion. The fuses were inspected, and the spectators exchanged bad jokes in their nervousness. What, asked one, if the explosion should go wrong? 'We shall all,' answered another, 'be swallowed up.' 'Swallowed down,' said a third. As two o'clock approached, the time for the detonation, a silence fell in which the choughs and crows were clearly heard. The sea was calm. Flags were hoisted. A warning shell was thrown over the cliff where it burst with an echoing report which bounced from the hills around like rifle-fire. The flags were hauled down. It was one minute to firing.

When it came the explosion was a dull, muffled boom, and the earth jolted. The foot of the cliff appeared to dissolve. The mass above slowly separated from the mainland and sank to the beach. In two minutes the cliff had gone. The volleys of ejected chalk rolled inwards upon themselves, great boulders crashed into the sea, broke, and then reappeared above the surface as crushed and coalescing bits, fermenting. There was no roaring explosion, no bursting out of fire, no wreath of smoke, for the gunpowder had exploded under a pressure which almost matched its energies, under a million tons of chalk. When the turf from the top of the cliff reached the level of the beach the stream of debris was 1,200 feet across and covered fifteen acres of sea and sand.

The most hazardous job of all was tunnelling. The miners worked deep in the earth, often soaked by muddy water, in constant peril from their own explosions, breathing foul air made fouler by the fumes of gunpowder, and working twelve hours a shift, day and night.

F. The horse gin

If the tunnel was short the miners bored in from one end, or from both ends; but in a longer tunnel work would also proceed from shafts bored vertically into the earth along the line of the tunnel. These shafts were bored by a machine called a gin, which was powered at first by horses attached to a great wheel, and later by steam engines. This boring of the shaft was itself a feat of engineering: most shafts were eight to ten feet across and some were as deep as 600 feet. When the bore was completed men descended to its foot in huge buckets and began to excavate the main tunnel, working in two directions at once from the bottom of the shaft. The soil and the men were brought up in the same buckets. When the tunnel was completed the shafts served as air holes, creating a strong draught, so that the men putting the finishing touches to the masonry of the tunnel worked in a constant gale of wind, a contrast to the fug in which they had laboured for so long before.

The first of the great railway tunnels was that bored under Liverpool in 1827. Henry Booth, treasurer of the Liverpool and Manchester Railway, wrote that in some places the substance excavated was a soft blue shale, with abundance of water; in other places a wet sand appeared, requiring great labour and contrivance to support until the masonry which was to form the roof was erected. Under Crown Street, near the Botanic Garden, the whole mass of earth above the tunnel fell in from the surface, to a depth of thirty feet of loose moss, earth, and sand. No one was hurt.

Sometimes the miners refused to go on, and the engineers had to chivvy them back to work. Nor, said Booth, was this surprising. The men bored their way almost in the dark, with the water streaming around them, and uncertain whether the props and stays would bear the pressure from above until the arch work was completed. Those who had been through the tunnel after it was completed, when it was lit by gaslight and traversed by horses, carriages, and crowds of passengers, could not, he said, easily picture to themselves the original dark and dangerous cavern, with the roof and sides supported by shores, while the miners worked by the light of a few candles, whose feeble glimmer, glancing on the water which ran down the sides, or which spread out in a sheet below, was barely enough to show the dreariness of the place.

The tunnel was a mile and a quarter long, and was the work of 300 miners. During its construction it was one amusement of the bolder citizens of Liverpool to walk part way through to see how the work was getting on. The *Liverpool Mercury* of 16 February 1827, after reporting that the shafts were sixty feet in depth, added that the visitor might descend them in one of the buckets with perfect safety, and that it was an interesting and novel sight to those who had never seen mining in its grander operations. Though numerous candles were burned by the workmen, 'the darkness of the cavern was but made visible', and the sound of busy hammer, and chisel, and pick-axe, the rumblings of the loaded wagons along the railway leading from the farther ends of the cavern to the pit, and the frequent blasting of the rock, mingling with the hoarse voices of the miners whose sombre figures were scarcely distinguish-able, formed, so the report said, an interesting *tout ensemble* of human daring, industry, and ingenuity.

One visitor said of the men that their numerous candles twinkled in the thick obscurity like stars on a gloomy night, marking out their figures here and there in dark profile while they flung about their brawny arms – all this, together with the frequent explosions and the fumes of gunpowder, 'conveying no contemptible idea of some infernal operation in the region of Pluto'. This same observer, James Scott Walker, afterwards wrote that parties of workmen were employed at each of the six shafts and at each end of the tunnel, and that, guided by the mariner's compass, they met each other with astonishing precision at the lines of cutting. Though each party had cut about five hundred yards, the levels of the tunnels seldom varied above an inch at the joins. 'And the sensations,' said Walker,

of the workmen and contractors when, after so long and perilous a working in 'the bowels of the harmless earth', they were enabled by the removal of the stone barriers between them to shake hands with each other in regions never visited by the light of day, may be more easily conceived than described.

The methods of tunnelling remained, throughout the cen-tury, much the same as they were at Liverpool. A visitor who went down a shaft of the Belsize Tunnel, London, in 1865, said that at the bottom you could see a kind of light and hear strange sounds from both sides. He followed the newly exca-vated tunnel in one direction and after about eighty yards reached the lights and found a dozen men at work, half of them with pickaxes, tearing away at the rough clay and accompany-ing every stroke with a noise that was half grunt, half groan. After these navvies had cleared away a length of twelve feet the centre supports were put up and the bricklayers took over.

All these men worked day and night in relays, some of the labourers working for two days and the intervening night without more than an occasional break for food.

Tunnels were the hardest work, but out in the open country a viaduct is perhaps the most spectacular kind of railway engineering to look at. To create an embankment of much the same size would have been a greater labour, but such an embankment, after more than a hundred years, and covered with trees and shrubs, looks like a natural rise. Indeed, railway earthworks very soon became part of the landscape. In *A Laodicean*, a novel published in 1881, Thomas Hardy described the mouth of a tunnel which had been built only a few years before:

The popular commonplace that science, steam, and travel must always be unromantic and hideous, was not proven at this spot. On either slope of the deep cutting, green with long grass, grew drooping young trees of ash, beech, and other flexible varieties, their foliage almost concealing the actual railway which ran along the bottom, its thin steel rails gleaming like silver threads in the depths. The vertical front of the tunnel, faced with brick that had once been red, was now weather-stained, lichened, and mossed over in harmonious rusty-browns, pearly greys, and neutral greens, at the very base appearing a little blue-black spot like a mouse-hole – the tunnel's mouth. Mrs Goodman broke the silence by saying, 'If it were not a railway we should call it a lovely dell.'

But a viaduct is wood or stone or metal, and distinctly man made. Viaducts were, however, most frequently built in and near towns, where their advantages were many. In a built-up area the soil for embankments would have to be brought in from miles off, and the company would have to buy whole tracts of expensive land on which to put up its earthworks. Viaducts, on the other hand, were made of bricks and iron, materials easily got, and could be erected by masons and builders, who were also easily found. The company needed to buy only the narrow strip of land over which the line would pass. Many of the London lines, for instance that from London Bridge to Greenwich, were virtually viaduct lines all the way, and though they were more expensive to build than lines on level ground, they were less costly than embankment railways would have been, and were easier to maintain. There were other advantages. As one early railway historian said, the vacant spaces beneath the arches could be let for tenements, shops, or warehouses, fitted up as ragged schools or as nightly homes for the homeless, or used for other purposes. In 1849 a body calling itself The Samaritan Society of England set out to shelter and 'reclaim' destitute people and discharged prisoners. It announced that it would rent arches from London railway companies and fit them out with first, second, and third class compartments for men, and first and second for women. The tenements would be warmed by hot water, lit by gas, and supervised by the police. The first class would have iron bedsteads, flock mattresses, and blankets and cost twopence a night; the second class wooden boards, pillows, and rugs for a penny a night; and the third class clean straw, for nothing. It was proposed to turn some of the second class arches into day schools on the plan of the Rev. Mr Queckett, who had already leased three arches from the Blackwall Railway in which to teach 600 children.

Bridges were generally not navvy work, or, at least, they were not commonly erected by the same men who built the other works of a railway. The railway company often made the bridges itself, or, if these works were contracted out, they were retained by the principal contractor, who himself employed a separate force of masons, carpenters, and ironworkers to construct them.

In an age which well knew how to exploit mechanical inventions, and in which great works of engineering became commonplace, it seems at first astonishing that the chief tools used to build the railways were picks, shovels, and gunpowder. Powered tools of any kind were hardly used at all, and this is not because there were none to be had. As early as 1843, John Weale, in his book *Ensamples of Railway Making*, wrote about a steam shovel which – though it was, he admitted, not the English practice – he commended to the British and Irish public. He included an illustration of a newly patented excavator, originally an American invention, which could cut and level the earthwork for a railway at a cost considerably below that of manual labour, and which had the additional advantage, guaranteed by the patentee, of saving much time. These advantages would, he hoped, be proved when the machine was adopted in Britain. It would be an important consideration in the making of less costly railways and was 'a desirable object for immediate use'. With an engineman and his assistant, together with six men to cart away the removed earth, it could be made to excavate 1,500

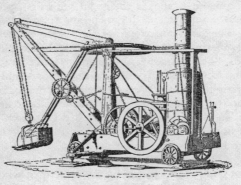

G. Mechanical digger, 1843

cubic yards in twelve hours, at a cost for fuel of twelve shillings a day. The machine itself cost £1,500.

Perhaps this capital cost is one reason why steam excavators were rarely used in Britain, but the principal reason is that, except for a few years of the first and second railway manias, labour was easy to come by, and contractors, who already took enough risks, preferred the traditional navvy to the untried machine. In the United States and Canada, where labour was scarce and expensive, mechanical diggers were used. In the States the machine tradition became so strong that today the word navvy is understood to mean not a man but a steam shovel. But in Britain and Europe men and spades were always there for the asking.

It was only at the tag end of the railway age that machines

were at all widely used here. In 1887 Frederick McDermott wrote in his biography of Joseph Firbank, the contractor, that the steam excavator was fast encroaching on the province of the navvy, and was to be seen working on many contracts. It had, he said, been estimated that one of these steam navvies could fill 240 wagons, nearly 1,000 cubic yards, in a day of ten hours. To excavate by hand only 600 yards a day, at the same rate as the steam navvy, would have taken 100 men, and since only thirty men were required to work with the machine, it could be said to do the work of seventy.

But this was at the end. Almost all the railways had been long built – with picks and shovels.

3

Navvy and Contractor

IT takes many men – with ideas, and engineering know-how, and shovels – to build a railway, and the method of executing works by contract and sub-contract was essential to the sudden and rapid growth of the mid nineteenth century. In the early years the railway company appointed an engineer, who surveyed the line himself and employed assistant engineers and navvies to man the works. This was how George Stephenson built the Liverpool and Manchester. But only a few years later, at the time of the first railway mania, greater speed, greater organization, greater division of labour, became essential. It was then that the first big contractors appeared, quoting so much a mile for a whole line, letting out a cutting at so much a yard, amassing fortunes or collapsing into bankruptcy.

The making of a railway was organized in this way: first the company, the London and Birmingham or the Great Western, appointed an engineer – say Robert Stephenson or Brunel – to devise the routes, specify the works to be done, superintend their construction, and to be responsible to the company for the whole venture. The company then invited tenders for part or whole of the work, and appointed a principal contractor, or contractors, to carry out these works. This main contractor was the Brassey or the Peto, the grand entrepreneur. The contractor himself then appointed agents for each section of the line, and these agents were empowered to let parcels of the work, a cutting here, an embankment there, to sub-contractors. These sub-contractors in turn appointed the gangers, the corporals of the enterprise, and the gangers took on the navvies.

There were variations, according to the size of the work and the capacity of the main contractor. Some sub-contractors engaged gangers as their employees at a fixed wage, and paid the navvies, whom they took on through the gangers, by the day. Others sub-contracted again, so that the gangers were not their employees but their agents. Often the navvies worked not for a fixed day rate but on piece work, for so much a foot, or so much a set. Sometimes the navvies were employed neither on a daily rate nor on piece work, but rather formed themselves into butty gangs, and struck a bargain with the sub-contractor to do a piece of work for a certain sum, in effect becoming sub-sub-contractors. One trouble with butty gangs was that, since the pay was generally shared equally, each man was expected to do equal work. It sometimes happened that one man, not so strong as the others, overstrained himself trying to keep pace with them. And there were often squabbles about pay. Which one of the gang of ten or twelve men should collect the wages at the pay table? Was the leader of the butty to get something extra? Each man in a butty gang mistrusted the others in a fine spirit of comradeship. Thomas Eaton, navvy, said he had often known disputes – 'One man will want to take an advantage of the others; they generally settle it with an odd blow on the head.'

But in spite of its drawbacks the butty system was the one Brassey preferred. He could maintain reasonable discipline on his works, and it was his strong belief that the best way to get things done was to give the men a personal interest in doing a decent amount of work and finishing contracts on time. So the system of sub-contract was used wherever possible. On the L.S.W.R. between Winchester and Basingstoke, where Brassey contracted for part of the work under Joseph Locke, the engineer, there was an unusual proportion of excavation, about 3,250,000 cubic yards on a seventeen-mile stretch. The works were heavy and costly, and the time allowed for completion was so short that the works had to be pursued with the greatest diligence, day and night. Eleven hundred men were employed. They earned high wages and they did the work by the date agreed.

The amount of work let to a sub-contractor varied according to his capital and past record. One man would be allowed to take a contract for £10,000, another for twice that amount, and some would employ up to 200 men. When the work was organized in this way the function of the principal contractor was rather that of a practical engineer overlooking the execution of the works by a number of smaller contractors. The principal contractor himself remained responsible to the company's engineer. On this system the main contractor was *not* the employer of the navvies. This then was the classical method which ensured expedition and profit, and kept the main contractor free from any direct responsibility for the navvies. Only a few contractors preferred to superintend the work more closely, not to sub-contract it out, but to employ men directly. One of these was Samuel Morton Peto,* the Baptist, who in the extent of his railway works was second only to Brassey. Often his way was to take a big contract and then to appoint a chief agent who would superintend the work entirely, and through whom he would pass all his orders. This agent had under him on the contract, say, for the line between Ely and Peterborough, four sub-agents, each of whom had charge of about eight or nine miles of the line. Under these again, to every two miles, was a timekeeper, who kept a record of the time worked by every man in his own section. The work was then let to gangers who employed the men. The timekeeper's duty was to report to the sub-agent on the Saturday morning the hours the men had worked up to Friday night, and they were paid every Saturday. In this weekly payment, as in his concern for the sobriety and safety of his men, Peto was unusual. But though he preferred to employ men directly, and to exercise a closer control over the work, he could not always do this. In 1846, the year of the Ely to Peterborough line, he was employing 9,000 men, many of them on the sixty-one miles of the Southampton to Dorchester route, but of these only 3,700 were in his direct employment, the others being engaged by sub-contractors.

Nevertheless, a large and powerful contractor such as Peto or Brassey could impose what conditions he wanted on the

---

* Peto (1809–89) never used his first name, generally signed himself S. Morton Peto, and after he was created a baronet in 1855 – for his services in building an army railway in the Crimea and in acting as one of the commissioners of the 1851 exhibition – he took the style of Sir Morton Peto.

sub-contractors. Some of the larger railway companies, too, reserved to themselves, on paper at least, a substantial right to superintend working methods. In many agreements with a contractor the price of the work, and a list of any additional works to be completed, was given. The time for completion and the fines for being late were stated, with the condition that all payments were subject to the engineer's approval of the work done. The contractor found tools, labour, and materials, constructed all foundations, excavations, shafts, culverts, drains, and roads, and provided pumps, scaffolding, fencing, and other details, according to the specifications, plans, and drawings, and the instructions which he received from the engineer. He laid the permanent way, the materials for which were found by the company. If the contractor did not employ enough men on the works the engineer had a right to take on more after giving the contractor a week's notice of this. These men could use the contractor's material, and their wages would be deducted from the contract price. The engineer generally had the right to sack any of the contractor's men doing their work badly. The contractor was also bound to take down or alter any work not approved by the engineer. All materials, from the moment they were brought on the site, became the railway company's property and the contractor could not remove them without permission. Payments were usually made in monthly instalments, 10 per cent being kept back and not paid to the contractor until twelve months after completion, during which time he had to maintain the works.

The sub-contracting system gave a man a chance, with diligence and luck, to make his fortune. Self-help was more than a cant expression: men could make themselves, and many are the tales of those who did. One was Sir Edward Banks, who started as an agricultural labourer. He left home, so the story goes, with two shillings and two shirts, one rather inferior to the other. All the clothes he had were on his back, except for the good shirt, which he carried in his pocket. He could not read a word. He first went to Scotland, laboured on canals there, and afterwards became a small contractor. He did well, went on to build bridges over the Thames, to take some part in early railway works, and to undertake nearly all the government works at Sheerness, under the celebrated engineer Sir John Rennie. He accumulated a large fortune and was knighted. And all this by an illiterate, penniless labourer from Yorkshire.

So goes the story. Perhaps it is a tall story, particularly the bit about the two shillings and two shirts. But Banks's was a mild success compared with that of George Stephenson, the colliery engine boy who created half the railway revolution. And the history of Joseph Firbank, which is well documented, is little less spectacular than that of Banks. Firbank was born in 1819 at Bishop Auckland, and at the age of seven joined his father down the mine. In 1840 he was working on the Bishop Auckland and Weardale branch of the Stockton and Darlington Railway, and when he was only twenty-two he took a sub-contract on the Woodhead Tunnel of the Sheffield and Manchester Railway. From there he went to the York and Scarborough Railway, and amassed enough capital to take a contract on the Nottingham and Lincoln line of the Midland Railway. He survived the panic of the mid-1840s, then lost nearly everything on the Rugby to Market Harborough contract in 1848, but again recovered, and went from profit to profit until he ended his contracting career on the Settle and Carlisle line in the 1870s. He became a Justice of the Peace and Deputy Lieutenant, and died a rich man in 1886. He was one of the few contractors to offer his men not only bread but sympathy. On his works he gave his men water and oatmeal instead of beer, and they liked him in spite of it.

The way was always open for a navvy who could save enough to buy a few horses and carts and take a small sub-contract. Brassey for one encouraged this, and some men worked with him for forty years, as labourer, ganger, and sub-contractor. He had a way with his men. He would visit the works, talk with sub-contractors, and even take the advice of navvies. He was anxious to make a profit, but also to keep good men with him, so he dealt fairly. On his visits of inspection along the line he would listen to his sub-contractors and gangers. If a sub-contractor was obviously going to lose on one contract – if, say, the cutting he had taken thinking it to be sand turned out to be tricky shale – Brassey might alter the terms and pay a bit more, or see the man got a better deal on the next contract he took farther down the line. Those who saw Brassey on these visits were impressed by his genial manner towards his old followers. He used to recognize many of the old navvies, even some he had not seen for years, and call them by their Christian names. He shook hands with gangers and stopped for a few moments to talk over old times and ask after common acquaintances who had worked on previous contracts. Brassey's son put it this way: 'A small manifestation of kindness like this, how little it costs, how much it is valued.'

When Brassey was dying, in December 1870, his men remembered him and many of them came, some from abroad, to see their old master. Some had been his agents on great contracts, others navvies who had followed his works for thirty years. They did not intrude upon his illness, but asked to be allowed to wait in the hall of his house, hoping to see him as he was helped out to his carriage, and to shake his hand once again.

It was not only in Brassey's nature to treat his men decently: it was also in his own interests. A fly-by-night contractor, and there were many, could grind his men as hard as they would tolerate, not caring how they lived or ate, concerned only to finish a particular contract, take his profit on it, and move on. Brassey, on the other hand, had to maintain an establishment. To assemble a temporary rabble of navvies was not difficult, but he wanted a standing army which could travel from one railway to another, and from one country to another. He preferred the men he knew, looked after them, and was respected by them.

Peto, too, was much liked by his men. In the late 1840s, when he visited Portugal to inspect some works there, he rode down the new line on the tender of an engine, sitting on coal bags. All along the line he was greeted by the navvies who were at work, and at the end of the line, where there were many men who had worked for him on previous contracts, the

cheers followed faster and faster, until, to the astonishment of
Portuguese bystanders, Peto was lifted shoulder high and
carried to his hotel.

For both contractor and sub-contractor life was perilous. A
man needed luck. Of the thirty main contractors who undertook to construct parts of the London and Birmingham Railway, ten failed completely. Jackson and Seddon lasted only a
few months on the Primrose Hill contract, and T. Townsend
about a year at Tring before the company took over. William
Soars gave up after about nine months at Wolverton, and
again the company took over the uncompleted works. At
Kilsby, Jos. Nowell & Sons found they could not go on, and
surrendered the contract in February 1836. Mr Lecount,
assistant engineer to the company, explained that these contractors failed because the cost of labour and materials rose
soon after the biggest contracts were let. It became plain to
these contractors that they could not carry on except at great
loss, and after this, said Lecount,

a complete want of energy soon became apparent, and the company
were under the necessity, at whatever cost, of getting the contracts
into their own, or some other person's hands as quickly as possible,
as it was clear that whatever additional outlay might become necessary on this account, would be more than counterbalanced by the
time which would be gained.

The method of tendering was frequently chancy, particularly
in the early years. Firbank himself used to tell a story of one
Mr Wythes (probably George Wythes, who undertook,
among other lines, that from Dorchester to Maiden Newton)
who was thinking of submitting an offer for a contract. He
first thought £18,000 would be reasonable, but then consulted
his wife and agreed it should be £20,000. Thinking it over, he
decided not to take any risk, so made it £40,000. They slept
on it and the next morning his wife said she thought he had
better make it £80,000. He did; it turned out to be the lowest
tender notwithstanding, and he founded his fortune on it.

Few were so lucky. Robert Rawlinson, an engineer who
had worked on canals and then on the London and Birming-

ham Railway, said that in a wet season, and particularly with night work, no contractor could estimate within 25 per cent, and might be out by thousands of pounds. Look, he said, at such a contract. The new broken ground in the excavations was worked by man and horse into an adhesive mud, knee deep. The new embankment was in an even worse state. The horses' feet were cut by rails and sleepers, and the mud and wet produced diseases in their legs. The temporary railways buckled, the newly formed embankment slipped at the base and subsided at the top. The end of the embankment, at the tiphead, could not be kept up to its level; the wet earth was shaken in its wagon ride over bumpy rails into the consistency of birdlime and stuck to the inside of the trucks, making it impossible to tip. Frequently rails, wagons, and horses fell over the tiphead and were buried. Men and horses were almost powerless and became dispirited, and the poor contractor was bewildered or wrapped in despair. The savings of a life could be lost in a month or so.

Many more contractors went broke than made a fortune. The career of Benjamin Bailey is typical of many. He was a sub-contractor on the London and Birmingham, and rose to be what he called 'first contractor under Mr Brunel' on stretches of the Great Western, with 'horses, materials for work, wagons and carts and everything'. Then he failed and in 1846 was back at labouring.

On the whole, sub-contractors did not enjoy a reputation for the greatest integrity. As Thomas Walker, missionary, put it:

The Devil has a lot of sub-contractors: a bad lot I tell you; like some I have known who have drawn £500 or £1,000 and sloped to America and left the poor men nothing.

Benley and Leech, sub-contractors on the East Lancashire Railway at Hepton, near Burnley, sound as if they had gone over to the devil. One Saturday in the middle of September 1846 the rumour went round that they were planning to leave the district without paying the labourers the month's wages they were owed. The monthly pay was at a pub called the

Angel, where the sub-contractors had taken rooms. On the Saturday morning only some men were paid, and then the money stopped. It then became clear why Benley and Leech had been quietly removing their furniture from the inn during Friday night, and the navvies took the law into their own hands. A great crowd surrounded the Angel and shouted out that the two bilkers would be kept inside until the remaining wages were paid. The navvies lived from hand to mouth, and because there was no pay they had no food for themselves or their families. They decided that if they were going to starve so should Benley and Leech, so the innkeeper was ordered to give the two men nothing to eat or drink. Throughout Saturday night and Sunday a large concourse of people assembled in front of the Angel. Inside, the two contractors were detained in a billiard room by a large posse of labourers, who made what money they could by showing their prisoners to all who cared to pay a halfpenny for the sight of them, and collected seventeen shillings in this way.

Later on Sunday the magistrates became alarmed, and persuaded the navvies to allow the two men to be taken to the police station, on the understanding that they should appear in court on Monday to answer summonses against them. The court was crowded with navvies. A witness explained that the main contractor on the line paid the sub-contractors only once a month, and that they then paid the men, who had been hired at a fixed day rate. But the sub-contractors had fallen behind with the work and did not have the money to pay the wages. It was an old and familiar tale, and the magistrates could do nothing. The navvies could take their remedy at civil law and sue the sub-contractors for debt, but that was all. The two bilkers had committed no crime. So there was nothing left but for the magistrates to be sympathetic, to praise the forbearance of the navvies, and to say how sorry they were that some men and their wives and children had not eaten since Saturday. The bench had no power to enforce payment, and in any case the sub-contractors were broke.

When he was taken back, for his own safety, to the officers' day room at the police station, Leech climbed through the

window and ran, but the navvies saw him, chased him, and
conducted him in triumph to his old quarters at the Angel.
To protect him, and to prevent a breach of the peace, four
policemen rescued Leech and escorted him back to the police
station amid the shouts and threats of the mob. But the navvies
were really powerless. They stood around arguing that if the
sub-contractor could not pay them the main contractor should,
but he would accept no obligation. He had not hired the men.
They were nothing to do with him. So the mob dispersed, as
many had done before and many would after. The navvies
drifted off to other work, and when things quieted down Benley and Leech slipped out of the police station and left town.

In no profession, perhaps, were there so many bold,
rapacious quacks as among railway contractors and civil
engineers. Benley and Leech were among the rapacious. But
generally the contractors and sub-contractors not only paid
their men, they paid well. Throughout the century a railway
navvy could earn more than, say, a farm labourer – sometimes
two or three times as much. The contractors were not philan-
thropists. They were out to make not friends but profits, and
paid well because they had to. The work was always heavy and
dangerous, and a man had to abandon the comfort of his home
and live in a shanty by the line. There had to be something to
induce a farm labourer to leave the land and go for a navvy,
and that something was money. The contractors needed the
better labourers and had to pay for them. A contractor chose
his men as he chose his horses; there was a certain limit below
which neither cheap horses nor cheap men were any good to
him. He had to finish the line on time or pay a money penalty,
so men who could not work hard and fast were useless and
just got in the way.

Once he had got his navvies by paying well, the contractor
had to keep them by paying better than the man building the
next stretch of line. The railways were not built rationally,
according to a system, one main line at a time. They were
thrown up all together in periods of intense competition, so
in 1838, say, if a man was not paid handsomely enough on one
contract of the London and Birmingham he could tramp a

few miles north and work for another master, or go on a longer tramp and try his luck on the Great Western. There were few strikes, and this is because, in days of prosperity, the navvies had a more powerful argument – they could jack up and go elsewhere. In times of unemployment, in the quiet years of the early 1840s when there was for the while little railway-building, the men stood to gain little by strikes, but even then wages never fell as low as in factories. Even in slack times the contractors had to maintain their armies, perhaps at some immediate loss to themselves.

It was all a matter of supply and demand. Wages increased because of great and sudden demands for labour. This was particularly true of foreign lines. When the Grand Trunk of Canada was being constructed Brassey had to send out men from England. They were engaged in Lancashire and Cheshire, and on landing in Canada were paid 40 per cent more than at home for doing the same work. As the work went on, with the hardships becoming greater and some men returning home, the wages rose from 3s. 6d. a day to 6s. Masons whose pay in England was 5s., and who were taken to Canada at the contractors' expense, were paid 7s. 6d., although the cost of living was not higher in Canada than in England. The point was that there was a ready supply of men in England: in Canada there was not.

To build a railway in New South Wales 2,000 men were sent out from England at the joint expense of the contractors and the government. The cost of living for a single navvy was 10s. a week as compared with 8s. at home, but although this difference was so small, and although the contractors paid for the passage out and back, navvies were so scarce that men who had been paid 3s. to 3s. 6d. a day in England could earn 7s. 6d. and more in Australia. Some masons and bricklayers earned as much as 12s. to 13s. a day. When native labourers were used their pay always rose too. On the Bilbao and Tudela line men were receiving a mere shilling a day at the start, but this had risen to 3s. a day before the railway was completed. On the same line the masons' wages increased from 1s. 4d. to 5s. a day.

The fall in wages after a commercial panic, when there was less building and work was scarce, shows how closely the rate of wages depended on supply and demand. After the railway panic of 1847–8 labour on the Royston and Hitchin Railway was cheaper than it ever was afterwards. Men who on the North Staffordshire, shortly before the panic, had earned 3s. 6d. a day, accepted half a crown on the Royston line. Brassey found that after the panic the navvies' wages, which had risen as high as 6s. a day in the mania of 1846, declined so that on the Cheshire junction line the cost of the whole works fell by 15 per cent.

Mackay, one of Brassey's staff, worked out a comparative table of weekly wages from 1843 to 1869.

	1843	1846	1849	1851	1855	1857	1860	1863	1866	1869
Masons	21/–	33/–	24/–	21/–	25/6	24/–	22/6	24/–	27/–	27/–
Bricklayers	21/–	30/–	24/–	21/–	25/6	22/6	22/6	24/–	27/–	25/6
Carpenters and Blacksmiths	21/–	30/–	24/–	21/–	25/6	22/6	22/6	24/–	25/6	24/–
Navvies, getters (pickmen)	16/6	24/–	18/–	15/–	19/–	18/–	17/–	19/–	20/–	18/–
Navvies, fitters (shovellers)	15/–	22/6	16/6	14/–	17/–	17/–	16/–	17/–	18/–	17/–
Cost of labour only per cube yard:										
of brickwork	2/3	3/9	2/9	2/3	2/6	2/6	2/4	2/6	2/9	2/6
of earthwork	/4½	/7½	/5	/4	/5½	/5¼	/5	/5½	/5¼	/5½

He explained that in 1843, which was a period of general depression, excellent workmen were plentiful, and provisions for men and horses cheap. The Gloucester and Bristol Railway was built at this time, and so was the Gloucester to Stonehouse Line, where clay cuttings were taken out at the low cost of sixpence a yard, inclusive of horse labour. Three years later, when Brassey's English contracts included the Lancaster and Carlisle, Trent Valley, Caledonian, North Staffordshire, and Eastern Union Railways, things were different. This year, 1846, was the height of the second railway mania, the demand for men was great, and good navvies were scarce. In Lancashire and the north farmers complained that most of their

men had gone to the railways but even so the contractors
needed more. Beer was given to the men as well as wages.
Lookouts were placed on the roads to intercept men tramping,
and take them to the nearest beer shop to be treated and induced to start work. Work went on day and night, and
sometimes the same men worked continuously for several days
and nights on end. A few men were paid for as many as
forty-seven days in one lunar month. Provisions were dear and
wages high, higher than they ever were again until the Settle
and Carlisle line of the seventies. This was the year after the
first Woodhead Tunnel was finished. Mackay wrote:

> Excessively high wages, excessive work, excessive drinking, in-
> different lodgings, caused great demoralization, and gave the death-
> blow to the good old navvy already on the decline. He died out a
> few years after this period.

(Mackay was not the only one to mourn the death of the
genuine navvy, but these complaints meant little. Contractors
and engineers were always moaning that navvies weren't what
they used to be, but still went on boasting that the English
navvy was the best in the world.) In 1849 when the Great
Northern, Oxford, Worcester, and Wolverhampton, and
Chester and Holyhead lines were being constructed, wages
and costs were much lower. The general uneasiness caused by
the financial crash of 1847 was aggravated by the political
turmoils and European revolutions of 1848. Many contracts
started in 1846 were not yet finished. Works were stopped in
1847 and were only partly resumed in 1848. The late forties
and early fifties were a bad time for the navvies, many of
whom went abroad. In 1855, though railway work was still
slack, wages rose because men were harder to come by. The
best had gone to France, Spain, Belgium, Switzerland, Italy,
and Canada with Brassey's contracts. Other experienced
navvies had gone to the Crimea, and at home the militia were
all under arms. Wages were higher, and food dearer. It cost
5s. a day to feed a horse. Thereafter wages remained steady
throughout the later fifties and sixties, except for a year or so
at the time of the 1866 panic. Shortly before this the men on

the Kensington and Richmond line had become almost un-manageable. But then came Black Friday, 11 May 1866, when after a great run on the banks the City financiers Overend and Gurney went bankrupt, Peto failed and 30,000 of his men found themselves out of work, Brassey barely survived, and railway shares dropped two-thirds of their value in a day. Immediately the men's tone was much changed and their demands became more reasonable.

In 1872 Thomas Brassey Jnr (who was the son of the contractor and later became Earl Brassey), expounding the classical doctrine of supply and demand, said there were strict limits within which wages could fluctuate. They could not long continue so high as to deprive capital of its fair return, because if they did the capitalists would find something else in which to invest their money more profitably. Nor could wages long remain below the amount necessary to keep the labourer and his family. At about this time too, it became fashionable for classical economists to point out that whether cheap or dear labour was used, the cost of railway construction remained the same. Mr John Hawkshaw, a consulting en-gineer with experience in South America, Russia, Holland, India, and Britain, said that he was perfectly well acquainted with the value of 'Hindoo and other labour', and that though an English labourer would do more work in a given time than a Creole or a Hindoo, yet the Englishman had to be paid higher wages. Therefore it didn't matter which the con-tractor used. This is not an argument that would have ap-pealed to the contractors of the great days of British and West European railway building, before about 1855. It forgets that speed was the essence of these early contracts. No doubt Hawkshaw's theory worked out well enough on the later railways of South America and India, where the cost of taking out British navvies and paying their higher wages would not have been justified, particularly when it hardly mattered within a few months when the line was completed.

But in the early days, though some of the more unscru-pulous did their best to sell their men rotten food at the tommy shops, the better contractors looked after their people because they had no use for depressed and dispirited navvies. Brassey several times opposed suggestions that he should economize by reducing the pay of his men, partly perhaps because he was humane, partly no doubt because he knew they would work worse for worse pay. And in 1851 Peto (who became an M.P. in 1847), seconding the Address to the Crown at the opening of Parliament, said of the labouring man:

I know from personal experience that if you pay him well, and show you care for him, he is the most faithful and hardworking creature in existence; but if you find him working for fourpence a day, and that paid in potatoes and meal, can we wonder that the results are as we find them? [He was referring to the wretchedness of Irish navvies on some Irish lines at the time.] But give him legitimate occupation, and remuneration for his services, show him you appreciate those services, and you may be sure you put an end to all agitation. He will be your faithful servant.

4

Death and Disaster

We are pained to state that a labourer, who was working in the excavation of the rail-road, at Edgehill, where the tunnel is intended to come out and join the surface of the ground, was killed on Monday last. The poor fellow was in the act of undermining a heavy head of clay, fourteen or fifteen feet high, when the mass fell upon him, and literally crushed his bowels out of his body.

Liverpool Mercury, 10 August 1827

THIS is the first recorded death of a railway navvy. But this unnamed labourer killed on the Liverpool and Manchester was only the first of many thousands. The work was inherently dangerous. Gangs of men, half disciplined if at all, hacked away at great banks of earth and at sheer cliffs of rock, or blasted out tunnels hundreds of feet below ground. Deaths were expected, and the navvies increased the ever-present hazard by their own recklessness. It was a sort of bravado with many of them not to take care. A contractor said he knew one fellow who would smoke a pipe near an open barrel of gunpowder.

Gangs repeatedly undermined too great a height of earth, too great a 'lift' as it was called, exposing themselves to a constant risk of being buried, because they could earn more that way than by doing a bit at a time. Some excavations could be safely worked with a lift of ten or twelve feet, to bring down a fall of fifty tons, but in other soils a lift of not more than six or eight feet was prudent. The technique was to burrow into a face of earth – 'knocking its legs from under it' – and then to blast away the overhanging mass. Often the soil would not need blasting, but would fall of its own weight when sharpened iron bars and piles were driven in from above, and much of the skill of the excavator lay in knowing when he had burrowed far enough in, and when he should climb up on to the bank and hack away at the overhang to cave it in. In properly organized gangs one man would be stationed on top of the excavation to watch the soil over the burrow hole and shout a warning if it showed signs of shifting or cracking. But often the men did not bother with the lookout, or they worked at night when it was impossible to see. Blasting in tunnels was always perilous, and often seems to have been done by common navvies without any supervision.

As if the work were not hazardous enough (and as if enough of them did not die anyway from dysentery, consumption, inflammation of the lungs, smallpox, cholera, and – like two men at Woodbridge in 1856 – sunstroke), the navvies also took risks for risks' sake. At Blisworth the men had taken to riding on a rickety temporary tramway which was designed to take wagons of soil from a cutting to an embankment. One man was killed when a truck was derailed, but this did not deter others, and a few days later a gang of navvies riding down to their dinner were thrown off and buried beneath the derailed trucks and their load of earth. One young man emerged from the rubble, looked at his arm, said, 'It's broke, I maun go home,' and walked six miles to his old village.

A few navvies grew wise. One older man described a certain cutting to Elizabeth Garnett, the missionary:

I went to look at it and I saw a spot that looked queer. It was about fifty feet overhead. I chucked a stone up and down came a bit of muck as big as a horse, so I jacked.

Another man told her:

I went round by Eston. We call it the slaughterhouse, you know, because every day nearly there's a accident, and nigh every week, at the farthest, a death. Well, I stood and looked down, and there were the chaps, ever so far below, and the cuttings so narrow. And a lot of stone fell, it was always falling, they were bound to be hurt. There was no room to get away nor mostly no warning. One chap I saw killed while I was there, anyhow he died as soon as they got him home. So, I said, 'Good money's all right, but I'd sooner keep my head on,' so I never asked to be put on, but came away again.

But most navvies came to accept the risk of injury. They

were callous when others were hurt. One ganger told a boy whose foot was crushed: 'Crying'll do thee no good, lad. Thou'dst better have it cut off above the knee.' And when a man was himself injured it was the fashion – if contemporary accounts are to be believed, and perhaps they are not always – to display great resignation and fortitude. Theirs was a stoicism very like that of William Huskisson, one of the promoters of the Liverpool and Manchester Railway and a former President of the Board of Trade, after he was run over by a locomotive at the ceremonial opening of that railway in September 1830. Later that afternoon, after he had been given 240 drops of laudanum, he asked how long he had to live, and the surgeon told him at most six hours. Huskisson thanked him, and then made a will, which he signed W Huskisson. 'It is an extraordinary fact,' said the *Manchester Guardian*,

and evinces the uncommon firmness and self-possession of the right hon. gentleman under such awful circumstances, that after he had signed the papers he turned back, as it were, to place a dot over the i, and another between the W. and the H.

If navvies had made wills they would have dotted the i's.

Even the most apparently humane of engineers resigned themselves – or rather their navvies – to the risk of the work. Brunel was once shown a list of 131 navvies on the Great Western, not including those slightly injured, who had been taken to Bath Hospital from 30 September 1839 to 24 June 1841. 'I think it is a small list,' he replied,

considering the very heavy works and the immense amount of powder used, and some of the heaviest and most difficult works; I am afraid it does not show the whole extent of accidents incurred in that district.

Asked again if he did not consider that such a list was, on the face of it, startling, he repeated that he did not. The number of accidents was small, considering so many men had been at work for two or three years.

The great number of casualties became something of a burden to hospitals. At Salisbury Infirmary between 23 June 1845 and 30 May 1846 there were fifty-two navvy in-patients.

The weekly cost of keeping each man was twelve shillings, and the total cost to the hospital was £177. Towards this the South-Western Railway Company contributed £5, and the contractor six guineas, leaving the hospital to find the other £165 14s. Not only the men suffered. Boys were often used to lead soil wagons and many died when they fell beneath the wheels. Edward Higham, aged five, was luckier. On 17 July 1845 he was discharged from the Manchester Royal Infirmary after being cured, so the hospital records say, of a fractured skull.

Because the companies and contractors were so mean the labourers had to help themselves by setting up sick clubs. About sixpence a week was collected at the pays, and an injured navvy was allowed twelve shillings a week. Sometimes this was found to be too much as it encouraged a man to stay ill when he could have returned to work, and if a man was suspected of malingering his money was cut to eight shillings a week. If a man died the contractor generally gave something to his wife and children, but not much. 'If a man is killed,' said Peto, 'and I give his wife £5 or something of that kind, she is only temporarily relieved.' Sometimes the navvies themselves were more generous; on one line of the Midland Railway in the late 1870s the men collected £80 for the widow of one of their gang. Not until 1904, long after there was any great need for it, did a few contractors set up an Aged Navvies' Pension Fund, giving five shillings a week to navvies over sixty-five and seven shillings and sixpence to married couples. Even then only 200 received these pensions, a derisory number.

In a way, with so many huge works being flung up at so great a rate, it is surprising that men were killed only one or two at a time and not in whole gangs. It had been confidently predicted, when the London and Birmingham Railway was proposed, that in not so many years the viaducts and embankments would crumble and become just so many picturesque ruins to decorate the landscape. But most of the railway works stood, and still stand. There were few disasters.

One of these few was at Ashton under Lyne in 1845, where

the Stalybridge to Ashton line was carried over the River Tame by a nine-arch viaduct. At about quarter past three on 19 April, a Saturday afternoon, an old man called William Kemp was sitting on the battlements of the arches watching a group of labourers putting the finishing touches to the viaduct which was due to be opened soon. He saw a crack, stuck his stick into it, and then went down into the valley below to have another look from there. He saw what looked like a steady stream of black mortar falling from one arch. At the same time Henry Morton, a navvy, up on the viaduct, saw the crack too, and pointed it out to his mates. 'It's nothing,' they said, and laughed at it. Beneath them, Kemp heard the men laughing, looked up again, and was knocked over by a baulk of timber falling from the top. This was the beginning. The arches fell one after another, quickly, until they came to the centre of the viaduct; then there was a pause for a second or so, before the arches toppled from the farther bank in orderly succession. Of the twenty or so men on the arches, five jumped or were thrown clear, Henry Morton among them: the rest were buried in the collapsing rubble. It was twenty past three.

The noise was like so many gun-shots. Panic spread through the town of Ashton, women ran about shrieking in the streets and others clawed about in the debris to find their men. The contractor's other navvies hacked away at the wreckage, trying to rescue their fellows, but the curious crowd so impeded them that James Lord, a magistrate, called in the military. Twenty or thirty men of the 56th Regiment of Foot arrived to keep the mob back. Joseph Fowler, one of the sub-contractors, who had been on the second arch, escaped with a sprained ankle and stayed all Saturday night helping to direct the rescue. Another man who escaped ran three miles to Hyde, without stopping, to tell his wife he was all right.

Throughout Saturday 200 navvies toiled at the rescue, but they got in each other's way and so the numbers were reduced to 150. All through Sunday immense crowds of people congregated on every height and spot commanding a view of the fallen arches and gazed for hours at the labourers digging.

The *Manchester Guardian* reported that 20,000 to 25,000 stood and watched.

Gradually the men were found. Richard Critchley and Thomas Brown were brought out alive and not badly hurt. George Collier, aged forty-five, and James Bradbury, aged twenty-three or four, both excavators, were found dead, lying across each other. Abraham Nowell was also dead. He left four children and a widow soon expecting a fifth. William Birchenough survived, and was fit enough to go back to work on Monday. William Hardwick, called Trump, was dead. So was Michael Kelty, an Irishman, who was about to emigrate to America, and only waiting for a letter from the captain of the ship in which he was to cross the Atlantic. His widow, almost distracted, wandered about the ruins during Saturday, Sunday, and Monday. The body was uncovered on Tuesday, at four in the afternoon. Then there was a York-shireman, believed to come from some place within two miles of Leeds, perhaps the village of Holbeck, but who had never given his name and was written down in the contractor's books as 'York'. Later someone identified the body as that of John Hufferton.

Altogether fifteen died. All the bodies bore marks of severe contusion on the face, but in no instance was the head crushed or the features mutilated. On Sunday, 27 April, the workmen assembled in Park Parade, Ashton, at ten o'clock, where they were joined by the engineer and manager of the company, and then marched to the parish church to hear the Rev. J. Handforth preach on a text from the thirty-third chapter of Ezekiel, 'Say unto them, as I live, saith the Lord God, I have no pleasure in the death of the wicked: but that the wicked turn from his way and live: turn ye, turn ye, from your evil ways; for why will ye die, O house of Israel?' The navvies were all neatly dressed, behaved with great propriety, and seemed to feel the force of the gentleman's statement that he had no pleasure in the death of their colleagues and that they themselves should turn from their wicked ways. They went on building the railway.

Why had the viaduct fallen? There were reports that it had

been built only fifteen yards north of a coal pit which had been abandoned twenty-five years before, and that the foundations might have subsided into old pit workings. Not true, said the railway engineers. The pit was there, but everything was safe enough. No one was to blame. The company said it had been up to the engineers to build the viaduct, the engineers said it was up to the contractors, and the contractors in turn said the engineers had supervised the work anyway, and had been satisfied enough with it. The report of three experts given at the inquest was damning. 'The rubble stone filling,' the report said, 'together with the improper workmanship, were alike unfitted to the purpose to which they were destined.' The piers had been erected with an outer shell of ashlar stone, and the whole of the interior was a mass of rubble and scabblings, neither bedded with care, nor flushed, nor grouted, but full of cracks. 'Not the slightest adhesion had taken place between the mortar and the masonry, in any one part.' The coroner was unhappy. What, he asked, if such an accident had happened at a time when thousands of the workpeople of Ashton had been packed into an excursion train on its way to Manchester on a holiday? The jury brought in a rider which spoke of negligence in both construction and superintendence, but their formal verdict was 'accidental death'. The railway works were put back by three months but they went on.

Generally, though they were brutalized by constant risk and death, the men were fastidious in their mourning and made an event of a funeral. It was sometimes wondered why men so coarsened should show such grief as they commonly did for their dead comrades. One man was killed on a beautiful summer evening. The weight of earth that fell on him snapped in two a knife he was carrying in his pocket, though the man himself, when they dug him out, was scarcely grazed. It was, said John Shedlock, engineer, a light evening and the men could have worked several hours longer, but so strong was their sympathy with their dead mate that they refused to, and went home. Mr Shedlock was astonished.

There is one less gentle tale of a ganger on the London and North-Western Railway in the late 1830s who raffled the body

of one of his navvies. Nearly 300 men joined in, at sixpence a
time, the proceeds to go towards a drinking bout. The raffle
took place, and so did the revel, but the man who won the
body did not welcome it, and the funeral, after a fortnight's
delay, was performed by the parish. It is not clear how true
this story is, because it was recounted, more than forty years
later, by the Rev. D. W. Barrett, who was doing his best to
suppress drunkenness among the navvies by recounting
horrific tales of the loathsome results of drink. If it is true it
is untypical. Navvies were usually devout at a funeral. On 27
April 1846 a young man called Clerrett was working as a
tip-driver on the Southampton and Dorset Railway at Can-
ford Bridge, in Dorset, when he fell so that the horse and
wagon crushed him to death. He was only seventeen. At the
funeral nearly 140 navvies, each wearing a white favour in his
coat, followed the body to the grave. 'The becoming de-
meanour of these stalwart and untutored men,' said a newspaper report, 'bespoke of the utmost sincerity of regret at
the untimely fate of their comrade.' The contractor arranged
the funeral, and the men agreed to pay for it out of their next
week's wages.

But what happened after a funeral was often a different
story. In the same week as Clerrett's death another young
man died on the works at Maiden Newton in the same
county. The *Poole and Dorsetshire Herald* said:

A large number of the fellow workmen of the deceased followed
the body, but although the funeral was conducted in the most im-
pressive manner by the Hon. and Rev. W. H. Scott, rector, but
little effect was produced on some, as at twelve o'clock the same
night, a body of these persons made a most wanton attack on
various persons connected with the White Horse Inn, breaking the
windows and all things capable of being destroyed. Mr W. Thomas
the constable was assailed and so much injured as to require
medical assistance. Other persons attempting to keep the peace
were also beaten. We are sorry to say that the neighbourhood is in
danger of constant disturbance by these lawless fellows, and unless
an efficient force be kept near other outrages may be expected.

There are many such stories, of mourners being so drunk

they nearly fell into the grave themselves, of funeral cele-
brations conducted to the terror of the neighbouring villagers,
but at the same time there was attributed to the navvy a
gentle, gruff, romantic reputation of being friendly and
courteous towards corpses. In *Self-Help*, in a chapter entitled,
'The True Gentleman', Samuel Smiles tells the story of the
Emperor of Austria who found himself strolling about the
streets of Vienna at the time of a cholera epidemic, and en-
countered a corpse on a litter with no mourner. The relations
were too afraid of the infection to attend the funeral. 'Then
we,' said the Emperor, 'will supply their place; for none of
my poor people should go to the grave without that last
mark of respect.' Smiles then comments that fine though that
illustration might be of the qualities of the gentleman, he
could match it with another equally good, of two English
navvies in Paris. One day a hearse was observed ascending
the steep Rue de Clichy on its way to Montmartre, bearing a
coffin of poplar wood with its old corpse. 'Not a soul followed, not even the living dog of the dead man, if he had
one.' The day was rainy and dismal; passers-by lifted the hat,
as was usual when a funeral passed, and that was all. At
length it passed two English navvies, who found themselves
in Paris on their way from Spain.

A right feeling spoke from beneath their serge jackets. 'Poor
wretch,' said one to the other, 'no one follows him; let us follow.'
And the two took off their hats, and walked bareheaded after the
corpse of a stranger to the cemetery of Montmartre.

5

Shanties and Truck

NAVVIES not only worked together; they also lived together. Even a thousand labourers working today on one site do not become a single body of men because they leave work at the end of the day and go home. But the railway navvies cut across open country, miles from anywhere, and after work they returned to their own shanty towns, away from the settled pattern of the villages from which they had come perhaps years before, and far from the civilizing and sobering influence of family and home.

The clearest picture of shanty life in the early days is given by a boy, whose name is unknown, who ran away from home in March 1835 and tramped thirty miles to the nearest railway works. Later he wrote about his experiences in the magazine *Household Words*. At first he was taken on, as boys frequently were, as a tip-driver, but he drove horse and truck together over the tiphead, and got the sack. Again he went off on the tramp, until he was employed as a bucket-steerer in one of the shafts of the Watford Tunnel, and later as a member of a regular gang of navvies there. There were forty men in this gang, each with a nickname – Happy Jack, Long Bob, Dusty Tom, Billygoat, Frying Pan, Redhead, and others. The boy, who because of his new clothes and new tools was called Dandy Dick, was put to work with Kick Daddy, made friends with Canting George, and they all worked under a ganger called Bullhead.

The boy himself lived in a small hut, but he knew the larger shanties well. Most were built of stone, brick, mud, and timber, roofed with tile and tarpaulin, and consisted of one large oblong room. There were sixty gangs working on the tunnel and almost all of them lived in these shanties, which the boy called dens of wild men. Each shanty was looked after by an old crone who was expected to cook, make beds, and wash and mend the clothes of her masters, who beat her fearfully, mostly for entertainment. These women took part in all the obscenity and blasphemy, and lent a hand in the fighting. Their features were disfigured, their heads and hands cut and bandaged, and they were quite at home.

In his spare time the boy was teaching George Hatley to read, and one Sunday morning in early May, when it was too wet to go to church, he strolled over to George's shanty and asked for him. The man was out, but Old Peg, the presiding crone, said he would be back by eleven o'clock. The boy said he would wait, the woman cursed him in a way intended to be very friendly, and he sat down on a three-legged stool and looked around the place. The open door was about midway in one of the walls, with a window on either side. Near one of the windows were rough benches, and on these sprawled four or five navvies who were already up. Two others were lying on the earth floor playing cards, and another was sitting on a stool mending his boots. They all nodded to the boy and offered him a drink. Near the other window stood three barrels of beer, all in tap, the keys of which were chained to a strong leather girdle round Peg's waist. She was the tapster and sat in an old armchair near the barrels.

The opposite end of the shanty was fitted up with bunks from floor to roof like the between-decks of an emigrant ship, and in each bunk lay one or two men, drunk or asleep, with their heads pillowed on their kit. This was their knock-off Sunday, the one Sunday in perhaps two or three on which they did not work. Nestling with many of the navvies were dogs and litters of puppies, mostly bullhounds or lurchers, which the men used for fighting or poaching.

One end of the room was a kitchen. There was a rough dresser in one corner, and a rickety table on which stood tin, wood, or earthenware dishes, each holding a cup, basin, or bowl. Against the wall was fixed a double row of cupboards or lockers, one for each man, and below them, on hooks, were several large pots and pans. Over the central fireplace hung half a dozen guns. In another corner was a large copper, beneath which a fire was roaring. Old Peg, muttering and spluttering, threw on coals to keep it boiling. Hanging over this copper were several strings, which disappeared into the steaming water. To the top of each string a bit of wood was attached, and the boy asked what this was for.

'Them,' said Peg in her broad Lancashire dialect, and taking one stick in her hand and pulling its string out of the copper, 'why sith'ee lad, this bit o' stick has four nicks in't, well it's Billygoat's dinner, he's a bed yond. Now this,' taking up another stick with six nicks, 'is that divil Redhead's, and this,' seizing a third with ten nicks, 'is Happy Jack's. Well, thee knowst he's got a bit o' beef; Redhead's nowt but taters, he's a gradely brute is Redhead. And Billygoat's got a pun or so o' bacon an' a cabbage. Now, thee sees, I've got a matter o' twenty dinners or so to bile every day, which I biles in nets, and if I dinna fix em in this rooad, I sud ha niver tell where to find em, and then there ud be sich a row as niver yet was heered on.'

Soon after this, Red Whippet came in bringing with him a leveret, which he tossed to Peg. 'Get it ready an put it along o' the rest, and look sharp or thee's head may be broken.' Then the man took off his jacket and boots and tumbled into a berth.

Such shanties were more civilized than many. On the South Devon Railway at Totnes in the middle forties the huts were made of mud or turf. The most usual way of throwing them up was to burrow a short way into a bank, so that the back and part of the sides of the hut would be formed by solid earth, and then make a roof of spare rafters and timbers. On the Hawick branch of the North British line twenty to thirty men slept in huts twenty-eight feet by twelve, two or three navvies sharing a bed. Alexander Ramsay, an engineer, said that the huts were often verminous; he knew of one man who had found twenty-four fleas on himself. There was no separation between the beds. In one slept a man and his wife and one or two children; in another a couple of young men; in a third in the same hut another man and his wife and family. In some of the huts, he said, a humane man would hardly put a pig. As late as 1887, at Brere Ferris, near Devonport, some old hulks of men-o'-war were bought by the contractors and towed up river for the navvies to live in. To this day, near Four Marks in Hampshire, a large wooden building stands by the side of the A.31, only a hundred yards or so from the London to Southampton line. It is now a pub, and its sign-board bears the name of 'The Shant'.

The luckier navvies sometimes found billets in the villages along the line, but they were still fearfully crowded and over-charged, and were apt, in return, to slope off, that is leave without paying. Because of this the landladies sometimes asked to be paid direct by the contractor rather than take the chance that the navvies would forget to pay for lodgings. The navvies opposed this. Richard Pearce, who in 1846 had been a labourer for thirty-two years, having started on the Lancaster Canal, was asked by the 1846 Commons Committee if it might not be better for the masters to pay for the men's lodgings.

He was downright in his answer. 'That would not do at all.'

'Why not?'

'Because some of the landlords' wives would take one half of your victuals, if they were sure to get your money. They are not all honest, the lodging-keepers are not.'

'On the other hand, the landlady is sometimes sloped?'

'Sometimes,' argued Pearce, thinking a little sloping a good thing, 'there is such a case as this, which is, a landlady taking the lodger's victuals, and if the man is going to *pay* the woman as well she would be paid twice.'

Later in the century the navvies who drove railways over wild, open country – in the north-west of England and the Highlands of Scotland – lived as barbarously as they had ever done. Hovels remained hovels. But on lines taken through populated country, where there were at least villages along the line and towns not too far away, things got better. When the Manton to Kettering line was begun by the Midland Railway in the mid 1870s the navvies did not tramp in with nothing but two shirts and two shillings; they came in organized train loads with their families and possessions. At the railway stations little knots gathered together discussing the best way to get to the new works, or crowded round railway officials asking directions. Bundles of bedding, household stuff, furniture, bedsteads, frying-pans, birdcages, prams, and clocks were strewn over the platforms. There was not enough room for all in the villages, so soon the hills and dales for fifteen miles echoed with the sound of mattocks, hammers, and axes as the men built their own hut encampments. Hundreds of huts sprang up, mostly of wood, but a few of earth or bricks. A cluster of six appeared by the roadside here, a group of fifty across the hilltop there, another fifty in a valley by the riverside, and a little colony in the midst of a wood. Seaton Hill was crowned with a cluster which was given the name of Cyprus. Along the fifteen miles of the new line 2,500 men, not counting their families, lived in huts, and another 1,000 or 1,500 in villages. Prices went up. Trade followed the navvies. Brewers' drays, hucksters, packmen, cheapjacks, milkmen, book-hawkers, shoemakers, tailors, and likeness-takers descended on the works.

The Rev. D. W. Barrett, who was curate in charge of the Bishop of Peterborough's railway mission, described the encampments in detail. While the huts were there, he said, they gave the countryside a colonial flavour. They might have been set in the Canadian backwoods or the Australian bush rather than in the English Midlands. The huts varied. Some were no more than primitive burrowed caverns in the side of a bank, covered over with bits of tarpaulin scrounged around the works. Others were small timber sheds, in which the men often sat and smoked as they waited to go down the tunnel shafts.

Then there were those shacks with four walls of turf, made by piling sods of earth one on top of the other up to a height of about six feet, and by stretching across the top a sagging roof of timber. It appeared to Mr Barrett that all these huts needed was the hills of Connemara in the background and Paddy and his pig at the door to make the scene complete – and then you could have imagined yourself in what he called the wild regions of the Emerald Isle. Indeed, he said, the pig was often there. He found one of these hovels which had been made into a two-storeyed dwelling, though not by the usual method of adding a floor. The occupants had erected a huge wooden meat safe and hung it from the rafters. This was reached by a movable ladder. When he asked what it was he was told, 'Oh, that be where the brats sleep.' It was a brat cage.

The largest huts were the shanties, wooden erections whose timbers were tar coated and then perhaps whitewashed, and whose roofs were made of felt. These large huts were divided into three parts. The central hall, with doors at the front and back, was the common living-room for the whole family and the lodgers. To the left was the bedroom of the man, his wife, and his children; and to the right the lodgers' room. Some shanties could hold ten people, others many more. All were crowded, as many as 120 being crammed into a building that was meant for eighty. When the work was pressing on and extra men were taken on for a few weeks, the shanty-keepers did a great trade, charging fourpence a night for a bed, a penny to sleep on a table, and a halfpenny for the floor.

As you walked into one of these wooden huts you would see half a dozen empty spirit bottles, and walls covered with cuttings from *Police News* and other penny dreadfuls, or else papered with patchwork squares from a paper-hanger's sample book. Birdcages and boots hung from the beams. In some, not many, said Mr Barrett, you might have thought you had walked into an officer's quarters in an army camp because of the handsome clocks, cases of stuffed birds and animals, small objects of vertu, sewing machines, and musical instruments. This was the respectable side of the navvy society. These better huts were often named: The West End, The Hermitage, or Rose Cottage. One encampment took its civilization so far as to support a resident poetess whose verses were printed and circulated but not read. None survive.

Whether they lived in ditches, shanties, or Rose Cottage, the navvies ate and drank enormously. One policeman who visited the works near Edinburgh in 1846 remarked that provisions were abundant. He saw fifty loaves in one hut.

When they wanted some bread they would, he complained (and this seems to have offended his Scots frugality), just take a new loaf and cut into it. Joseph Firbank mentions quite casually that his navvies consumed on average two pounds of meat, two pounds of bread, and five quarts of ale a day. He once knew a man drink seventeen quarts in an afternoon. Rawlinson said that on the London and Birmingham Railway crowds of people followed the navvies to sell them ale and whisky, and that some of the men carried their own kegs round with them.

Ale was the most common drink: whisky and gin, when the money would stretch to them, the favourites. Thomas Beggs of the Scottish Temperance League was disheartened to find, on the Muirkirk and Ayr Railway at Crumnock, that the publicans were thriving as never before, one boasting that he had recently had the pleasure of ordering a 125-gallon cask of whisky. The publicans near a settlement looked on the navvies as their natural victims and did all they could, by doctoring their beer to make it seem stronger, by offering prizes, or hiring music and getting up clubs, to induce the men to spend more. Some men would sell their shovels for cider: and there was one woman publican who would pull the boots off a drunken man's feet and take them instead of money when he called for more beer and could not pay. Beer could drink up almost all a man's pay. One navvy, in a fit of Christian remorse, told a woman missionary how beer had dominated his life. The man had first worked on a farm, but had fallen to drink and dissolution, and by the time he was eighteen he was so desperate, having pawned all his clothes and being too ashamed to beg from his parents, that he enlisted in the Royal Marines for five years. But the Marines found him to be a bad character and an habitual drunkard and turned him out as a disgrace to the corps, so there was nothing left for him but navvying and more drink. 'In fact I was in one hut for two and a half years,' he said, 'and was not sober one week of the whole time. We have been at many other places, too, and I have starved my wife and children and clothed them in rags, all through the cursed drink.' Another

man told the same missionary that he had saved £212, and
then spent all but a shilling of it on drink in one month at
Barnsley. This was in the early eighties. On the Kettering and
Manton line it was estimated that in one year 312,000 gallons
of beer and 5,200 gallons of spirits were drunk, at a cost of
£36,000 altogether. Williams, the railway historian, said in
1852 that a sum equal to £1,000 a mile on all the railways of
Britain had been spent on drink.

All this needs to be put in perspective. In those days beer
was much more freely drunk, particularly by the labouring
classes, than now. On a railway works, where the water was
not good, beer might be expected to be the customary drink.
But, even so, any figures must be only cautiously accepted. At
the best they are estimates. More likely they are guesses, and
often guesses by teetotal clergymen who had a motive in
exaggerating.

But drink, certainly, was one of the navvies' consolations.
On one occasion at least they had champagne, at the ceremony of digging the first sod at Yeovil Pen Mill station in
1846. When a line was being made near Ashford, Kent, a
strong wooden building was put up, known as The Cage, in
which tiresome navvies were locked up. This did not deprive
them of their drink. Friends poked pipes through the barred
windows, and the prisoners sucked in their beer. All sorts
of events were an excuse for a drink – pay days, of course, and
funerals – and where there was no ready pretext one could be
invented. The navvy custom of putting a man in the gauging
box was only an excuse for a drink. If a man broke any of the
traditional and unwritten laws existing among his fellow
workmen, if he flouted his landlady's rules, or committed a
breach of the navvies' freemasonry, the cry would go up,
'Put him in the gauging box.' A rough court was then con-
stituted, the offender solemnly arraigned and invariably found
guilty, fined, often heavily, and the money spent in drinks all
round, or else put in an accumulating fund until there was
enough for a big drink on a day off.

One navvy story crops up again and again, slightly different each time. One version, ascribed to Sir Francis Head,

tells the tale of a shanty landlady at Hillmorton, near Rugby, a woman of very sharp business practice who boasted that no navvy should ever do her down. One morning a labourer walked in carrying a huge stone bottle and asked for half a gallon of gin. She poured in the gin and then asked a high price, which he declined to pay. Right, she said, pour it back. Quietly he returned into her measure the half-gallon, and walked off. But since he had previously poured into his bottle half a gallon of water, both navvy and landlady eventually found themselves with half a gallon of gin and water.

But more often it was the navvy who was done. Brewers would sometimes allow gangers a commission on every barrel of ale they could induce the men to drink, and the beer consequently cost dearer. This was only a mild form of exploitation. A much greater evil was truck.

Truck is payment not in money but in goods or in tickets which can be exchanged for goods. On the face of it this seems reasonable enough. Bands of men working together miles from the nearest towns, away from the ordinary markets, could perhaps be best supplied by their employers, who could bring up the food in bulk, distribute it among the men, and deduct the cost from their wages. This way the men could get food cheaper than they could buy it singly. But this supposes honest dealing. In fact, truck became a system of plunder. Often contractors made more profit from truck than from the railway works themselves. Edwin Chadwick, the social reformer, said that contracts were often undertaken at prices which a competent engineer or contractor must have known to be too low to yield a profit. He gave the example of one piece of work taken by some contractors of a sort not much above the labourers they employed, who would lose by the work itself, but make more than £7,000 out of the truck of beer and bad food to the workmen. Here the interests of the contractors in the sale of beer were greater than in the proper execution of the work, and so their navvies often worked in a drunken state, and were encouraged to. Peto also knew of contractors who made their greatest profit from truck. One such man, he said, had made £1,400 in four weeks in this way.

The racket was run like this. The men were paid at long intervals, generally once a month. They were not given to saving, and more often than not had no money of their own until they were paid, so in the weeks before the pay they had to live on credit. If a man was earning, say, five shillings a day he could, at the end of his first day on the works, ask the ganger for a sub, a subsistence allowance, up to the value of the money he had earned. This sub was given in the form of a ticket which could be exchanged for goods only at the truck shop, where the man was swindled left, right, and centre. First, the goods offered there were generally bad – rank butter, poor bacon, watered beer – but the man had no choice. The ticket was good there and nowhere else, so he could shop there or starve. Second, prices were higher and short weight was given: again the man had no choice but to pay. Third, the ticket was often not worth its face value even in tommy goods: it was the practice to deduct a commission, up to 10 per cent, so that the navvy's five-shilling chit was really worth only four-and-sixpence. The deducted sixpence was the ganger's or contractor's cut. So the navvy lived on truck for a month until the pay day, when the value of all the tickets he had received was taken away from the wages due to him. Often he was left with little. On the North British lines in the mid forties, where masons were earning four shillings a day, they were so robbed by the shop-owners that at the end of a month they often had less than ten shillings to come in cash.

Benjamin Bailey, an unsuccessful sub-contractor who once kept a truck shop on the London and Birmingham Railway, said he did not consider a sovereign worth more than fifteen shillings at such shops. If they wanted cash before the pay day men would sell the tickets they got from the ganger, but they did not expect to get more than two shillings or half a crown for a three- or four-shilling ticket. Often tickets were accepted at pubs. John Deacon, another failed sub-contractor who turned publican, kept a house at Ramsgate where he took tickets from the men and cashed them by arrangement with the shopkeepers. To compensate himself for his trouble he charged the men a halfpenny a pot extra.

At a small shop a man's name was just written down in the shopman's book, but at larger works tickets were printed. Here is the form of a truck ticket used on a Scottish line in 1846:

Borthwick............184......

Mr Govan,

At the request of............ No............, give him goods to the amount of............, to account, or in advance of wages which may be owed to him by Messrs Wilson and Moor, and place the same to their debit.

Truck shops, sometimes also called tally shops or tommy shops, were owned either directly by the contractor or sub-contractor or were let out to shopkeepers on the understanding that a certain proportion of the profits went back to the contractor. Systems varied, but the effect of all of them was to exploit the navvy for the greater profit of his employers. Even if a man had ready money it would not help him. Labourers were often taken on only on the say-so of the tally shopkeeper, and a man would find that somehow or other he could not keep his job unless he took the ganger's tickets and spent them at the tommy. But all this was done in an under-the-counter way. As Chadwick said, contractors and even railway company directors had been seen in the back parlours of tally shops looking over the account books. But who could swear that they were not looking over their own accounts, or performing some act of disinterested kindness to the shopkeepers? How to prove what was well known, that they owned the places?

The law offered no remedy. Truck Acts had made the system illegal in factories, though because there was no inspection the factory owners continued to do as they pleased, but even these ineffectual acts did not extend to railway works. The men had no legal redress, as four navvies working at Barnes on the Richmond Railway found in November 1845 when they attempted to take out summonses against a ganger called

Davis, who had taken them on at two shillings and sixpence a day and then refused to pay them in anything but tickets for his tommy shop. They had to eat, so at first they accepted the tickets, but then they demanded to be paid in money. John Nagle, who spoke for the four men, told the magistrate that he was certain one shilling in money was worth more than two shillings in tickets, and asked the court to order Davis to pay in cash. The magistrate explained that he could do little. They had accepted the tickets and that was that. He could issue a summons requiring Davis to pay cash in future, but that would cost two shillings in legal fees. The men said they had not got a farthing in the world and left the court. Even if they had got their summonses they would have been hardly better off, because Davis could thereupon have dismissed them.

A more effective answer was to strike. At the village of Quidhampton, two miles from Salisbury, navvies were given tickets to the value as they supposed of about half their wages, but when they came to be paid some were found to have less than a shilling coming to them. So they struck, and left to go to the Basingstoke and Salisbury line which was then being started. This was in April 1846, and the men were lucky, because it was a time of great railway-building in the south and south-west, when men were scarce.

Many liberal-minded people deprecated the evils of truck. Brunel did, but he was not a contractor, and they were the ones who stood to gain by truck and who therefore defended it against what they called interference in their private affairs. Some reformers did what they could to put an end to the evils of the system. But it was not easy. Peto, though he detested truck and would not allow it on his own contracts, doubted whether the system could be done away with. He said,

It has been the custom for the last hundred years, ever since they commenced making canals, to pay the men in this way; and I think it requires a very strong hand indeed to bring about a transformation.

Nevertheless, he did his best to suppress the racket. In 1854, when he was one of the Members of Parliament for Norwich, he supported the Payment of Wages Bill, which was designed to make the Truck Acts more effective. He told the House that when he first became connected with public works the payment of money was the exception and not the rule, but from twenty-five years' experience he could conceive no reason why there should be a departure from the rule that a man's wages should be paid in the current coin of the realm. The firms with which he had been connected had employed 30,000 navvies in England, Canada, Denmark, Norway, and various parts of the Continent, and never paid their wages other than in money. Let Parliament make the Act as stringent as it could.

A few years earlier John Roberton, a Manchester surgeon, had also urged rigorous laws against truck. Many contractors, he said, made a profit, often an enormous profit, out of the bowels, as it were, of their navvies. The Government should teach such people that the law was their master, and had an arm long enough to compel them to cease this plundering of their own workmen.

But throughout the century truck continued to flourish to the greater glory of the contractors. Truck Acts were passed but never properly enforced. Men on railway works continued to have no option but to take their ticket to the tommy where they paid long prices for short weight, and where the food, anyway, was mostly tommy rot.

6

Riots and Randies

During these trials the utmost interest prevailed in court – and among the spectators were to be seen a great number of navigators. They seemed much surprised at the severity of the sentence on Hobday – fifteen years transportation for maiming another navvy – but that worthy turned around and laughed at them. The prisoner Hobday is a remarkable man, and may be considered a type of the class to which he belongs. His stature is rather below the common height, but his broad frame gives evidence of immense strength. His countenance is forbidding in the extreme. Every feature indicates habitual crime.

> For evil passions, cherished long,
> Have ploughed them with expressions strong,

while his rough matted hair completed the aspect of the finished ruffian. We understand he has said that for nine years he has never slept in a bed, or worn a hat; that his custom was to put on his boots when new, and never remove them until they fell to pieces, and his clothes were treated very much in the same way, except that his shirt was changed once a week.

Carlisle Patriot, 27 February 1846

THE *Patriot* was not a bad newspaper, but these were difficult times up near the Scottish border, and in printing this hodge-podge of abuse and hearsay the editor was only expressing popular feeling. Navvy riots had become habitual, had constantly to be put down by the military, and the local population lived so much in fear that it must have seemed no more than reasonable to condemn a navvy because, among other things, he had never worn a hat for nine years.

Throughout the previous year the railways had been extending through the English border country and into Scotland. A third of the navvies were Irish, a third Scots, and a third English: that was the beginning of the trouble. Easy-going Roman Catholic Irish, Presbyterian Scots, and impartially belligerent English. The Irish did not look for a fight. As the *Scottish Herald* reported, they camped, with their women and children, in some of the most secluded glades, and although

most of the huts showed an amazing disregard of comfort,
'the hereditary glee of their occupants seemed not a whit
impaired'. This glee enraged the Scots, who then added to
their one genuine grievance (the fact that the Irishmen would
work for less pay and so tended to bring down wages) their
sanctified outrage that the Irish should regard the Sabbath as
a holiday, a day of recreation on which they sang and lazed
about. As for the Scots, all they did on a Sunday was drink
often and pray occasionally, and it needed only an odd quart
of whisky and a small prayer to make them half daft with
Presbyterian fervour. They then beat up the godless Irish.
The Irish defended themselves and this further annoyed the
Scots, so that by the middle of 1845 there was near civil war
among the railway labourers. The English, mainly from
Yorkshire and Lancashire, would fight anyone, but they
preferred to attack the Irish. The contractors tried to keep the
men, particularly the Irish and Scots, apart, employing them
on different parts of the line, but the Scots were not so easily
turned from their religious purposes. At Kinghorn, near
Dunfermline, these posters were put up around the town:

NOTICE IS GIVEN

that all the Irish men on the line of railway in Fife Share must be off
the grownd and owt of the countey on Monday th 11th of this
month or els we must by the strenth of our armes and a good pick
shaft put them off

Your humbel servants, Schots men.

Letters were also sent to the contractors and sub-contractors. One read:

Sir, – You must warn all your Irish men to be of the grownd on
Monday the 11 of this month at 12 o'cloack or els we must put
them by forse

FOR WE
ARE DETERMINED
TO DOW IT.

The sheriff turned up and warned the Scots against doing
anything of the sort. Two hundred navvies met on the beach,

but in the face of a warning from the sheriff they proved not so determined to do it, and the Irish were left in peace for a while.

But in other places the riots were savage. Seven thousand men were working on the Caledonian line, and 1,100 of these were paid monthly at a village called Lockerby, in Dumfriesshire. Their conduct was a great scandal to the inhabitants of a quiet Scottish village. John Baird, Deputy Clerk of the Peace for the county, lamented that the local little boys got completely into the habits of the men – 'drinking, swearing, fighting, and smoking tobacco and all those sorts of things'. Mr Baird thought that on a pay day, with constant drunkenness and disturbance, the village was quite uninhabitable.

A minority of the navvies were Irish, and they were attacked now and again, as was the custom. After one pay day a mob of 300 or 400, armed with pitchforks and scythes, marched on the Irish, who were saved only because the magistrates intervened and kept both sides talking until a force of militia came up from Carlisle, twenty-three miles away.

The worst of the riots were to come a few months later, at Penrith in Cumberland, and at Gorebridge, ten miles from Edinburgh, both in February 1846. The Penrith disturbances started in a trivial way. Reports conflict, but it seems that an Irish navvy was told by an English ganger to use a shovel instead of a pick. He refused to be ordered about by an Englishman, and this so inflamed national feeling that the English, who were in the majority, promptly drove all the Irish off the excavations, wrecked and burned their huts, and turned out their wives and children into a cold February to find shelter where they could. Next day 500 Irishmen assembled from neighbouring works around Penrith and marched with their shovels and picks towards the English, to avenge the defeat of the day before. The English prudently fled, so that when the Irish came to the navvy encampment there was no one there. They then acted with great moderation – not burning and destroying as the English had done, but just resigning themselves to the sad fact that there was no one to fight – and returned to Penrith. On the way back they met a couple of stray Englishmen, but these they let go, saying they would not be bothered with only one or two.

This was on a Tuesday. That evening, and through the night, the English assembled their forces, and Yorkshire and Lancashire labourers marched on Penrith in bodies of 300 at a time. They came from as far away as Shap, ten miles off, and even from Kendal, which is twenty. Before nine o'clock on Wednesday morning, to the great alarm of the inhabitants of Penrith, more than 2,000 Englishmen had assembled in the town to thrash the Irish. The Irish had fled, or most of them. Only a few remained, and they hid. The invaders ransacked the town, routing them out. Twelve or fifteen were found in a lodging house and then, said the *Carlisle Patriot*, a scene of cruelty ensued such as had never been witnessed in Penrith since the Border Incursions. The house was broken into, the lurking Irishmen pulled out from their hiding places, and beaten with bludgeons so that their lives were despaired of. A bystander said, 'It was a regular butchery; and could be compared with nothing else than turning rats into a box, and as many laying on with sticks as could get near them.' One of the Englishmen was John Hobday, and he laid into Denis Salmon, an Irishman, with a pick shaft. Salmon called out for mercy, but Hobday just urged the others to join in the beating. 'Pitch into the bugger,' he said, 'he has life enough in him yet.' When Salmon was lying on the ground, unmoving, a farmer tried to intervene and begged Hobday not to kill the man. Hobday took no notice. Salmon, he said, was shamming, and it was well known an Irishman would sulk for an hour before he was killed.

It took the Westmorland Yeomanry to restore order. Hobday and some others were arrested, but this was not the end of the affair. In the next two weeks, while Hobday and his fellow prisoners were awaiting trial at Cumberland Assizes at Carlisle, the Irish twice tried to avenge themselves on the English. They were dispersed, the first time by cavalry, the second time by a force of yeomanry. The Irish only hesitated when they first saw the yeomanry, but ran off when the soldiers were ordered to load their carbines.

The riots spread as far south as Kendal, also on the Lancaster and Carlisle line. There a body of about fifty Irishmen appealed to the Mayor of Kendal, Cornelius Nicholson, for protection. They told the usual story – they had been driven from their work by the Scots and their huts had been pillaged or set fire to. The mayor and magistrates assembled and did what they could to help, and had a handbill printed saying that strict measures would be taken to protect the peaceable in their lawful calling and to bring offenders to justice. The Irish were sent back to work again, under cover of the mayor and magistrates, who stood by on horseback, attended by the police force of the town.

A few days later, over the border into Scotland, great masses of rioting navvies were on the march again, this time on the Edinburgh to Hawick line being built by the North British Railway. Between nine and ten o'clock one morning more than 1,000 Scots patriots, led by a piper and a bugler, were marching northwards in the direction of Edinburgh to beat up 200 Irishmen. The discontent had been seething for a long time. The navvies were living two to a bed in timber huts which resembled nothing so much as prison hulks. The food was terrible and the men complained bitterly that they were swindled at the tommy shops – as was only natural because the contractors were also the truckmen. The gangers were worthless, dissipated bullies, chosen indeed because they were bullies and thus could force their men to work. As for the contractors, they were just as much afraid of their men as the local population were, and had no control over the navvies. The work had been more hazardous than usual, many had been killed, and tunnelling had been pushed on day and night with a haste which the sheriff for the county of Edinburgh, Graham Speirs, considered inconsistent with safety. Sheriff Speirs was most unhappy: he not only deplored the way the navvy rabble lived, but he feared 'the effect that such an exhibition of social life may have on the population of Scotland'. He argued vigorously that railway companies who brought large bodies of workmen on to their lines should be obliged in some way to bring with them the means of preserving order, morality, and religion among the people. The contractors, however, were not greatly concerned with such things and Sheriff Speirs had to preserve what order he could with a force of four or five policemen on the whole line.

On top of all this, the navvies were the usual mixed lot – Scots, English, and Irish. They were segregated, of course (they had to be or no work would ever have been done), the Irish being employed on that part of the line nearer Edinburgh, and the Scots and English to the south of them. The greatest danger was always at a pay day. Trouble was bound to come, and it came on a pay day on the last Saturday of February.

At Gorebridge, about ten miles south of Edinburgh, the gangs of Irish navvies had been paid in a pub. Many of them were angry because they had received less than they thought was due to them: they were illiterate and had not kept any count of the past month's tickets which all mounted up and consumed a great part of their wages. But they had enough to get drunk on. In the course of the long drinking evening a packman arrived at the village and went to the pub. The Irish were there, by now thoroughly happy, but still with some money left. Would they like, asked the packman, to see some watches, good watches? All right, said the navvies, and two watches were handed round for inspection. That was the last the packman saw of them. When he asked for the watches back they laughed at him. What watches? There was no point in arguing with a gang of drunken Irishmen, so the packman went to the village police station and complained. Two of the carousing navvies were dragged out of the pub, arrested, and locked in one of the cells at the station.

For a while the Irish muttered to each other. Look what those damned Scots policemen had done. The news spread, the navvies gathered, the muttering grew into a universal grievance against the generality of damned Scots, and some-one began a collection, which his colleagues rapidly took up, of all the pickaxes, bludgeons, and hedge-bills to be found. By half past one in the morning there were nearly 200 Irishmen, suitably armed, and they moved off to make their representations to the police.

The two policemen who happened to be in charge at the time, Sergeant Brown and Constable Christie, tried at first to reason with the men and to prevent them from entering, but they soon saw that the Irishmen were determined and that it was impossible to stand against such a mob. For fear of their lives they gave way, and even then Sergeant Brown had his left arm disabled by a blow with the back of an axe. The rabble crowded into the station and found the cells. One of the mob then ordered the sergeant to unlock the prisoners and, when he refused, presented a pistol at his head and threatened to kill him there and then unless he did what he was told. The sergeant still refused, so the men left him alone and pulled down the cell door themselves, freed the two prisoners, and marched off with them towards Fushie Bridge, about half a mile off.

They had gone only a short distance when they met two policemen on their ordinary round, the district constable, Richard Pace, and John Veitch of the railway police. Pace and Veitch heard the rabble and tried to save themselves by hiding in a hedge, but it was too late. They were seen, pounced on, and dragged out. Veitch escaped in the scramble, but Pace was knocked senseless by a severe blow on the head from a pick handle. The Irishmen laughed at him, put the boot in as he lay on the ground, and then left him. He was all but dead. Two lads who had heard the shouts of the mob from a distance, crept up when the navvies had gone, and found the constable lying on the road only a hundred yards or so from his own house. The alarm was given, Pace was carried home, and a doctor got out of bed. But Pace was so badly hurt that he never spoke again, and at six o'clock on Sunday evening he died. He was a married man, but had no children. Veitch, the policeman who got away, was hurt about the head, but was well enough to go back on duty on Monday. By mid morning on Sunday the news had reached Edinburgh, where Alfred List, superintendent of the county police, hastily consulted with the sheriff and agreed to send a contingent of the county force, together with twenty-four of the city police, to Gorebridge. This force reached the village at midday but by then the rioters had dispersed and all was quiet.

But not for long. News of the outrages had also reached the navvies working on a stretch of the same line to the south, and these men were Scots, mostly Highlanders, and English. They hated the Irish, and resolved to extirpate the Paddies, burn their huts and be rid of them at last. All this was to be done, so it was afterwards explained, to avenge the dead policeman, who was a Scot. The rest of Sunday was given up to planning and drinking and threatening, and then, early on the Monday morning, the Scots and English moved, more than 1,000 of them by now, towards the Irish huts. The local policeman saw this gathering and sent a rider off to Edinburgh. Another detachment of the city police was sent out from Edinburgh in a coach and four, and the cavalry at Piershill barracks were alerted. But by this time the navvies were well on their way, gathering numbers as they went. At Newbattle paper mills, which they reached between nine and ten o'clock, they were joined by 150 of the Marquis of Lothian's colliers, also keen to rout the Irish. There were now nearly 1,500 on the march, and they drew themselves up in proper array, with colours flying, with a piper and bugler at their head, and armed with bludgeons and shafts which they had wrenched from the hammers and other tools belonging to the railway, not one of which remained intact.

At Chrichton Muir, to the north, the Irish waited until they saw how many were coming against them, and then they fled, some leaving their families behind. So when the Scots reached the first huts they were unopposed. They smashed and burned, and the huts of wood and turf were soon so many heaps of smouldering ruins. On again they went, and burned the huts near Borthwick Castle. One solitary row, that nearest Edinburgh, was all that now remained, and this was soon levelled with the rest. 'It was truly pitiable,' said the reporter of the *Scottish Herald*,

to see several of the wives of the Irish labourers sitting, at short distance from the blazing huts, in the midst of a few articles of furniture, which they were able to save from the flames, wrapped up in the cloaks peculiar to their country, and watching with melancholy countenances the gradual demolition of their humble dwellings.

Having set fire to all the huts of the Irish, the rabble began to disperse, though on their way back to their own camps they were tempted to break into a house at Fushie Bridge where one of the Irish contractors had taken refuge. But there were fewer of them now, they felt they had already done a good day's work, and they allowed themselves to be persuaded to leave the contractor in one piece. By four o'clock in the afternoon, after it was all over, Sheriff Speirs and his men arrived in time to inspect the ruins. Later still sixty dragoons rode in from Edinburgh. There was nothing to do except leave a large force of police and military behind to keep the precarious peace.

Next day, Tuesday, the 200 Irishmen from Edinburgh tried to march out to meet the Scots, but this time Sheriff Speirs, with his police and dragoons, got there first and persuaded them to go quietly. The Irish looked warily at the cavalry drawn up in front of them, reflected on the superior force of Scots which they would have to meet even if they got through, and walked back into the city.

The incident was over. The contractors met the homeless Irish labourers, sacked many of them, and helped the others to rebuild their huts and start work again. The new huts were put up in the same old style, in spite of the grave displeasure of the *Scottish Herald*, which, after condemning the riots, went on to say that there was, as the editors put it, another subject to which they must advert, namely, the degrading practice of having the huts of the labourers fitted up so as to accommodate the greatest number in the smallest possible space, without regard either to decency or the health and comfort of the parties occupying them. 'We were told,' said the paper,

that in each of the huts which were destroyed, the beds were ranged above one another like the berths on board ship, and that from seventeen to twenty-four families were accommodated in this manner in a temporary building of very small dimensions. The immorality which such a system is calculated to produce must be obvious to all; and it is not to be expected, that people who are subjected to such a degrading condition, and familiarized with all the indecent habits incident to it, will feel any great respect for the laws enacted for the preservation of social order.

Order was something the *Scottish Herald* greatly prized. Immediately underneath a report of the riots was an account of a temperance dinner given that same Saturday of the riots, at which

the Chairman rose and proposed, as the introductory sentiment of the evening, 'the Queen and the Royal Family'; and, in doing so, took occasion to pay a warm and well-merited tribute to Queen Victoria for the temperance, economy, punctuality, and order which characterized her court, which in this respect was so different from the Courts of some of her predecessors. The sentiment was received and applauded with great cordiality.

Sheriff Speirs searched for the murderers, but they had escaped him. With the burning of the huts by the Scots he was not unduly concerned. He seemed to think the provocation sufficient to justify the demolition of a few shanties. Afterwards he told a questioner,

I did not form a very unfavourable opinion, particularly of the Scottish labourers, on that occasion: I thought they acted under some mistaken view of the law.

A month later the sheriff still had no murderer, but someone had talked, and he had the names of two men. So he offered a reward of £50 for Peter Clark and Patrick Reilly, Irish labourers since absconded, and wanted for the murder of Constable Pace. Clark was described as thirty-five or forty, five feet eight or nine inches, stout, fair with sandy hair and whiskers, last seen wearing a blue jacket, dark greyish trousers, drab vest, green velvet shooting coat, and 'large navie boots'. Reilly was about forty, stout, five feet seven or eight, dark, with black hair, and black whiskers mixed with a few grey ones, dressed in a blue bonnet, moleskin jacket, vest, and trousers, and also wearing 'large navie boots'. But this

was a month after the murder, and by then the large navvy
boots had tramped a long way off. The murderers were not
caught.

But after a much smaller and less dangerous riot at Bathampton, near Bath, the next year, one navvy was caught and
tried for his life. One evening some labourers on the Wilts
and Somerset Railway were interrupted in a brawl by one
John Bailey, who was not in uniform but said he was a
constable and told them to stop fighting. They knocked him
about, he fell down, and died later of his injuries. Only one
of the navvies was recognized and arrested – Maurice Perry –
and he stood his trial for murder before Chief Justice Wilde.
The evidence was hardly conclusive, and the jury, returning
their verdict, said they found Perry 'guilty of being a party
concerned', but added, 'we have no evidence of his having
given the fatal blow'.

The Chief Justice said, 'Guilty of being concerned in what,
gentlemen?'

One of the jurors, 'In the murder, my lord.'

The Chief Justice, 'If he was there, with others, having a
common object to prevent the peace officer from putting an
end to the fight, that amounts to the crime of murder.'

The jury again consulted for some time, and when they
turned round many of them were in tears. The foreman then
returned a verdict of guilty, and the Chief Justice, after a little
sermon, sentenced Perry to death.

Organized riots like those at Penrith gave the navvy an
awesome name. When the memory of Napoleon grew dim,
mothers threatened to give fractious children not to him but
to a figure of equal terror – a navvy. A legend was created, and
nourished with sensational tit-bits of rumour and half-truth
dished up as news. In September 1846, the *Poole and Dorsetshire Herald* carried a paragraph about a navvy working on the
line at Ely, 170 miles away. This news item had probably
travelled from newspaper to newspaper, being copied intact
without checking, as the custom then was. This navvy, it was
said, had once been convicted of highway robbery and sentenced to hang. He was on the scaffold when a messenger with

a reprieve galloped up. 'In ten minutes the horse died from exhaustion.' The sentence was commuted to transportation for life. After ten years and nine months the man who had claimed he was robbed confessed on his death bed to the mayor, 'that he had the money in his pocket all the time, having been led to this atrocious crime by feelings of revenge'. The accused was brought back to England, granted a free pardon and given £15 for his trouble.

The popular image of navvies was that of depravity and violence, but the truth of the matter seems to be that they were 'not vicious, rather drunken, and fond of spending their time in a public house'. These are the words of a missionary employed by the Pastoral Aid Society as a railway chaplain, and such missionaries and clergymen were not commonly lenient in their judgement of the godless. The most serious disturbances were in fact religious riots, which occurred whenever Presbyterian could get at Catholic. But apart from this the affrays were little and local, and the violence casual and aimless. The trouble, as the missionary said, was nearly always drink.

Navvies drank every day at their work, but this regular drinking, though it caused many accidents, was not so great an evil as the monthly randy after the pay day. Time and time again the magistrates and police urged the railway contractors to pay weekly, to avoid the inevitable disorder which followed when the navvies were let loose with any large sum in their pockets. Again and again the contractors refused. If the men were paid weekly, they said, there would be four randies a month instead of one. This sounds a plausible argument, but in fact where the men were paid weekly, as they were by a very few contractors, the riots were fewer and the men began to save a little. The real reasons for monthly pays were first that it was less trouble for the contractors, who had to do less bookwork: and second, and much more important, that a long interval between pays was essential to a thriving truck system. If the men had ready money, as they would have if they were paid more frequently, they might buy elsewhere, for cash. But if they were paid only monthly they had no option but to live on credit from the tommy shop. It suited the contractors to pay once a month, and they could not be expected to change their ways to avoid a few riots among the lower orders. So the pays remained a perpetual danger. The men assembled in rabbles, often at the contractor's public house, and drank their accumulated wages. On the North British line, on a pay night, the whole county was a scene of riot and disorder. Sir Thomas Acland, a Member of Parliament who concerned himself with the condition of railway labourers, once asked a railway missionary:

'Will you describe what a randy is?'

'A randy is a drunken frolic.'

'Which not uncommonly terminates in a serious fight?'

'Yes.'

Robert Rawlinson, engineer, described how, when the London and Birmingham Railway was being built, the men went off on drawn-out randies:

In Northamptonshire, after midsummer, the annual feasts, first in one village, and then in another, go on for three months. Nothing would keep these men from the feasts, and joining in revelry and drunkenness, as long as they had a farthing to spare.

These were exceptionally long and lively randies, but contractors came to accept that after a monthly pay the men would not be back at work in any numbers until they had drunk themselves broke, and that generally took four or five days.

During a randy a wise man kept away. The Rev. James Gillies, chaplain on the notorious Lancaster and Carlisle line, that of the Penrith riots, usually took three services on a Sunday which he conducted in the tap-room of a place built for the navvies to drink in after the pays. It could hold 160 and the innkeeper kindly gave him the use of it on Sundays. But not every Sunday, as Mr Gillies explained: 'On the Sabbath after the monthly pay, I thought it prudent not to go near it; it was generally pretty full of those who were in a state of intemperance.'

The several days of a randy were devoted to a celebration of drunkenness, fighting, poaching, robbery, and, occasionally, high-spirited murder. The drunkenness was everywhere, and a sort of prize-fighting was common. Matches were arranged, preferably between men with a grudge against each other, and the navvies assembled to see the match fought with bare fists and until one man could go on no longer. These fights were generally long and bloody, but the fun at one scrap in the Marley Tunnel, on the South Devon line, was short. The two opponents were stripped and ready for the combat when one of them fell dead before a blow was struck.

Poaching was sport for the men, and helped provide the fresh meat that was seldom to be got at the tommy. Many navvies kept lurcher dogs and a few owned shotguns. At Bedfordshire Quarter Sessions, in the late 1870s, Mr Magniac, a magistrate, spoke urgently about a serious evil. The land-owners in the district were, he said, practically at the mercy of bands of navvies who were accustomed to go about in groups of eighteen or twenty, with guns and dogs, breaking down hedges and fences, and poaching. At other times they amused themselves by occasional assaults on the clergyman of one parish and on a building used for divine service. The men, he complained, were obviously not properly supervised – look at the way they were housed, 300 to 500 of them camped on swampy ground, with pools of green water in front of their wretched huts.

Landowners – many of whom were not in any case the best friends of the railway, whose construction they had sometimes bitterly opposed – often sat on the local bench of magistrates and imposed harsh sentences on the few poachers who were caught, thus doing one more thing to create a thriving enmity between the navvies and the ordinary people of the country-side.

When they were drunk packs of navvies were apt to steal or destroy for the delight of it, and at times their depredations were distinctly witty. Towards the end of 1845 at Katrine, on the Muirkirk and Ayr line, the Scottish population was en-raged, and the navvy camps vastly entertained, when some railway men enticed a wandering tinman into a pub, got him

drunk, and then ran away with eleven shillings from his
pockets and with the new shoes off his feet, for which they
substituted a worn old pair of boots. And at Ridgeway, in
Devon, when a party of thirty navvies fancied themselves
overcharged at the Old Ship Inn, they threatened to pull the
whole place down, and it took the under-sheriff of the county
and his forces to stop them.

As the missionary had said, more drunken than vicious. But
sometimes the mischief turned savage, as it did in June 1846
on the Leeds and Thirsk Railway. On one section there was
no pub near the works, so the shanty owners began to make
and sell beer without a licence. These mushroom beer houses
were run by the men themselves and not by the contractors,
who were therefore taking no cut, and when the men began to
spend more and more of the day drinking their own cut-
price brew, and less and less working on the line, the employers, fearing that the contract would never be finished on
time, gave orders that the illicit traffic should stop, and
locked up the barrels. The navvies were contumacious, broke
the dens open, staved in the barrels, and drank the lot. Having
got fearfully drunk, they then fell to fighting, to the terror of
the inhabitants of the village of Wescoe Hill, one of whom
told a newspaper reporter that they were all 'frightened out
of their wits at the horrible noise and reckless cruelty with
which the men prosecuted their savage conflict'. There were
hundreds all fighting together in a field of mowing grass, their
blood flowing in torrents and reminding the villagers, as they
afterwards put it, of what they had heard of the Battle of
Waterloo. When the navvies had enough they wandered off,
leaving a field of ruined grass and one dead man, whom a
villager, Joseph Cunliffe, of Otley, found lying on a heap of
stones. The navvy had two terribly bruised eyes and his face
was cut in an awful manner. No one knew at first who he was
or where he came from, but then one of his mates came forward. The poor man, he said, had been drinking all the week,
with the rest of them, but on Wednesday things went a bit
far and his companions amused themselves by stripping him
and pumping water all over him. Then they blacked him all

over with soot, and carried him about for a show. After that they sluiced him down once more, then blacked him a second time, and in the fight he was forgotten and left in the field, where he died.

This ready brutality is one side of the popular view of the navvy character. Many railway historians and newspaper reporters (like the one who wrote the report of the *Carlisle Patriot* given at the beginning of this chapter) seem unable to mention navvies without using words like forbidding coun- tenance, evil passions, finished ruffian. This you might call the Chartist-rabble doctrine. But at the same time there are other writers who, whenever they describe navvies, write of giant thews, right spirit, and fine fellows. This you might call the dignity-of-labour doctrine, and it stresses particularly the loyalty of these men to each other and to their employers. Peto said:

There is a feeling amongst all these men exceedingly creditable to them; any man who comes there, and is at all in want, his brother navvies will take care he shall have plenty of tommy. They will divide their dinner with him.

It was this same virtuous loyalty, leading men to help each other and rally round the common cause, that was one cause of many virtuous riots, particularly when the cause was religious or patriotic. And even when the men's loyalty was not to themselves but (and this was accounted an altogether higher thing) to their employers, the contractors, it often turned to violence.

Take the Norwich election riots of 1847. There were three candidates for the two seats: the Marquis of Douro, later to become the Duke of Wellington, put up by the Conservatives; Serjeant Parry, who stood as a Nonconformist; and Peto the contractor, whose supporters called him a Freetrader. The election campaign was long and vigorous, and Peto, whose liberal reputation had preceded him, became a favourite. On polling day, Thursday, 29 July, the state of the voting, which was in those days announced at hourly intervals, showed him to be leading comfortably, with the Marquis second, and

Serjeant Parry nowhere. As four o'clock drew near, the hour at which the poll would close, the roads in the centre of the city were crowded with thousands of people who had come to hear the result proclaimed. About this time a group of 200 navvies arrived from the Eastern Counties Railway where they were working for Peto. They paraded through the town, cheering their employer and boasting about his success, when a number of Parry's supporters, seeing their own candidate had lost, decided to take it out on the navvies, whom they began to hoot and hiss. Someone threw a stone, which struck a passer-by on the head, and this started a running riot, up St Andrews Street, up Post Office and Exchange Streets, into the market place. The police mixed in and made many arrests, but they could not hold the mob, which chased the navvies to the Castle Inn. The railway men saw themselves overpowered, and ran inside for shelter. This was the inn at which more than 150 people connected with the railway, contractors and share-holders, had already gathered to celebrate Peto's victory, so when the navvies crowded inside and barricaded the doors there was a regular siege – the railway party inside the inn, and the Parry mob outside. Showers of stones were hurled at the place, every window on the ground and first floors was broken, and furniture was damaged. No one was seriously hurt but in the mêlée several people in the crowd were hit by flying stones, and one was carried off with his head laid open.

This was just another navvy riot, but what is most revealing is the way it was reported in the Press. Two local papers, one of which had been markedly in favour of Peto during the election campaign, did not report the riots at all, as if wishing not to publish anything that would embarrass Peto. A third Norwich paper carried a full and sympathetic account, and *The Times* of London gave a report which fell over itself to be fair to the navvies and to vilify the town rabble. The railway men, it said, had come into the city

wishing probably to give an extra cheer to their master, Mr Peto . . . and as is frequently their wont, regaled themselves rather too plenti-fully with ale, till the jolly god, as he too often does, stole away their powers of self control, and they perambulated about the streets, shouting the most vociferous cheers for Mr Peto, keeping up their perambulations, their waving of hats, and their loud 'hurrahs', till the close of the poll.

The report goes on, after speaking of the 'ill blood of the Norwich mob' which attacked the railway men, to describe how the navvies ('jolly fellows') were belaboured somewhat unmercifully until they were rescued by the police who drove back the mob, took the navvies for their own safety to the police station, and then afterwards drove them in horse buses to the railway station, still followed by the infuriated mob, where they were packed into a special train and taken back to the railway works. The navvies' touching loyalty to their master seemed, in *The Times*' eyes, to excuse a mere riot. Peto paid for about £70 worth of damage said to have been caused by his men. Two days later, in a procession after which the two newly elected Members of Parliament were formally presented to the mayor, the navvies, now more loyal than ever, carried banners reading: 'Stand by the Queen who has Stood by You', and 'Peto, the Generous Employer'.

The best example of the navvies' lawless loyalty is that of the Battle of Mickleton. This village was on the Oxford, Worcester, and Wolverhampton Railway, and a tunnel there had caused constant trouble since it was begun in 1846. After only a few months, Brunel, who was engineer to the company, appointed a new contractor, but the work still went on slowly and in 1849 was suspended. Brunel's contractor, Marchant, started work again in 1851, but in June of that year a series of disputes between him and the company – over the exact terms of the contract, and the payment, and the ownership of the plant being used to build the tunnel – came to a head, and the company decided to take possession of the works and hand them over for completion to Peto & Betts, the contractors for the rest of the line. Marchant would have nothing of it. He declined to hand over the works or the plant, and kept his navvies on guard against the company's men. Whenever the new contractors tried to take possession they were driven off by Marchant's men, and after several such skirmishes Brunel resolved to finish the matter off himself. On Friday, 20 July, he and his assistant, Varden, went to the tunnel with a considerable body of men to take over. But the contractor had heard rumours of this and complained to the local magistrates, saying that if they did not attend and read the Riot Act there might be a fight. So when Brunel and his party arrived they were confronted by magistrates, who warned them not to commit a breach of the peace. Brunel retired until the next day, when he returned to the tunnel early in the morning, hoping that the magistrates would have considered their duty done and left. He was wrong. The magistrates were still there, and they had been joined by a large force of policemen armed with cutlasses. On one side stood Brunel and his navvies, on the other Marchant and his men guarding the works, and between them the law. A fight seemed inevitable, but a magistrate mumbled through the Riot Act twice, and under this threat and that of the police cutlasses the navvies again withdrew.

Later that Saturday Brunel and Varden, playing at generals, discussed how they could mount a surprise attack. They did not scruple to take the works by force from Marchant, but they thought it unwise to get into a fight with armed policemen. What they had to do now was what they had failed to do before – mislead the magistrates into thinking they had given up hope of taking the works and then, after the magistrates had gone happily home, swoop on Marchant and catch him on the hop. So that evening, and all day Sunday, Brunel's men made no move, and the magistrates left the tunnel. They were deceived, because although Brunel appeared to be doing nothing he used that Sunday to organize reinforcements. Navvies were marched up from other parts of the line, from the works of the Birmingham and Oxford Railway at Warwick, and from the Great Western. In the darkness of Sunday night and early Monday morning gangs of navvies awoke village after village as they tramped through, alarming the whole countryside but not stopping long enough to do any damage. Reports vary, but it seems likely that about 2,000 navvies assembled under Brunel's command. His idea was to overawe Marchant by a show of strength, and to persuade him to hand over the works. At three o'clock on Monday morning the navvies began to close in on the tunnel and the Battle of Mickleton began.

At the Worcester end of the tunnel, a Mr Cowderey and his band of 200 men from Evesham were met by Marchant, who brandished pistols and said he would shoot the first man who went any farther. In the face of the pistols Cowderey was discreet and told his men – who were ready to devour the handful of labouring boys escorting Marchant – on no account to strike a blow. The navvies waited with their pickaxes and shovels. Then Brunel gave his orders for a general attack on the works. The navvies dodged round Marchant, who did not shoot, and launched into the boys with fists, using spades only on one man who drew a pistol. They hit him on the head, but gently, so that he survived. In fact no one was killed, though several heads were broken and three men had shoulders dislocated.

Marchant retreated for the moment, leaving his opponents in full possession of the tunnel, but after an hour he came back with three dozen policemen, some privates of the Gloucestershire Artillery, and two magistrates, who immediately began reading the Riot Act again. While they were doing this a fight broke out on an embankment overlooking the tunnel. Several men suffered broken limbs, and one John M. Grant was nearly trampled to death but was rescued just in time. Brunel's reinforcements continued to increase. Another 200 from Warwick arrived, and a similar force from the Great Western. The main bodies just stood and faced each other, but odd fighting went on around the edges and in the half-darkness. The magistrates, who had all along favoured Marchant as the man who was being attacked, suggested that he might occupy his men by setting them to work. He did this, but the Peto men were immediately ordered to stop them, by force if necessary. Two small batches of navvies again met, and in the affray one little finger was bitten off and one head badly wounded. All day long little fights started and petered out, until Marchant saw at last that he was outnumbered, and gave in. He went to Brunel and they agreed to refer the whole dispute to the arbitration of the firm of Stephenson & Cubitt, celebrated railway contractors. The peace was concluded at four in the afternoon, just before the troops, called in to help the police, arrived from Coventry. The battle was over.

In their August report the directors of the company were mainly concerned about other things. The shareholders were critical of the way the company's financial affairs were being handled, and *The Times*' report of the meeting was punctuated by explanatory words in brackets like (Oh, oh! and confusion) and (Hear, hear, and shame). But the Battle of Mickleton Tunnel was mentioned, the directors reporting that the company had taken possession of the works, 'without absolute violence . . . although the menacing conduct of the contractor had at one time rendered such an issue probable'.

Once again great bands of navvies had rioted, but this time, as with the Norwich affair, it was all in the cause of loyalty to their employers and was therefore all right. The most telling point was made by poor Marchant in a letter printed in the *Railway Times*. He said that he and his partner had paid £10,000 for the plant at the works and that attempts had been made to take this plant from him violently; he denied that he had ever drawn a pistol in the fight, and then went on to say this:

I may leave Messrs Peto and Betts to defend themselves against the charge of having consented to the march of two thousand men on a Sunday for the purpose of taking possession of my property by force.

Just so. Did Peto, the good Baptist, know that his men were being marched about on a Sunday? Did Peto, the Member of Parliament, know that what was virtually a private army was being used to take the tunnel by an illegal show of force? And what of Brunel? Peto may not have known what was being done by his assistants, but Brunel was there. At the least he was promoting, organizing, and then leading a series of riots, playing soldiers to the great danger of some hundreds

of men and incurring casualties of several broken bones and
one little finger. The violence of navvies looks mighty innocent compared with this lawlessness of the men who used
them. But then, as the company directors said, the tunnel was
taken 'without absolute violence', whatever that may mean.

7

Woodhead

WOODHEAD is a small Cheshire village of never more than a few houses and now almost deserted, whose only distinction is that it gave its name to the most degraded adventure of the navvy age – the Woodhead Tunnel. The village is on a narrow peninsula of Cheshire which reaches out eastward through Lancashire and Derbyshire into Yorkshire. It is high and wild moorland where the wind is bitter even on a soft day. The only things that seem to belong to the place are sheep and railway tunnels – the sheep because the heath and bogs are good for nothing else, and the tunnels because Woodhead is midway between Sheffield and Manchester and because, although the engineering was almost impossibly hazardous, this was the easiest way to take the line through the Pennines. The first tunnel made there was three miles thirteen yards long, and at the time was the longest in Britain, more than twice the length of Brunel's magnificent Box Tunnel near Bath.

There have been three Woodhead tunnels. The first, for a single line of rail, was built from 1839 to 1845. The second, to take another single line for the uproad, was bored alongside the first in the years 1847 to 1852. The third tunnel, a modern work which takes a double electric line, was completed in June 1954. At the official opening ceremony on 3 June, the then Minister of Transport said, 'All of us here believe that the railways have a future as important as their very great past.' The story of the very great past at Woodhead is that of the two old tunnels, and that is a story of heroic savagery, magnificent profits, and devout hypocrisy.

The Sheffield, Ashton under Lyne, and Manchester Railway Company was formed in 1835, and its proposed line was authorized by an Act of Parliament of 1837. Plans were commissioned both from Charles Blacker Vignoles, a military engineer of high reputation, and from Joseph Locke, one of the finest railway engineers of the age, whom *The Times*, in his obituary, was to call one of the great triumvirate, the others being Robert Stephenson and Brunel. Vignoles's plans were preferred, he was appointed engineer to the company, and Lord Wharncliffe, the first chairman of the railway, cut the first sod with a ceremonial spade at Saltersbrook, a mile or so east of Woodhead, on 1 October 1838. The tunnel was to run from Woodhead in Cheshire on the western side, to Dunford Bridge in Yorkshire on the east. Vignoles estimated the cost first at £60,000 and then at £100,000. Things did not go well. There was animosity between Vignoles and Locke, who seems to have been retained as a consultant engineer, and between Vignoles and the board of the company, who were reluctant to spend anything more than they had to. It was only after a struggle that the company agreed to provide tents for the 400 men who had begun the first shaft at the western end, and who had been sleeping in the open. But most of the men had to look after themselves, and as the winter drew in they bivouacked in huts run up with loose stones and mud and thatched with ling from the moors, and slept on truckle-beds in groups of twenty.

For Vignoles nothing went happily. Often there was no money for the works, and when there was the constant rain made the mining difficult and the construction of access roads impossible. Vignoles was pursued by rain. In August 1839, at a house he had taken at Dinting Dale, a few miles away from the works, he gave a banquet in honour of the coming of age of his eldest son, Charles. All the county was invited, marquees were erected on the lawns, and the festivities were to spread over two days. It rained: for two days it rained.

By this time Vignoles was in serious difficulties with the board. Two years before, when the company had been in some financial distress, he had himself bought shares which were otherwise unsaleable. When the company recovered somewhat, he declined to sell these shares at a profit and retained them. In 1839 the company's affairs were again precarious and the shares were not only worthless but a liability. Vignoles was unable to pay the calls made by the company. He went to the chairman, Lord Wharncliffe, and they made a gentleman's agreement that Vignoles should renounce his shares, in effect that he should lose the money he had already paid for them but should be released from his liability to pay the calls which were due. But this agreement was repudiated by the board, Lord Wharncliffe resigned, and Vignoles, knowing he could not pay, also left the company. The directors did not forget their old animosity to the engineer and sued him, forcing him to assign all his property to pay what he could of the calls. In all he lost £80,000. In later years Vignoles was to recover his fortune, but in 1841 he was broken. He wrote in his diary for 15 January of that year: 'Good God, that men whom I had served so faithfully and for whose railway I had done so much, should act like this.'

Meanwhile Locke had been appointed in Vignoles's place, and the work went on with vigour. The new engineer dismissed the small contractors who had undertaken the work in the first years, and in 1842 let the western part of the work to Richard Hattersley, and the eastern to Thomas Nicholson. Wellington Purdon, the man engaged as assistant engineer by Vignoles, was retained, and his name and that of Nicholson crop up again and again in the history of the first tunnel. Nicholson was a self-made man. He began as a labourer, worked on the Stockton and Darlington Railway, and originally came to Woodhead as one of the company's supervisors of the works. The contract for the eastern tunnel was his first big venture as a contractor. He lived till the age of seventy, and died in 1861 when he was knocked down by an engine as he inspected a viaduct at Ingleton. Purdon was the only engineer to stay for the entire six years it took to complete the first Woodhead Tunnel, and he was later to achieve notoriety for his refusal to use safety fuses because they wasted time.

In 1842 the new contractors needed more navvies, and this is where conditions, which had always been bad, became much worse. The original force of 400 men had grown to nearly 1,000, who were living in something hardly less than out-and-out savagery. All the company had done was build about forty stone shelters for them. Most of these men had been working under the supervision of Nicholson at Woodhead on the western side, and when Nicholson got the contract for the eastern side at Dunford Bridge he took his men with him. These navvies were decidedly the better sort, because he had been able to pick them at a time when hands were plentiful and work scarce. They had had some time to settle in huts they built themselves, and perhaps to bring their families with them, and were by then experienced in the work.

But Hattersley, when he came to the Woodhead end, had to take what he could get. He advertised for labourers when jobs were plentiful and at a time when the works were getting a bad name because of the number of accidents. It was also being confidently predicted that the tunnel would never be finished. The tunnelling was proving more and more difficult; the first estimate of £60,000 had by then risen to £200,000, and this in a period of tight money when more and more shareholders were finding themselves, like poor Vignoles, unable to pay their calls. The sceptics were remembering George Stephenson's remark, made some years before when the plans were first drawn up, that he would eat the first locomotive to go through the tunnel.

So Hattersley had to pay higher wages to get anyone, and he assembled a rabble. The average number of navvies on the works is generally put at about 1,100, but at one time there were 1,500 and more, tunnelling into twelve different rock faces at once. One gang worked in from each end, and two (one eastward and the other westward) from the foot of each of the five shafts which had been bored down into the moorside. Some of the men suffered a sort of claustrophobia, because the shafts were only ten feet in diameter, and the tunnel only fifteen feet high and eighteen across.

At its highest point the moor above Woodhead is more than 1,500 feet above sea-level. The tunnel itself goes through the Pennines at a height of about 1,000 feet, and the depth of the longest shaft is 579 feet. The miners had to blast their way through millstone grit, shales, softer red sandstone, slate, and clay. Much of the rock was treacherous, and all but 1,000 yards of the tunnel had to be lined with masonry to prevent falls from the roof. All this was done by fits and starts. When there was no money there was no work; when the company had raised some more cash the work went on uninterrupted by day and night. Purdon explained the need for this night work.

In great railway works, the interest [upon the money borrowed] is so great when it is spread over a number of years, and the company sacrifice that interest until the line comes into operation, and they bind their contractors to knock off the work quickly to save the enormous amount of interest; this requires them to man the work in a very masterly style.

Shortage of money was one difficulty, but a far greater one was the isolation of the place. The nearest town of any size was Glossop, nine miles off, and even when the railway was built up to the two ends of the uncompleted tunnel, provisions had to be lugged up the steep hills on to the moors to the navvy encampments round the shafts. In his *Life of Joseph Locke*, published in 1862, Joseph Devey wrote that the difficulties of getting provisions to the place proved almost as great as those of victualling Balaclava. In June 1845 John Roberton, a Manchester surgeon, went to see these encampments. The huts, he said, were a curiosity, mostly of stones without mortar, or of mud, with a roof of thatch or flags, and generally put up by the men themselves. One workman would build a hut for his family, and also lodge some of his fellow navvies. Some huts contained as many as fourteen or fifteen men. Many were filthy dens.

While he was inspecting the huts at the Woodhead end of the tunnel Roberton met Henry Pomfret, also a surgeon, who lived at Hollingworth about eight miles away, and who went up to the tunnel three days a week to treat the injured. He also went up whenever he was called, often at night-time, if there had been an accident. He was retained not by the railway company or the contractors but by the men themselves, who paid so much a week as a voluntary contribution, and had

chosen Pomfret by a vote. The men liked him, and he faithfully slogged up to the tunnel in all weathers and at all hours,
but since he lived so far away it frequently took him two
hours to get there. He had contracted to treat the men for
ordinary sicknesses as well as for injuries, but he spent most
of his time operating on the smashed-up limbs of men caught
by rock falls. When he met Roberton that day Pomfret said
he did what he could, but that it was difficult to conceive of a
set of people more thoroughly depraved, degraded, and reckless. They were utterly drunken and dissolute – a man, he
said, would lend his wife for a gallon of beer – and more than
half of them, men and women, suffered from syphilis. Most
of the accidents, he said, were caused by the general recklessness and drunkenness; many men habitually went to work
drunk.

Before he left that day Roberton asked Pomfret for a list of
casualties, which he agreed to prepare, and Roberton returned to Manchester 'painfully impressed', as he said, and
went to tell his tale to a friend, the superintendent of the
Manchester and Salford Town Mission. The superintendent
went to the tunnel himself on the following two Sundays and
reported to Roberton that the men were indeed in a demoralized condition, 'for the work goes on by night as well
as day, and on Sunday the same as other days, and such has
been the case from the commencement'. The superintendent
went into the huts, talked to the men, whom he found in a
'most brutish state', and found himself agreeing with everything Roberton and Pomfret had said, except that he seemed
to find the wife-lending less serious than he had feared because, as he put it, 'many of the women in the huts were not
wives, but "tally-women", i.e. women who had followed the
men as their mistresses'.

Anyway, the superintendent thought the men's need was
great, so he sent a missionary to live among them for three
months. This man kept a journal, and from this and from
Roberton's remarks it is possible to piece together a detailed
picture of the way the navvies worked and lived during that
autumn of 1845.

As the superintendent had said, work went on as usual on Sundays, and the missionary was particularly concerned about this. It was not just the pumping of water from the shafts and other maintenance work which was done on the Sabbath – this was felt to be essential and therefore allowable – but the main work of blasting and digging. On Sunday, 3 August, the journal records:

Went into the tunnel, passed to No. 2 shaft, and saw about a hundred miners, labourers and others at work; also outside the tunnel at the Manchester end of the entrance, about eighteen or twenty men were employed boring and blasting the rock: a number of shots went off, and shook the school-house, at the time when we were engaged in prayer, at our afternoon meeting.

The work itself was not only dangerous but thoroughly miserable. The tunnel was generally ankle-deep in mud, sometimes knee-deep. Water ran down the side of the walls, and the men, parched by the work and the closeness of the tunnel, drank this muddy effluence and suffered from chronic diarrhoea. But the wages were good. Joiners earned five shillings and masons six shillings for a ten-hour day, miners four to five shillings for an eight-hour day. But when the work was urgent, and men scarce, navvies were asked to work double and treble shifts, and the horses, and the boys who drove them, worked on as well.

The men were paid once in nine weeks, sometimes once every thirteen weeks. Out of the wages the contractors withheld three halfpence a day from every man, to pay the surgeon, to help pay the schoolmaster (a school was at one time established at No. 3 shaft, but later abandoned because so few attended), and to pay into the sick fund, which provided a man with eight shillings a week when he was hurt or ill. Besides this it was the custom, when a navvy was killed, for each man to pay a shilling to cover the expenses of the funeral and to leave a bit over for the widow.

The navvies suffered greatly from the truck system. By 1845 the railway had already been built up to the mouth of the western end of the tunnel and so there was cheap and easy carriage of goods from Manchester and Ashton. Despite this, said Roberton, it was perhaps to be expected that a crowd of people camped on a desert moor should have to pay rather dear for their provisions, but he was astonished at the prices demanded at the tommy shops, 20 to 50 per cent above Manchester prices.

Flour was 2s. 8d. a stone, tub butter ('of very indifferent odour') 1s. 1d. a pound, but the most surprising thing was the price of potatoes, 1s. 2d. a score. At first Roberton doubted this, as the highest price in Manchester was only eightpence, but he asked at several huts and the story was the same everywhere. Beer, too – 'represented as very inferior' – cost dear, sixpence a quart. The shops belonged directly or indirectly to the contractors, and the interval of nine weeks or so between pays was so long that the men had to rely on tickets to get food. And at Woodhead the contractors, with their eye on the greater profit, made beer tickets easier to get than food tickets. A man could have a food ticket only at certain times, but a beer ticket could be had at any time of the day, up to the amount of a man's earnings and sometimes even beyond that, so that he was living on double credit. Roberton gave this example of the way beer tickets drained a man's earnings:

. . . A workman carries a five-shilling ticket to one of the beer shops, and asks to have out of it, a quart of beer. The drink is furnished, and the ticket with 'quart' written on the back of it goes up on the file of the publican. The man has, it may be, glass after glass, gets intoxicated, and at length, in this state, goes home. On returning again, the following day, trusting to the ticket in the file, it will often happen that he finds his credit exhausted; he must bring another ticket: altercation ensues, the man accuses the publican of cheating, and thus uproars, fights, and (it may be surmised) the grossest roguery, are of perpetual occurrence . . . It was evidently a sore subject with the workpeople, one of whom exclaimed to me, 'They give us great wages, sir, but they take it all from us again.' . . .

The men, women, and children, Roberton said, did not give the impression of enjoying vigorous, comfortable health, though there were some exceptions. Some of the younger children appeared flabby and others very pale, and the adults wore a look of exhaustion and dissipation which the mission

superintendent thought was caused by the universal drunkenness and irregular sleep. Many of the night workers, he said,
drank all day when they ought to have been in their beds. The
infrequent pays, which were conveniently made at a public
house, were followed by days of rout and rowdiness. July 11,
1845 was a pay night, and on the 14th the missionary wrote
in his journal that everywhere were fights, disorder, and
drunkenness. The six constables employed to keep order on
the whole works, kept their distance.

For days the men were so drunk they just reeled around and
were incapable of anything except casual violence. Asked if
he had seen any gambling among them, Pomfret replied: 'I
cannot say I did; I think they used to be too far gone to think
of that.' But there was, he said, plenty of fighting.

The men's exhaustion was not caused only by their own
drunkenness and brutality. Many had chronic coughs, which
they blamed on the moistness of the tunnel. Their clothes
became soaked before they had been at work a quarter of an
hour. Roberton asked a woman in one of the huts how ten or
fourteen lodgers in one hut could dry all their wet clothes by
a single fire. She answered that the clothes were seldom half
dry. Pomfret said the coughs were caused by this perpetual
dampness and also by the inhaling of dense gunpowder
smoke with which the tunnel was commonly filled.

The men also suffered most atrociously from accidents.
When Pomfret prepared the list he had promised Roberton,
it showed that thirty-two men had been killed, several
maimed, and what Roberton called an almost incredible
number less seriously injured. The list included:

23 cases of compound fracture, including two fractured skulls.
74 simple fractures, including three of the clavicle, two of the
   scapula, one of the patella and one of the astralagus.
140 serious cases, including burns from blasts, severe contusions,
   lacerations and dislocations.

One man, said Pomfret, lost both his eyes, and another half
his foot. One man had his arm broken by the blast, which also
burnt the arm, one eye, and all that side of his head and face.

Several men had broken ribs. There were also about 400 minor accidents, including trapped and broken fingers (seven of which had to be amputated), injuries to the feet, lacerations of the scalp, bruises and broken shins, though some of these smaller injuries were caused by the men fighting among themselves.

This is not a complete list of all injuries on the tunnel, because the men on the eastern end had, for two years out of the six, been attended by another surgeon. Furthermore, at the time Pomfret drew up his list, in July 1845, there was still another four months' work to be done.

Later Edwin Chadwick was to write:

Thirty-two killed out of such a body of labourers, and one hundred and forty wounded, besides the sick, nearly equal the proportionate casualties of a campaign or a severe battle. The losses in this one work may be stated as more than three per cent of killed, and fourteen per cent wounded. The deaths (according to the official returns) in the four battles, Talavera, Salamanca, Vittoria and Waterloo, were only 2·11 per cent of privates; and in the last forty-one months of the Peninsula war the mortality of privates in battle was 4·2 per cent, of disease 11·9 per cent.

An eminent engineer of mining works in Cornwall, where mining was still at this time a thriving industry, said that the number of lives lost on the Woodhead Tunnel was evidence of gross mismanagement.

One of the commonest causes of accidents was the use of iron stemmers in blasting. A stemmer is a ram used to pack first the powder and then the filling of clay into a drilled hole. Stemming was dangerous because sometimes the stemmer struck against the rock into which the bore hole had been made, and the sparks ignited the powder. After several men had been wounded two or three times each, Pomfret suggested to Purdon that the stemmers should be made of copper, which was softer and less likely to strike sparks. But Purdon only told him to mind his own business and leave that sort of thing to the engineers. Purdon had strange ideas of an engineer's responsibilities, and the next year, 1846, he was to have a rough time with the Commons Select Committee.

Towards the beginning of his evidence he was to tell them: 'An engineer should see that no improper materials are used, and no system of operation involving danger: he should not permit weak ropes in shafts; high lifts in tunnelling.'

But when he was questioned about stemmers he said the copper kind were too dear. Question and answer then went like this:

'You thought, on the part of the company, that it was worth while running the risk of two or three men's lives rather than go to the expense of more expensive tools?'

'You must prove to me that any man's life was lost.'

'I will read to you from Mr Nicholson's pamphlet [this was Thomas Nicholson, who had published a pamphlet defending himself and the company against allegations of neglect]: "William Jackson, miner, No. 5 shaft. He was looking over John Webb's shoulder, while he was stemming a hole charged with powder, when the blast went off, blowing the stemmer through Jackson's head and killed him on the spot."'

'The copper stemmers are so very soft on the head, that they are objectionable.'

The committee left the subject of stemmers. In response to other questions Purdon said he had taken a great aversion to 'anything like Government officers interfering with details in the case of engineers', and then that perhaps twenty-six deaths had occurred. 'I think it may be possible,' he said, 'one or two more or less, somewhere thereabouts.'

A few moments later he was asked if patent fuses were used in blasting. No, he said. The committee persisted. Wasn't this sort of fuse safer? Purdon made his celebrated reply.

'Perhaps it is; but it is attended with such a loss of time, and the difference is so very small, I would not recommend the loss of time for the sake of all the extra lives it would save.'

He was then asked:

'Would not a jar or two of acid, and a few yards of wire, be all that was required?'

'That is all the material but the application of it is a great loss of time.'

At Woodhead neither the contractors nor the company paid

any compensation to the families of men killed. Purdon, asked if he had ever made representation to the Board that they should make any such compensation, replied that he had found 'great unwillingness on the part of the Board to listen to such a thing; they did not wish to admit the principle'. The company admitted few principles, and the work was done to no known rules. Pomfret said: 'It has been said that there were certain rules (I never saw them or knew what they were) for the men to go by.'

So the men worked by day and night up to their knees in water, the injured were patched up and left to recover in the boiler houses at the shafts (the warmest places, though rain still dripped in on them as they lay), and the dead were given a hasty inquest and burial. These inquests were formal: in the six years he was surgeon at the tunnel, Pomfret was never once called upon to give medical evidence of the cause of death.

But among all this bodily misery it was the irreligion of the men which seems most to have concerned those who were prepared to be concerned at anything at all. Roberton said:

The forlorn condition, in a religious sense, of the hurt and the sick . . . cannot be imagined by those who are in the habit of regarding England as a Christian country. . . . There have been examples of destitution in this particular, such, it is probable, as would scarcely occur in one of our most remote colonies.

But the clergy, shocked by this religious destitution, did little about it. There was a small chapel of St James at Woodhead, about three miles from the western entrance to the tunnel; it was not a parish church in its own right, but a curate from Mottram in Longdendale, nine miles away, used to conduct services there. For a short time he lived at Woodhead and went occasionally to give lectures to the navvies, but he scarcely considered the men at the tunnel to be his parishioners. At the other, eastern, end of the tunnel, the nearest parish church was at Penistone, six miles away, where the vicar, from 1841 onwards, was Samuel Sunderland, who had the reputation of being a humane man. But over those

moors, and over the cart-tracks, six miles was a long way, and
Mr Sunderland appears to have done little but bury some of
the men. Only the nonconformists seem to have done more
than pray for the navvies. Devey wrote in his life of Locke:

They were visited by dissenting ministers who preached to them
in rainy weather under tarpauling canvas, and who appeared more
zealous in proportion as their eyes were opened to the utter hope-
lessness of their mission.

The services of a surgeon, said Devey, were far more in
request than those of his clerical colleagues.

Roberton said that until he told his friend the superintendent of the Manchester and Salford Town Mission – 'an
excellent Moravian' – of the moral state of the men, little had
been done to visit the sick or wounded, or to give the men
religious instruction. He said:

One or two clergymen, and the Methodists . . . have occasionally
done a little – nothing, however, worth mentioning. The missionary's journal, and the aspect and manners of the people, furnish
evidence of a state of neglect and destitution, in reference to all that
concerns religion, utterly disgraceful to the directors of the railway,
and to the conductors of the works; and to the public also, who
have for so many years heedlessly and criminally winked at it.

The Salford missionary did what he could. Of course he
sold bibles, and the navvies bought from him, 'at somewhat
reduced prices', twenty-two bibles, seventy Testaments, and
thirty-six prayer books. But he also visited and comforted the
men. In his journal for 8 July he writes:

Going over the moor, this morning, met two women. One said:
'Have you not sometimes been to pray for Johnson?' I said I had.
He is dead, said she; I have just laid him out; it is but little more
than six years since I came to live on these hills, and he is the
twenty-ninth man I have laid out, and the first of them who died a
natural death.

The deaths of most of these men are remembered only in
burial registers. That for Penistone church records the burial
there on 5 March 1845 of 'A Stranger (Excavator) from

Kendal'. The entry says he died in the workhouse, that the
burial was conducted by S. Sunderland, and guesses that the
unnamed man was fifty-five years old. There was not even a
nickname, or perhaps the nickname was not thought proper
for the register.

The register at Woodhead includes the names, among
others, of Robert Blackburne ('killed from the falling in of
earth from a cutting on the railroad'), John Young, John
Thorpe, Mark Shepley, John Elliot. The children died too.
Lucy Kenning (Tunnel, No. 3 shaft) aged one; Samuel
Ollerenshaw, infant; and many more.

Although the graves are today unmarked, and perhaps
there never were any headstones, the navvy funerals were
decently conducted. Thomas Nicholson wrote:

A good oak coffin, provided at my expense, and the person at
his death, if he had friends, was given up to them, to be interred
wherever they thought proper, the club paying the expenses. If they
had no friends they were buried either at Penistone or Woodhead:
and I have heard the public remark their entire satisfaction of the
way in which these men were interred. The usual allowance for
parties attending the funeral is a dinner and one quart of ale.

Nicholson was convinced not only of the public's entire
satisfaction, but also that there was 'no instance of any misconduct at a funeral'. Except, he added, at William Lee's.
Now the death of this man Lee concerned many people.
Only Nicholson mentioned him by name, but he had, as
Nicholson complained, been 'said much about'. Lee was a
miner, aged about fifty-five, and very corpulent. One day in
January 1842 he was walking near the capstan of the horse
gin. It was windy and he was walking with his head down
when one of the arms of the capstan struck him on the breast
and threw him to the ground, terribly injuring him. He lived
for ten days, until 28 January.

The first to mention the man was Roberton. 'Take the case,'
he said,

of a fine, powerful workman, who had the spine fractured in such
a way as to preclude all hope of recovery. Although this man

1. Excavation at Olive Mount on the Liverpool and Manchester, c. 1828

2. Navvies at work at the mouth of the Church Tunnel on the London and Birmingham

3. Barrow runs at Boxmoor on the London and Birmingham, c. 1837

4. Tring Cutting on the London and Birmingham

5. Wolverton Embankment on the London and Birmingham

6. A young navvy of the 1840s

7. Navvy on the tramp, 1855

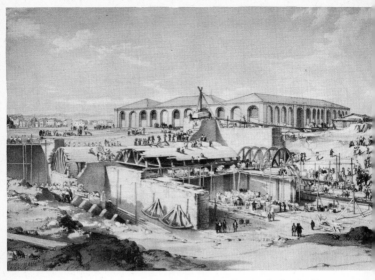

8. Building the engine shed at Camden on the London and Birmingham

9. Building the retaining wall at Camden on 17 September 1836, probably the scene described by Dickens in *Dombey and Son*

10. In the Kilsby Tunnel on the London and Birmingham

11. The Dutton Viaduct on the Grand Junction Railway

12. Memorial in the shape of a tunnel in the churchyard at Otley, Yorkshire, to navvies killed making the Bramhope Tunnel on the Leeds and Thirsk Railway, 1845–9. Mrs Elizabeth Garnett, the navvy missionary, came from Otley and knew this memorial as a child

13. Making a cutting on the Great Western, 1841

14. Blasting rocks near Linslade on the London and Birmingham

15. Brassey's navvies' feast in the open air at Maisons in 1843 after the Paris–Rouen Railway was finished. French cavalry were there to keep order

16. Roasting a whole ox for the feast. The three chefs were French. The spit turner, drinking from a bottle, was English

17. Navvy carrying his dinner, 1855

18 & 19. Men of the Crystal Palace gang at Sydenham in 1853. These are the first known photographs of navvies

20. Navvies in the waiting-room at Euston en route for Liverpool and the Crimea say good-bye to their families and, on the right, sign papers ordering part of their wage to be paid to their dependants

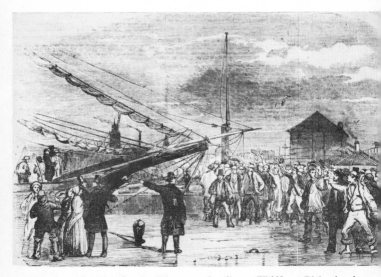

21. Navvies embarking for the Crimea on the clipper *Wildfire* at Birkenhead in December 1854

22 & 23. *Punch* cartoons of the winter of 1854–5 when navvies were shipped to the Crimea to build a supply railway which rescued the British Army. (22) the popular view of what the navvies would do to the Russians. (23): one navvy is saying to the other, 'Ah, Bill! It shows the forrard march of the age. Fust the brute force, such as 'im; and then the likes of us to do it scientific, and show the might of intellect.'

24. Alexander
Anderson,
navvy poet

25. Elizabeth
Garnett,
navvy missionary

26. Boys with tip-truck on the Wootton Underwood to Hadenham section of the Great Central, c. 1896

27. Navvies' dinner-time at Sulgrave on the Great Central

28. Breakfast in old cellars at Nottingham on the Great Central

29. Navvies on the Wootton Underwood section of the Great Central

pleaded again and again to have the scriptures read to him, with religious counsel, the request was in vain; for, after remaining many days in a sinking state, he was suffered to expire without having received the least attention of the nature he so earnestly craved.

The Commons Select Committee was to hear more. When Pomfret gave his evidence he said he remembered a man with a broken back who had for several days asked for a clergyman to visit him. No clergyman came, said Pomfret. The chairman of the committee then asked:

'How near does the clergyman reside to the place where this man lay?'

'Nine miles. I think the neglect may be attributed to this circumstance, there was some little disagreement about the district.'

'Do the clergymen ever think it their duty to attend?'

'I conveyed a message about this man myself to the clergyman, and he said he would attend, and I borrowed a horse for him, but he never availed himself of it.'

'Did you ever hear what reason was assigned for his not attending in the case you alluded to?'

'Engagements about home, I believe.'

'The result was that this man went without?'

'The result was that I went to a Methodist and offered him a day's wages to go, and the man died before he got to the house.'

Pomfret probably means, when he talks about a 'little disagreement about the district', that it was not certain in which parish the man lay. The boundary between Cheshire and Yorkshire runs across the moors between the two entrances to the tunnel, and neither the vicar of Penistone in Yorkshire, nor the vicar of Mottram in Cheshire, wanted to claim the man as his own.

Nicholson later became angry over all the fuss. After writing sorrowfully of Roberton's 'allusion' to Lee, he turned on Pomfret and criticized him, plainly in ignorance of what had happened. Writing of Lee's wish for a clergyman, Nicholson added: '... now, I ask, who was a more suitable person to

convey this wish to a minister than the surgeon who was
visiting him daily? Did the surgeon convey such a message?'

But Nicholson seems put out not so much because Lee died
unconsoled as because there was some misconduct at the
funeral. Lee had been living with his second wife. At the
funeral his two sons by his former wife caused 'some confusion' by insisting that the money paid by the sick club to
the dead man's relatives should be given to them and not to
the second wife. Nicholson refused and paid the woman.

Nicholson was altogether most indignant that the tunnel
should have got such a dreadful reputation, and in his
pamphlet, which he had printed in defence of his employers
and more particularly of his own character and that of the
workmen, he denied nearly everything. True, some men had
died, and he gave a list. Samuel Hawkins, a miner aged fifty,
had been coming up No. 4 shaft when he banged his head on
a horse tree (a cross-beam) and fell out of the bucket. He lived
fifteen hours afterwards. Then there were William Holt and
George Cook, and James Holt – who fell only eleven feet but
broke his neck – and Thomas Houghton and Neal Livingston
and Joseph Leaver, the last three killed all at once by one fall
of rock, but it was their own fault. Often, he said, the men
just did not look out for themselves – take the case of Richard
Moore. He was a labourer, and on 13 August 1844 he left a
pub at about ten at night and promptly killed himself by
falling down the west face of the tunnel. There had also, said
Nicholson, been some minor accidents, but the men hadn't
suffered much. James Derbyshire and William Chadwick,
miners at No. 1 shaft, had been drilling the stemming out of
a blast hole that had hung fire when the lot went off in their
faces. Derbyshire lost an eye but was able to go back to work
again later, and as for William Chadwick, he was 'one of the
greatest blackguards that ever came to the tunnel', and after
drawing pay from the sick club for eighteen months he was
sacked for getting drunk and fighting. Both his eyes had been
hurt and he was a little disfigured, but he could still see and
got work in Manchester as a bricklayer.

As for Pomfret, said Nicholson, that talented surgeon had

been so anxious to make up the number of injured that he had included a few men with scratched faces they had probably got from their wives. The Moravian missionary? – they might as well have sent a Moravian horse, which would have understood tunnelling just as well. And the woman who had told the missionary she had laid out twenty-nine men – Nicholson knew all about her. She was Sarah Alberson, a woman who used to get drunk with her husband while their children were left to fend for themselves. She would say anything for a glass of gin. Was she a woman whose word was to be trusted? Anyway, why send a missionary to a wilderness like Woodhead where about a thousand men were collected and expect to find them all perfect, well educated, and of religious habits? Clergymen should worry about the labourers of their own parishes, and not concern themselves with those working on a wild mountain.

The food, too, had been pretty good. Treacle, sugar, tea, flour, butter, cheese, bacon – Nicholson recited this list of wholesome things as if to convince the world that his navvies had lived off nothing but the best. The tobacco now, that had been supplied by Mr Smith of Sheffield; warranted genuine, threepence-halfpenny an ounce. The beef Nicholson had bought himself in Rotherham market, and he could bring some of the most respectable butchers to prove that it was the best in the market. He could also distinctly prove, and did most solemnly declare, that he had never had any connexion, direct or indirect, with any beer house and had never taken any percentage from beer sold to the men. Look what he had done in the case of Thackray, who kept a public house in Wakefield which was supported chiefly by the loose characters of the town. This man got a grant of land at Dunford Bridge from one George Hall, a religious man supposed to be a Methodist, and they applied for a licence. But Nicholson and Purdon used their influence with the magistrates, the licence was refused, and Thackray went back to Wakefield. 'Now mind you,' said Nicholson, still touchy about the accusations that the tunnel works had been dangerous, 'he did not work in the Sheffield Summit Tunnel, but he fell downstairs and broke his neck.' Thus was Thackray prevented from bringing with him the loose characters who frequented his place at Wakefield. But then one George Wilson, also from Wakefield, appeared on the works, having leased a bit of land from Hall. About a week before every pay, said Nicholson, Wilson brought a number of loose girls from Wakefield, but again the contractor used his influence to break this up and gave orders that any man who went there was to be discharged. 'We succeeded in smashing them,' he said, 'and the place is now a cow shade.'

Nicholson maintained that he had allowed only two pubs to be used by the men, Mr E. Taylor's at Saltersbrook, and Mr George Whitfield's at Dunford Bridge, and had never permitted any tickets to be given for beer except as a reward for extra services, such as working in wet weather. There had, however, been a great quantity of malt sold on the works. What with its being a wilderness, and with no milk to be got, he had encouraged brewing among the families.

Of course, there had been the occasional bad worker. He had known men who pinched themselves and their families for nine weeks so that they could have a good randy at the pay, and there was one Richard Kenyon who had drunk so excessively that he had starved his own family, though he had since reformed. But generally, Nicholson insisted, there never was a public work more respectably conducted, or with fewer depradations, insults, or crimes committed by the workmen, throughout any part of England.

Throughout the summer, autumn, and winter of 1845 the work dragged on until at last the tunnel, which had been thought impossible and which had cost so much, was completed. On 20 December 1845 the Board of Trade inspector rode through the tunnel, thought it a fine piece of work, and declared it fit to be opened to the public. The great day was fixed for the following Tuesday, the 23rd. The navvies had finished their work, and only a few would stay to maintain the tunnel. As the work came to an end, fewer and fewer men were needed and the navvies had drifted off to find work on other lines. But there were still 300 left on the western part of the tunnel, under Hattersley, and on Monday the 22nd they were, as the *Manchester Guardian* reported, 'treated by the railway company to a roasted bullock, with every other requisite for the making of a good and substantial dinner'.

The men assembled in a tent at Saltersbrook near a store shed in which the bullock, 'above the ordinary size', was roasted whole. The butchers also cooked it. They contrived to fix through the carcase one of the rails used on the railway, and with the help of the blacksmith, who fastened the carcase to it by means of large iron bolts, they made an excellent spit which was turned by two men, at intervals, from noon on Sunday until about one o'clock on Monday. Then it was cut up into large pieces and sent to tables put up in the tent. The *Guardian* said:

The workmen seemed much to enjoy themselves, having more provided for them than they could possibly eat or drink; and around the tent were fixed up various flags, which were left waving in the breeze in honour of the event.

Next day, at ten in the morning, a train of twenty carriages left the Sheffield terminus drawn by two new engines. In it rode the directors of the company, the engineers, the local gentry, the shareholders, and various mayors. It had snowed, and it was cold. The train reached Dunford Bridge, about eighteen miles, in three-quarters of an hour, and stayed there for twenty minutes to take on water. Then it entered the tunnel. The *Illustrated London News* said:

It was $10\frac{1}{4}$ minutes in passing through this great subterranean bore; and on entering into the 'region of light' at Woodhead, the passengers gave three hearty cheers, making the mountains ring. It speedily passed over the wonderful viaduct at Dinting, and arrived at Manchester at a quarter past twelve, the band playing, 'See, the Conquering Hero Comes'.

That night, back at Sheffield, the directors and their friends banqueted at the Cutlers' Hall. Having worked so long and anxiously for their profits, they sang 'Non Nobis Domine'; having broken poor Vignoles and afterwards completed the line substantially according to his plan, they toasted his

successor Locke; having scattered the lives and health of their
army of navvies, they never mentioned the men. But Purdon
was mentioned. The great tunnel, said John Parker, Esq.,
M.P., chairman of the company, had been under the special
superintendence of Mr Purdon, and he must say the work
did him the greatest credit. Mr Appleby, one of the directors,
then gave the health of the assistant engineer, without whose
services he believed they would not have been able to celebrate
the opening of the line that day. (Applause.) Mr Purdon, in
acknowledging the compliment, said that the work just
finished, and with which he was more than immediately connected, had certainly been a very stiff job. (Applause and
laughter.)

*

The first tunnel was built. But this was far from the end of the
Woodhead story. The miserable history continued. On 10
July 1846, a rumour went round Manchester that the tunnel
had caved in, but it was only a landslide. The Manchester to
Saltersbrook turnpike road, which ran thirty yards above the
western entrance to the tunnel, had been washed down by a
stream on to the line, taking with it several small huts built
on the side of the hill, in which some excavators lived. The
landslide happened at two o'clock in the morning and the
men in the huts escaped and were reported to have run about
in a state of near nudity.

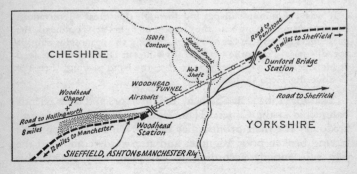

The next year, 1847, the second tunnel was started. Although the first had originally been planned for two lines of track, it had soon been decided to economize and make do with a narrower tunnel to take a single line. The making of the second tunnel, immediately to one side of the first, was much less hazardous and costly than the first. The soil and rock formation was known, and no new shafts were necessary because the engineers of the first tunnel, foreseeing that one day it might be necessary to widen the tunnel, had driven twenty-five arches at intervals into the side walls of the first tunnel, and the excavations for the new one were made from these arches. The second bore was completed in 1852. Working conditions were better and fewer men were killed, but in 1849 the cholera, which was epidemic over much of England that summer, came to Woodhead. The outbreak at the tunnel, in which twenty-eight people died, is still remembered by the inhabitants of Woodhead and Dunford Bridge as 'the plague': they do not know it was cholera and think of it rather as some black death. It was a sudden and violent outbreak, 'evidently originating [said the *Manchester Guardian*] in the grossest imprudence and intemperance'. Altogether 750 men were at work on the tunnel, in three shifts, working day and night. Saturday, 26 May, was the first pay day for eight weeks, and as the next week was Whitsun the works were closed to give the labourers a holiday. Many went off to Ashton and other places where they drank themselves stupid and had no regular meals, some of them eating only once or twice during the whole eight or ten days. When they returned to the tunnel, sober because they were now too broke to buy more drink, they were so weak from lack of nourishment that many developed what was at first thought to be dysentery. It was not. A few died, others sickened daily, and a doctor was called in. He diagnosed cholera. More men died, and when the navvies saw an extra supply of coffins which had been thoughtfully brought up to Woodhead to meet the expected need, they fled in panic to Ashton, Dukinfield, and other towns. Only 100 men remained by the Tuesday.

Dr J. G. Harrison of Manchester – whose principal

qualification seems to have been that he had once, in the 1832 epidemic, seen forty people die of cholera in one night – went round renewing his old acquaintance with such symptoms as vomiting, cramp, collapse, shrivelling of the fingers, sinking of the eyes, and rice-water evacuations, and doing his best to help by prescribing port wine as a remedy. One by one the men died. John Collins, aged twenty-five, who had been on the tramp and worked only one night at the excavations, died in a few hours. James Green, aged twenty-two, an able and sober young man, was found dying in a barn and lasted only until the next morning. The corpses were rapidly buried, and even the residents of the village began to leave in a hurry. Dr Harrison prescribed another preventive – hot coffee and brandy.

A married woman named Foulkes, from the Dunford Bridge end of the tunnel, volunteered to act as nurse, the previous nurse – called Peg Leg because of her wooden leg – having just died of the disease. Mrs Foulkes came forward on a Friday, in the second week of the epidemic, when she seemed in good health, but on the Sunday morning she became almost without pulse, turned blue, and died the next morning. Why she volunteered is not clear, for she was terribly afraid from the moment she came. Rachel Foulkes, aged thirty-six, was buried at St James's, Woodhead, on 18 June, the day she died. She is No. 248 in the burial register. Her last patient, Thomas Fidler, is No. 247.

By then the place was nearly deserted. Even the foremen and overseers had gone, which was thought to be unmanly conduct, as they at least should have had the strength of character to remain. Throughout the epidemic, in which twenty-eight people died, medical opinion was that regular meals, a little port wine, and above all strength of character, could ward off cholera. It was frequently explained with satisfaction that those who died were drinkers, as if such moral weakness induced the disease. When a steady, sober man died this was noted with surprise.

A week or so after the epidemic died away the men straggled back to the village. But because the gangers and supervisors had gone the works were still closed, and the navvies hung around, played leapfrog, and were then condemned not only for want of character in having gone but also for laziness when they returned.

Because of this epidemic, and for much else, the two old tunnels have a dark reputation among the moorland villages. While the first tunnel was being built a man could look through it on a fine day and see, more than three miles away, a needle point of light at the other end. Not until the tunnel was closed, in 1956, could this light be seen again, because while the tunnel was in use the smoke of trains gathered so densely and lingered so long that it was often difficult for the gangers maintaining the line to find their way through even with lamps. Many of these men suffered from silicosis, and some became invalids after as little as six years in the damp and smoke and darkness 'under the hill'.

The engineers of the third tunnel, which was completed in June 1954, after five and a half years, had a great respect for the makers of the first tunnels, and used a geological map made in 1846 for the second bore. After all, said one of the modern contractors, why shouldn't they rely on the map: the man who made it had been an engineer, hadn't he?

Now the old tunnels are disused and have long been closed off by metal bulkheads. At the Woodhead end you can still open a heavy trap door in the bulkhead and see into the tunnel. The wind roars through, and up the old shafts, and the floor is littered with fallen masonry.

Above the Woodhead entrance, where the Manchester road curves steeply round to Saltersbrook, the old public house, called by some the Angel and by others the Crown, where the navvies drank and rioted after the pays, is now derelict. Of the three gargoyles above the old arches, one is gone altogether, the face of the second is broken, and the third looks out on its own. In the wall of the cutting leading up to the tunnel mouth there still remains a powder magazine, built in stone eight feet deep into the rock. Nothing is found in it these days except, now and again, a dead sheep.

The place is deserted. But the wretched spirit of the tunnel remains. It is the spirit of the contractors manning the work in very masterly style; the spirit of the engineer who would not use the safety fuse, for all the extra lives it would save; the spirit of the public remarking their entire satisfaction of the way in which these men, except for William Lee of course, were interred; the spirit of the directors singing 'Non Nobis Domine' and agreeing, after dinner, that it had certainly been a very stiff job. (Laughter and applause.)

8

Chadwick, Parliament, and Do-Nothing

SOME good did come out of the building of the first Wood-head Tunnel. It created a scandal which at least brought to the notice of Parliament and public the wretched life of the navvies. The protest was led by Edwin Chadwick, barrister, civil servant, one of the Commissioners of Inquiry into the labour of young persons in factories, one of the Commissioners of Inquiry also into the means of establishing an efficient police force, and the man who was to secure after ten years of agitation the Public Health Act of 1848, the first in a series of sanitary reforms.

Chadwick was a friend of John Roberton, the surgeon who was also president of the Manchester Statistical Society. When Roberton found the men at Woodhead in a state of brute de-gradation he told Chadwick, who was eager to agitate for reform. He had long thought the State should have built the railways as a rational system and not left them to be created haphazardly and run for profit by individual companies. The railway labourers were among the most exploited and least protected of all workers; their employers were not bound even by the early Factory Acts. Chadwick knew that on average half the capital spent in building railways went on the earth works and tunnelling, and in late 1845, at the beginning of the second railway boom, he foresaw that if the sanction of Parlia-ment was given for any considerable proportion of the new railway works presented for its consideration, and if no new precautions were taken in the way these new lines were built, then both the works and the men would suffer. Some £8,000,000, £10,000,000, or £12,000,000 a year, or as much as the annual cost of the Army and Navy put together, would soon be paid in navvies' wages. A great number of new works would be thrown up all at the same time. Competent railway engineers and managers were already scarce and there would not be enough to go round, nor would there be enough experienced navvies. Rabbles of new men would have to be quickly assembled, and they would work under equally inexperienced engineers. The result would be greater disorder and evil than ever before. And after these works had been completed, what then? The men, said Chadwick, drawing on his long experience of the working of the Poor Law, would be discharged penniless. Some would return discontented to their villages, reckless, deteriorated in body and mind; others would join the dangerous and increasing swarm of able-bodied mendicant vagrants and depredators who had been cluttering up the workhouses.

On 13 November Roberton wrote a long circumstantial letter to Chadwick setting out the number of dead and injured at the tunnel, and describing the evils of drink and truck and filthy huts. Soon after, Chadwick wrote to the Prime Minister, Sir Robert Peel, and received this reply:

He [Peel] fears that the accounts sent by Mr Chadwick as to the demoralization which is the result of such Employment have but too much foundation – but no satisfactory solution of the great difficulties which would attend Legislation on such a Subject has at present occurred to Sir Robert Peel.

Chadwick was also friendly with Robert Rawlinson, who was engineer to the Bridgewater Trust and had formerly worked on the London and Birmingham Railway. On 27 December Rawlinson wrote a long letter in which he told Chadwick of his experience with navvies. The question to be decided, he said, was whether the crime, disease, misery, and danger then attendant on public works could be abated, and, if so, how. He described a typical contract, with the contractor pushing on regardless of safety because he stood to lose a lot if he did not complete on time, and the men wretched and reckless and diseased – 'I have seen men with smallpox thick out upon them wandering about in the lanes, having no place of shelter to go into.' All this degradation was not, Rawlinson argued, a necessary consequence of public works. If the spiritual and temporal welfare of the men were looked after they would become as orderly as any other part of the community. Abundance of work, and money to pay for it, ought to be a blessing to the whole community; but readily earned money spent in vicious pursuits was the greatest curse that could afflict a civilized society. Large bodies of uncontrolled men were a scourge to each other and a terror to the countryside.

Chadwick took the two letters from Roberton and Rawlinson, added a long commentary of his own, and combined them into a paper which he sent to the Statistical Society of Manchester, where it was read on 16 January 1846 by Dr Philip Holland. In his part of the paper Chadwick argued the need for legislation to control the railway works. At that time there was only a statute of 1838 – 'An Act for the Payment of Constables for Keeping the Peace near Public Works' (1 and 2 Vict c 80). This recited that

great mischiefs have arisen by the outrageous and unlawful behaviour of labourers and others employed on railroads, canals, and other public works, by reason whereof the appointment of special constables is often necessary for keeping the peace, and for the protection of the inhabitants, and the security of the property in the neighbourhood of such public works, whereby great expenses have been cast upon the public rates of counties, and the districts chargeable with expenses,

and went on to make the railway directors and shareholders liable to pay the cost of any special constables appointed by the magistrates. But this power was little used, and at best it was only a way of repressing a riot once it had started. Chadwick was more interested in regulating railway works so that riots would never begin.

He also proposed a form of workmen's compensation, in which the employer should *prima facie* be responsible for accidents and liable to compensate the injured man or a dead man's family. If the company had to bear the expenses of maintaining and educating orphan children of men killed on their works, the directors would pass this responsibility on,

by means of a term in the contract, to the person best capable
of avoiding accidents, the contractor. Seeing it was in his own
pecuniary interest to work safely, the contractor would enforce proper precautions and superintend the work closely.

Chadwick estimated the value of a labourer, by what he
called contract prices for maintenance and education, at four
shillings and sixpence a week from birth. Thus the capital in-
vested in a man of twenty was £245, and in one of thirty,
£350. 'In general,' he said, 'every adult trained labourer may
be said to be, in this pecuniary point of view, as valuable as
two hunters, or two race horses, or a pair of first rate carriage
horses.'

Both in France and the United States, he said, the employers
had been made responsible for accidents, and this had checked
recklessness. Much the same principle had been most effective
in Britain, not on the railways but in the shipping of convicts
to Botany Bay. When the first prisoners were shipped out as
many as half of them died on the voyage. The shippers were
no doubt honourable merchants, who didn't mean to kill any-
body; but because they were interested in profit they packed
in as much freight as they could, not seeing it mattered that
convicts should put up with mere inconvenience. Unfortu-
nately the convicts were so inconvenienced that half of them
died, and this was regretted. But then, by a practical adjust-
ment of the shipowners' interests, things were entirely
changed; by a small change in the terms of the contract, the
shippers were paid not for the number embarked in Britain
but for the number who reached Australia alive, whereupon
the mortality rate wonderfully declined to as low as 1½ per
cent. The shipowners, without any law to compel them, paid
medical officers and put the whole conduct of the transports in
their charge.

It worked. When the doctors themselves were paid according to the number of prisoners delivered whole, the passengers
suddenly found they had room to breathe. The doctors not
only took great trouble to treat illness, but also did all they
could to prevent it, going so far as to take the wet clothes off
exhausted convicts so that they should not catch cold. And

when there was an unavoidable casualty, the percentage of his salary thereby lost to the doctor ensured the dead man at least one sincere mourner.

Chadwick proposed that the Parliamentary committees who examined new railway Bills should impose upon the companies the responsibility of controlling and caring for the men who would carry out the works. The companies should be required to answer these questions:

How many labourers will be needed, where will they and their wives and children live, and at what rent?

How will they be fed? What will be done to prevent drunkenness? How will the sub-contractors be prevented from running a truck racket?

What will be done to educate the men's children?

Will the promoters provide medical care for men who are injured or fall ill?

How will the company keep the peace on the works?

Chadwick proposed that Parliament should oblige a company to care for its men in all these ways, and appoint an inspector to see that it did. He knew the companies would say all these regulations would be impediments to public works, and inconsistent with the spirit of such enterprises. Reckless enterprises, he admitted, they certainly would clog, but on the whole proper regulations would improve the works. To take one example – working on Sundays. Quite apart from religious objections, it was inefficient to work men without a break.

Merely considering the labourer as a machine, it is as improvident a waste of power as running post horses every day in the week is found to be.

The night the pamphlet was read to the Statistical Society the directors of the Sheffield and Manchester Railway were invited to attend, but they did not. Chadwick then had 2,000 copies of the paper (*Demoralization and Injuries occasioned by the want of proper regulations of labourers engaged in the construction and working of railways*) printed at his own expense, and spent £30 distributing them to members of both Houses of Parliament and to the Press. The newspapers took little notice: as Lord

Campbell said in a letter to Chadwick in February, legislation could not be long delayed, but at the moment, 'only Corn was attended to'. This was a time of great agitation against the Corn Laws, and of famine in Ireland. Later in the year Peel was to repeal the Corn Laws and split his own party. The politicians and Press were also more concerned about a resurgence of Chartism than about the condition of navvies.

But the *Manchester Guardian* was concerned. Woodhead, after all, was only ten miles away. On 7 March that newspaper said in a leading article:

The contractors, being exposed to fierce competition, are tempted to adopt the cheapest method of working, without any close reference to the danger to which the men will be exposed. . . . Life is now recklessly sacrificed: needless misery is inflicted; innocent women and children are unnecessarily rendered widows and orphans; and such evils must be not allowed to continue, even though it should be profitable. The rights of property are very sacred, and must not be uselessly encroached upon; but life is holier still.

Four days later, on 11 March, another leader appeared, which said, after mentioning the mock wedding ceremony described in the pamphlet, in which navvy and woman jumped over a broomstick and were thereupon put to bed while the wedding party caroused in the same room, that a large body of people could not be allowed to live in a state of such fearful savagery without inflicting serious mischief upon society. The leader went on:

We are glad to learn that it is probable the matter will be formally brought under the notice of parliament, and that a petition on the subject is in course of preparation; towards promoting which, we shall be happy to give all the aid in our power.

In the meantime Chadwick went on collecting evidence. After the pamphlet was published, Thomas Beggs, a scripture reader on the Muirkirk and Ayr line, wrote to say that the contractor on that stretch of railway was 'a tall powerful Highlander, a man of mere brute passions, who drinks, dances and fights with the men . . . he often incites the men to drink and provokes them in that state to fight, in which amusement he seems to take an intense delight'.

The directors of the Sheffield and Manchester Railway defended themselves. In one breath they claimed that nothing improper had happened at Woodhead; in another they conceded that rather a lot of men had died (though not so many as thirty-two, they said) and then blamed the contractors for it. The sub-contractors, they said, had been particularly difficult to handle, and two of them had been killed by their own carelessness – one when he stuck a candle in a barrel of loose gunpowder, another when he stood under a block of stone as it was being hoisted and it fell on him. They were furious with Pomfret, the surgeon who had given the accident tables to the Statistical Society. He was written to, called upon, and threatened with every kind of punishment, for having, as the directors said, shamefully betrayed his employers. On 30 March Roberton wrote to Chadwick that he had received such a letter from Pomfret that he had ridden over to Hollingworth to see him early in the morning, to console him. But Roberton found things even more tangled than he had supposed – 'His wife's uncle is one of the Directors of the Sheffield Railway, his father-in-law a large proprietor, and many of his friends besides interested parties'. But, in fact, Pomfret could not be accused of any disloyalty: he had not been the employee of the company, but had been retained directly by the men.

Eventually the matter came to Parliament. In the Commons, on 30 April, the Hon. Edward Pleydell Bouverie, member for Kilmarnock, moved for a Select Committee. Sir James Graham, the Home Secretary, said he would save the Speaker the trouble of putting the question by at once stating that it was not his intention to oppose the inquiry.

He was obliged to the hon. Member for bringing the matter under the consideration of the House, although he did not anticipate that anything very important would result from the inquiries of a committee. He considered that the companies did not sufficiently avail themselves of the powers with which they were vested, in keeping an efficient police force along their respective lines; and he thought they should be compelled to do so. He must say, that in many districts it was absolutely necessary that the payments made to the labourers should be in kind, and not in money. He mentioned more particularly Westmorland, where railway labourers were sometimes eight or ten miles from any town, and could not possibly get even the common necessaries of life unless they were paid in that way. He knew, however, that the system was open to great abuse; he altogether condemned the principle of paying the people in paper notes, and he hoped that something might be done to put an end to it. He also admitted that the subject was of great importance, and worth inquiring into before a Committee; whatever suggestions they should make on the subject, it would be his duty to attend to.

It sounded very much as if the Government was not greatly concerned, and considered the easiest way out was to set up a committee and then take no notice of it.

Viscount Ebrington, Member for Plymouth, said he considered the inquiry absolutely necessary, if for no other reason than because of the large number of labourers recently killed or wounded on one public undertaking. (He seems to have meant Woodhead.) From the immense number of these people who were congregated together, away from their friends and relatives, and without possessing any tie to connect them with their superiors, except that of receiving their weekly payments, and being, as he might add, altogether devoid of control and discipline, they possessed all the evils, without any of the benefits, of a standing army.

Mr T. Wakley, Member for Finsbury, did not know what was to be gained by the inquiry. The people themselves had not complained of their condition, and if they had, he would venture to say, this complaint would not have been attended to – as he knew that when the people petitioned the House for the redress of any grievance, their petitions were never taken notice of; but when there was no petition from the people themselves, then the greatest alacrity was displayed in granting any motion made by an hon. Member. They had business enough before the House already, without superadding this discussion. The Member for the West Riding of Yorkshire, Mr E. Beckett Denison, a railway promoter who had won an independent route for his Great Northern Railway direct from

London to York after incurring Parliamentary expenses of £400,000, did not agree. These poor men, he said, ought to be protected. Though they received high wages, they worked harder and exhausted themselves faster than any other class.

The general feeling of the House was probably expressed by George Hudson, king of railway promoters and then Member for Sunderland, when he said he had no objection to the inquiry because he was satisfied that it would redound to the credit of those gentlemen who had the honour to be connected with public works. He believed that it was the wish of these gentlemen to improve not only the social but also the moral conditions of their labourers. The Government did not oppose the motion and it was ordered: 'That a Select Committee be appointed to inquire into the Condition of the Labourers employed in the Construction of Railways and other Public Works, and into the Remedies which may be calculated to lessen the peculiar Evils, if any, of that Condition.'

A week later the fifteen members of the committee were named. They included Mr Bouverie who was chairman, Viscount Ebrington, and George Hudson. In eight long meetings the committee heard thirty-two witnesses. Pomfret the surgeon, Purdon the engineer, Thomas Eaton the navvy – all gave evidence of the Woodhead disaster. The Sheriff of Edinburgh, the superintendent of Edinburgh police, and the deputy clerk of the peace for Dumfriesshire all told the same story of drunkenness and riots on Scottish lines. Three clergymen and two scripture readers told a sad tale of sexual immorality and religious infidelity on the works. One railway director, three contractors, two labourers, and one tommy shopkeeper were called to Westminster to face the committee. Among the more celebrated witnesses were Brunel, who spoke against truck – 'If you can trust a man with a shilling's worth of provision you may as well trust him with a shilling' – and Peto, whom the committee had earlier heard described by Brunel as probably the largest contractor in the world, though Brassey is usually thought to have been the bigger of the two. Robert Rawlinson gave evidence also, and told the committee much the same as he had written in his part of the Statistical Society pamphlet.

Chadwick, who urged the committee to recommend legislation for workmen's compensation on the French style, gave evidence that on the Paris and Le Havre line, where reasonable compensation was paid as a matter of right whenever a man was killed or injured on the works, only £5,000 had been paid out of a total expenditure of £1,000,000. Supposing the earthworks to have cost half the total (this was the usual proportion), then the money expended in compensation amounted to no more than one per cent of the navvies' wages. The wages were 22s. a week, so compensation had cost the company only about twopence-halfpenny a week for each man. At Woodhead, he said, thirty-two men had been killed and 140 seriously injured in six years. Suppose £200 had been given to the relatives of each man killed, and £50 to each man maimed, this would have cost only £13,400 out of £343,200 paid in wages. About sixpence per week for each man would have paid the insurance charge for 'this work of excessive danger, conducted in an excessively dangerous manner'.

Then he addressed himself to the principle of employers' liability, which he said Brunel opposed as interfering with the temper, boldness, and freedom of action of Englishmen and tending to put them in leading strings. 'Now the complaint is,' said Chadwick, 'that they are strings pulled, at the risk of life, by irresponsible persons, whom it is necessary to make responsible.'

Bouverie vacated the chair to give evidence before his own committee about the number of labourers he estimated would be working on the railways in the next three or four years. Sir Robert Peel, he said, had stated at the beginning of the session that an expenditure of £23 millions on railways had already been authorized, and if half went in navvies' wages that would be £11,500,000. There were also many more schemes which would be submitted to Parliament, and he assumed that these would add, say, another £5,000,000 in wages, making £16,500,000 in all. The average pay of a navvy was 20s. to 22s. a week, but the increased demand might make this 30s.

Allowing for that, £16,500,000 would give employment to nearly 200,000 men – exactly 198,717. The total effective force of the Army, Navy, and Ordnance was only 160,000.

Bouverie was asked why he thought the Truck Act did not apply to railway works. He explained that at the time the Act was passed (1831) there was hardly any railway work going on. One clause of the Act enumerated all the classes of labourer to which it was intended to apply; all the rest, therefore, were not caught by its provisions, and railway labourers were not among those named. The main provisions of the 1831 Act as it applied to other workers were very much the same as witnesses before the committee had proposed should govern the employment of railway navvies. Contracts had to be made in terms of money; the men had to be paid in money; goods could not be supplied in payment of wages; a set-off for goods supplied would not be allowed against a claim for wages; and an employer who did so supply goods was liable to a fine. Asked if he knew of any objection to extending the Act to cover railway labourers, Bouverie replied: 'The chief objection I have heard stated is, that it might be evaded.'

The committee members asked 3,115 questions, and the answers they received, taken together, revealed the navvies as drunken and perpetual rioters and yet as men who, for all that they were condemned by some witnesses as savages and the refuse of the community, and by the commissioner of Liverpool police as persistent utterers of forged sixpences, were not vicious. The contractors, with few exceptions, were revealed as men who happily fed their men on rotten food, got them drunk on truck beer, and worked them seven days a week.

The abuses and evils stood out plain. The need for reform was obvious. The committee was convinced. Its report was a strong one and made these recommendations:

1. The Truck Act should be extended to the railways, and the men should be paid in money, weekly.

2. Before a new line was constructed a railway company should notify a Public Board where the men were to live and how they were to be looked after if they were ill or injured,

and the work should not begin until the Board was satisfied. Inspectors should be appointed to supervise the works.

3. Magistrates should be given wider powers to enforce payment of wages. Contractors should be obliged to guarantee the navvies' pay, so that if a sub-contractor ran off the men would not be left penniless.

4. Wider powers should be created to appoint special constables to prevent rioting.

5. Companies should be made *prima facie* liable for all deaths and injuries on their lines. The burden of proof would be shifted from the person injured to the company, which would be held liable unless it could prove the victim had been wilfully careless.

6. Railway companies should make periodic reports on the welfare of the navvies to a public authority.

[The principle of workmen's compensation seems particularly bold, but some years earlier the Factory Acts had made employers absolutely liable for injuries done to workmen by unfenced machinery.]

On 28 July the report was ordered by the House of Commons to be printed. The recommendations covered twelve pages, there were two hundred and two pages of minutes and evidence, and an index which took another fifty-four pages. The case was well stated and cried out for action.

Nothing was done.

The report was formally received. It was not even debated. There was no public outcry. It was as Sir James Graham had said – nothing very important was expected to come out of it. And probably George Hudson, who had attended only the first of the committee's eight meetings, still preserved his satisfaction that everything redounded to the credit of those gentlemen who had the honour to be connected with public works.

Nothing was done. But then, what was to be expected of a House of Commons where one railway company alone was said to have eighty Members in its pocket?

9

Wellington, Cat's Meat, and Mary Ann

THEY called him Contrairy York. York because that was where he came from, and Contrairy because that was what he was. He was a character on the railways for many years, and the landlady of any hut where he had lodged could always tell a few tales about him. One day when there was bread and milk for breakfast – a strange breakfast for a navvy, but so the story goes – all the others had theirs boiled into a sort of pap, except Contrairy, who insisted on having his fried, as he called it. Another day, on the tramp, he and his mates came to a river which was quite deep. They looked for a bridge farther upstream, but not Contrairy; he waded through. As the same men climbed the hill beyond, Yorky was conspicuous again, not only because his clothes were dripping from the stream, but because now his trousers were rolled up, showing one blue sock and one white. And peeping over his shoulder was the cat he usually carried out with him – because most other navvies, if they had a pet, preferred a dog.

Nicknames like Contrairy's were part of the navvy character. It was not just that navvies, like any other body of men, used such names familiarly among themselves. It was more than that. The historian Williams, after calling navvies herds of brutes, went on to say that

the last relics of civilization seemed to disappear as they even changed their names into the uncouth and barbarous epithets by which they preferred to be known.

The navvies were in a real sense outside society, shunned and feared and living apart, and because of this they built up a freemasonry of their own, of which the names were part. John Smith, when he left the farm to work for better wages on the railway, became, after a time, a navvy. He was then no longer

just John Smith. He left that name behind when he became
one of a body of men who worked, lived, and occasionally
rioted, together. He now had a new identity. His true name
now became the one given him by his colleagues. He became
Hedgehog, because he looked like one, or Gorger, because he
gorged, or Gentleman Sydney for no discoverable reason, and
would hardly be recognized by his fellows if he was caught
poaching and written down on the magistrates' charge sheet as
John William Smith. Once, when a visitor wanted to see a
navvy whom he knew as Richard Millwood, he searched the
wholy navvy village without finding anyone who knew the
man, and was about to give up when a woman told him: 'Hang
it, thou means my feyther. Why doesn't thee ask for Old
Blackbird?'

Some men kept one nickname throughout their working
lives, but others were given a new name at every works they
came to. There was nothing sinister in aliases, or in constantly
changing names. It could happen that two men, coming new
to a contract, would tell the timekeeper that their names were,
say, Smith and Jones. The timekeeper already had more than
a hundred men on his books, and several Smiths and Joneses
among them. So look, he would say to them, you're Lock and
you're Key. Or the men might choose their own nicknames.
One timekeeper told a story of two men who when they were
asked their names gave those of the contractors, Lucas and
Aird, which the clerk refused to write down because the two
newcomers were known rough characters and he thought it
improper for them to take their employers' names in vain.

Some names, then, were given off-hand, without any reason,
and were the more striking for that. Coffee Joe so little deserved his name that he was dismissed for drunkenness, and a
navvy had to be far gone in drink before he was sacked for it.
But most were given for a reason, which might be a man's
looks, the way he talked, some tale about him, or the place he
came from. The Punches, the Slens, and the Nobbies were as
common among navvies as the Robinsons, Browns, and
Smiths among other people.

Punch was not usually one who drank punch, or a comic,

but just any man who was shorter than usual. And if he was in any other way peculiar he could expect to have a prefix tacked on as well. If he was nearly as broad as he was high it might be Ten-ton Punch; or if he came to a works with his hair long it might be Pigtail Punch; if short and thin, then Fanny Punch; or it might be Sore-eyed Punch, Chattering Punch, Teapot Punch, or Jack Brett's Punch, if he happened to be in the gang overseen by Brett. There was one Dolly-legged Punch, and this is how he got his name. The washing in many of the huts was done in a dolly tub, in the bottom of which the clothes were twirled around by a three-legged wooden instrument called a dolly. Punch objected to his landlady washing his belongings with this instrument because he was certain it would wear out the clothes. The woman laughed at him, so one night he quietly took a saw and cut the legs off the dolly, and was ever after known as Dolly-legged Punch. The Slens were the thin ones, the name itself being short for Slenderman. There were also other names for such men. Two brothers, both thin, were given the titles of Shadow and Bones, and others were called Straight-up Gip and Starch-'em Stiff. Nobby, a name given for no particular reason, became so common that its possessors needed another added to it to give them their full identity of Sumphole Nobby or Scented-soap Nobby.

If a man had lost a leg or an arm he was likely to be Peggy or Wingy. One man was called Rainbow Peg, not because he had painted his wooden leg in many colours but because whenever he stood he put all his weight on his one sound leg, which was somewhat bowed in the first place and later became, with the constant pressure on it, curved like a rainbow.

The colour of a man's whiskers could get him called Streaky Dick, Ginger Bill, or Black and Tan. But perhaps the most common sort of nickname was that which revealed where a man had come from. There were Bristol Jacks, Brummagem Joes, Devon Bills, and Yankee Toms. Navvies who came from Lancashire or Yorkshire were called Lanks or Yorkeys. Bacca Lank smoked hugely, and Contrairy was the most famous of the Yorkeys.

On the Kettering and Manton line there was a marvellous

assortment of names. Among them were Skeedicks, Moon-raker, Mountainpecker, Concertina Cockney, Jimmy-the-new-man, Johnny-come-lately, Beer, Brandy, Fatbuck, Scandalous, Rainbow Ratty, and Reeky Hoile, who had one day looked down a shaft at the fumes which rose after a blast had been set off, and exclaimed in his Yorkshire accent, 'What a reeky hoile.' That was in the 1870s. But the most famous of all navvy names were those borne thirty years before by three men who were known on public works all over England as Wellington, Cat's Meat, and Mary Ann – the first because of a fine nose, the second because of a previous profession, and the last because of an effeminate voice.

The different gangs also attracted nicknames. On one line two gangs lodged at an inn called the 'Horse Shoes', and were known as the Horse Shoe Gang and the Horse Shoe Shoe Blacks. A celebrated gang in the early days was the Old Ninety-fifth – perhaps they were old soldiers. New men were often called the Boys' Gang, and a gang which did its work fast might be known as the Fly Away Gang. Clergymen were called the Billycock Gang.

Nicknames had their drawbacks. A scripture reader called Dennis, at Worsthorne, appealed to navvies in June 1887, asking those who gave wrong names at the office to carry their proper names and addresses on a piece of paper in their pockets. Mr Dennis had had a lot of trouble with a man who had been killed on the works. He had given his name as Charles Fisher, and was also known as Reed. He had in his pocket a ticket for a pair of trousers pawned at Skipton, made out to J. Wilson. Eventually his real name was found to be Peter Lendall, from Askham.

Then there was another navvy, the son of a widow, who left home and found work on a line only twelve miles off. He took a new name, was unknown by his old one, and when he fell ill with fever was nursed and then buried by strangers. After he had been away for some time the widow became alarmed and asked a clergyman to help find her son, and they eventually traced the man. But it was too late, and the only consolation the priest could offer the mother was to show her the grave to which her son had been carried six weeks before. Another navvy lost his inheritance because of his nickname. An old man died leaving a considerable sum to be divided among his nephews and nieces. But one nephew had not been heard of for many years. He had become a navvy and adopted an alias, and so could not be traced. When the man did hear of his uncle's death many years had gone by, he had been presumed dead, his share had been apportioned among the others, and he had lost a thousand pounds.

But the strangest story is that of a navvy called Warren, who had taken the harmless alias of George Brown. In the autumn of 1882 he was working on the Midland Railway, widening the line near Irchester. On 29 August he was injured by a fall of earth and taken back to his lodgings, opposite the Dog and Duck at Wellingborough, where he died a few days later. An inquest was held, a verdict of accidental death returned, and two days later the man was buried. Then, as the *Northampton Herald* put it, 'an event took place which proved that truth was stranger than fiction'. Under the headline, 'A Strange Occurrence', the newspaper report read:

Soon after the funeral a man named George Warren, from Kislingbury, presented himself, and said he believed that, from what he had heard, the deceased was his son. He said he had not seen his son for a number of years, but he should know him by a peculiar scar on the breast, received from a scald during childhood, and he expressed a strong desire to see the body. An application was made to the Coroner, but he said he could not interfere. Other officials were applied to with the same result, and at last the grave-digger at the cemetery re-opened the newly-closed grave between eleven and twelve o'clock on Saturday night. The carpenter who made the coffin took off the lid, and the father by means of a ladder descended into the grave, removed the clothes, and there saw the scar which proclaimed the dead man to be his long-lost son.

Apart from these nicknames, the navvies also had a talent for slang, some of it very like the rhyming slang of Cockney tradition. 'Now, Jack,' says one navvy to another, 'I'm going to get a tiddly wink of a pig's ear, so keep your mince pies on the Billy Gorman' – meaning he is going to get a drink of beer and wants Jack to keep an eye on the foreman. If he had wanted something stronger than beer he might have spoken of 'Bryan o'Lin', or, 'Tommy get out, and let your father in', meaning gin.

At the end of a contract one man might say to another, 'Well, you've jacked up, what's your little game?'

'I'm going to get my kit and be off on the frog and toad.'

Frog and toad is road; as one clergyman put it, 'The motion of the two reptiles is suggestive, I suppose, of a man on tramp.'

Before the man started on the tramp he might blackbird and thrush his daisy roots – black and brush his hobnail boots.

Sometimes this strange language was used to baffle new-comers to the works, who were always good for a joke. So the ganger might say, 'Now then, my china plate, out with your cherry ripe, off with your steam packet, and set your bark and growl a going.' This meant, 'Now then, mate, out with your pipe, off with your jacket, and set your trowel going.' This is bricklayers' lingo. Their slang was by tradition the most picturesque, involved, and unintelligible of the lot.

If a man ran short of bricks he called to his mate for more Dublin tricks, if he wanted water he demanded fisherman's daughter, and if he was drunk he said he was elephant's trunk. The same clergyman who explained frog and toad surmised that elephant's trunk not only rhymed with drunk but also indicated, in the capacity of the trunk for sucking up water, the amount of beer the man had taken.

A man who was tired of the long walk he had to make to his work, and intended to get his money and go on to another job, might say, 'I can't stand this Duke of York to my Russian Turk; I shall go and get my sugar and honey and be off to another Solomon.' Solomon meant job.

There was a huge vocabulary of rhyming slang: 'bird lime' was time; 'Johnny Randle', candle; 'Charley Frisky', whisky; 'Charley Prescott', waistcoat; 'Jimmy Skinner', dinner; 'pen-neth o'bread', head; 'weeping willow', pillow; 'bo-peep', sleep; and 'Lord Lovel', shovel. In another system, which did not rely on rhyme, a shovel was generally called the 'navvy's prayer book'. The earth carted away was called crock or muck, and the men spoke of each other as muck-shifters or thick-legs. When the Sheffield, Ashton under Lyne, and Manchester Railway was building the Sheffield to Penistone line in the mid 1840s, a pub was opened for the navvies just north of the Thurgoland tunnel and called the Rest and Be Thankful. The navvies soon changed this name to the 'Rompticle', the near-by viaduct was named after it, and is still known as the Rompticle viaduct.

You might think that men who spoke such a flourishing lingo of their own, and showed such a gift for words, might also have had many worksongs. But it seems there were few – spectators often remarked on the concentrated silence as a gang of navvies got down to their work – and those few have disappeared. The following navvy song comes not from Britain but from America, where it was bellowed by Irishmen as they pressed on across the continent.

> Every morning at seven o'clock
> There were twenty tarriers working on the rock
> And the boss comes along and he says, kape still
> And come down heavy on the cast iron drill,
>
> CHORUS:
> And drill, ye tarriers, drill.
> Drill, ye tarriers, drill,
> It's work all day for the sugar in your tay,
> Down behind the railway,
> And drill, ye tarriers, drill!
> And blast! And fire!

The new foreman was Jean McCann,
By God, he was a blame mean man,
Last week a premature blast went off,
And a mile in the air went big Jim Goff,
> [Chorus]

When the next pay day came round,
Jim Goff a dollar short was found.
When he asked what for, came this reply,
'You're docked for the time you was up in the sky.'
> [Chorus]

There is another, of which only the refrain has been recorded. It lasted until the First World War and was sung in the trenches. The refrain goes:

> I'm a navvy, I'm a navvy, workin' on the line,
> Choppin' up the worms, makin' one worm into nine.
> Some jobs is rotten jobs, other jobs is fine,
> But I'm a navvy, I'm a navvy, working on the line.

Probably the truth is that there were songs, but they were considered unprintable and so were lost. In Britain the only line where much singing is recorded was the Chester and Holyhead, where many of the men were Welshmen, a most devout and un-navvylike lot who supported six scripture readers, went to chapel on Sunday, and sang fervent hymns, in Welsh, as they travelled to their work on weekdays. In the later years of the century, when missionary ladies began to take an interest in the salvation of the navvies, abstinence songs were printed and distributed along the works. One of them, which was published in 1880, ran:

> I am an English navvy, and I tell the tale with glee,
> Though thousands curl their lip in scorn, and mock at chaps like me;
> But round and round our kingly isle, on meadow, glen and hill,
> Ten thousand mighty monuments proclaim our strength and skill.

> Yes, I'm an English navvy; but, oh, not an English sot,
> I have run my pick through alcohol, in bottle, glass or pot,
> And with the spade of abstinence, and all the power I can
> I am spreading out a better road for every working man.

But it is unlikely that this song commended itself to more than a few.

There were two navvy poets whose work has survived – Alexander Anderson, who wrote in the 1870s, and Patrick MacGill, who published his first book in 1910. Anderson, from Kirkconnel in Dumfriesshire, worked as a labourer on the Glasgow and South Western Railway. He published several books of verse, notably *Song of Labour*, and a few years later,

in 1878, *Songs of the Rail,* which he dedicated to his fellow
workers on the railway in the hope that it might heighten their
pride in the service and help them 'to look upon the iron
horse as the embodiment of a force as noble as gigantic . . . a
power destined, beyond doubt, to be one of the civilizers of
the world'.

At his worst Anderson becomes all mystical and litters his
work with German quotations and allusions. In 'A Song for
my Fellows', under the title of which he places the explanatory
line '*Ambos oder Hammer sein* – Goethe', he writes:

> Then brothers let us rise up from our fears,
> No anvils are we, but men
> Who can wield the sledge-hammer, like mystic Thor,
> For the daily battle again.

In much the same tone he describes the whistle of an engine
as the 'great nineteenth century watch-cry for the world to go
ahead', but he could also do a most vigorous descriptive piece
of a locomotive:

> Hurrah for the mighty engine;
> As he bounds along his track;
> Hurrah, for the life that is in him,
> And his breath so thick and black.
> And hurrah for our fellows, who in their need
> Could fashion a thing like him –
> With a heart of fire, and a soul of steel
> And a Samson in every limb.

He wrote his best when he forgot this 'joy through strength'
philosophy of his and just wrote about what he had seen.
Even then he is inclined to be melodramatic, writing one poem
about an engine-driver who runs over the woman he loves as
she stands by the line to wave to him on the night before their
wedding day, and another in which an engineman runs over
his brother, whose severed head is then dragged along on the
front of the engine. But violent death was common on the
railway and, as Anderson explains, nearly all his poems were
based upon facts, on real incidents on the line where he
worked.

His verses received what might be called mixed reviews. The *Ayr Observer* said:

An educated surfaceman, a polished and gentle-minded wielder of hammer, pick and shovel, is truly a *rara avis in terra*; as remarkable a producer of verse as any that our century has seen.

The *Scotsman* said:

He is apparently familiar with German literature, talking glibly of Schiller and Goethe, and prefixing to his pieces German quotations, which we presume him able to translate ...

The *Chicago Tribune* merely remarked that Anderson's poetry had a hearty earnestness.

It also had, at times, a hearty bathos, as in 'The Wires', in which telegraph wires along the line talk about the messages they are carrying. The sixth stanza reads:

> A sound of bells is in my tone,
> Of marriage bells so glad and gay,
> It comes straight from the heart of one
> A thousand weary miles away.
> O sweet to see in a foreign land
> An English bride by the altar stand,
> Her eyelids wet with tears that seem
> Like dews that herald some sweet dream,
> As, blushing, she falters forth the 'Yes'
> That opens a world of happiness;
> But hush, this is all I have got to say,
> 'Harry and I were married today'.

The best of Anderson is probably 'Old Wylie's Stone'. The stone of the title stood by the rail and commemorated a man's death.

> We stood clear of both lines, and were watching the train
> Coming up with a full head of steam on the strain,
> When all at once one of our men gave a shout –
> There's a shovel against the rail! Look out!
> The shovel was Wylie's, and swift as a wink,
> He sprang into the four feet with never a shrink;
> Clutched it; but ere he could clear the track,
> The buffer beam hit him right in the back.

> In a moment poor Wylie was over the slope
> And we after him, but with little of hope;
> Found him close by the stone, with his grip firm set
> On the shovel that cost him his life to get.

Patrick MacGill wrote much later. He was born in Ulster about 1890, left school at twelve, began work as a navvy a year or two later, came to England and Scotland where he worked on railways and waterworks, and then in 1910 published his first book of verse, *Gleanings from a Navvy's Scrapbook.* This cost sixpence, and contained translations of La Fontaine's fables made with the aid of a dictionary, and many navvy verses. A typical poem, and one reminiscent of Anderson, is called 'The Greater Love'. Jim the navvy sees a seven-year-old child on the line and knows a train is coming. He runs to the child, but the engine is upon them.

> He thought as he would poor fellow, his life was a useless one,
> Many another to labour when he was buried and gone,
> Men were so very plenty, an' work was so sparin', or
> Since life had so little to give him, what was he livin' for;
> An' the child might have brighter prospects. . . .

So Jim throws the child aside, and is himself run down. In the introduction, MacGill says:

Some day – when I become famous – I will take immense pleasure in reminding the world, like Mr Carnegie, that I started on the lowest rung of the ladder, or, as is more correct, in looking for the spot where the ladder was placed. . . . I hope you will have more pleasure in reading these verses than I have had in writing some of them. Imagine a navvies hut, fill it with men shaggy as bears, dressed in moleskin and leather, reeking of beer and tobacco. In a dark corner of the hut aforesaid place your humble servant scribbling for dear life on a notebook as black as his Satanic Majesty, while on one side a trio of experts in fisticuffs discuss the Johnson–Jeffries match and on the other side a dozen gamblers argue and curse over a game of banker, and you have a faint idea of the trials of a versifier.

This first book got a few good reviews. Harry Beswick in *The Clarion* asked, 'How the deuce did this versifier find himself in a navvies' hut instead of a literary salon?' The *Illustrated*

London News said MacGill had a considerable gift, the *Daily Express* that he was not afraid to be original, and the *Westminster Gazette* found his verses racy and virile. Then in 1912 his second book appeared, called *Songs of a Navvy*. Like the first it was printed by the *Derry Journal*, but this time it is also described on the title page as 'published by himself from Windsor'. In its pages MacGill remarks that swearing is not a habit but a gift, says that all that glitters is not mud, and writes of navvies 'padding it' on tramp. He writes of his navvy shovel, which has the grace of a woman and the strength of an oak, and says the time is near when the shovel will rise over sword and sceptre as a mighty power in the land. At times he has the gift of a vivid phrase: in his verses lots of navvies are run over, and one is 'burst like a flea by the wheel'. Here is a poem entitled 'The Navvy Chorus'.

> And the demon took in hand
>   Moleskin, leather, and clay,
> Oaths embryonic and
>   A longing for Saturday,
> Kneestraps and blood and flesh,
>   A chest exceedingly stout,
> A soul – (which is a question
>   Open to many a doubt),
> And fashioned with pick and shovel,
>   And shapened in mire and mud,
> With life of the road and the hovel,
>   And death of the line or hod,
> With fury and frenzy and fear,
>   That his strength might endure for a span,
> From birth, through beer to bier,
>   The link twixt the ape and the man.

His best pieces all have this bitterness. Take a stanza of 'Played Out'.

> As a bullock falls in the crooked ruts,
>   he fell when the day was o'er,
> The hunger gripping his stinted guts,
>   his body shaken and sore.

> They pulled it out of the ditch in the dark,
>   as a brute is pulled from its lair,
> The corpse of a navvy, stiff and stark,
>   with the clay on its face and hair.

Or consider 'L'Envoi – To My Pick and Shovel'.

When the last, long shift will be laboured, and the lying time will
  be burst,
And we go as picks and shovels, navvies or nabobs must,
When you go up on the scrap heap and I go down to the dust

Will ever a one remember the times our voices rung,
When you were limber and lissom, and I was lusty and young?
Remember the jobs we've laboured, the beautiful songs we've sung?

Perhaps some mortal in speaking will give us a kindly thought –
'There is a muckpile they shifted, here is a place where they
  wrought',
But maybe our straining and striving and singing will go for
  nought.

Then in 1914 MacGill published *Children of the Dead End:
the autobiography of a navvy*. Once, he says, when he was on the
tramp, he met Moleskin Joe outside Paisley:

He had knee-straps around his knees, and a long skiver of tin
wedged between the straps and the legs of his trousers, which were
heavy with red muck frozen on the cloth. The cloth itself was hard,
and rattled like wood against the necks of his boots. He was very
curiously dressed. He wore a pea-jacket, which bore marks of the
earth of many strange sleeping places. A grey cap covered a heavy
cluster of thick dark hair. But the man's waistcoat was the most
noticeable article of apparel. It was made of velvet, ornamented
with large ivory buttons which ran down the front in parallel rows.
Each of his boots was of different colour; and they were also
different in size and shape. In later years I often wore similar boots
myself. We navvies call them 'subs', and they can be bought very
cheaply in rag stores and second-hand clothes shops. One boot has
always the knack of wearing better than its fellow. The odd good
boot is usually picked up by a rag-picker, and in course of time it
finds its way into a rag-store, whence it is thrown amongst hundreds of others, which are always ready for further use at their old

trade. A pair of odd boots may be got for a shilling or less, and most navvies wear them.

He met Tom MacGuire who was sitting on the roadside reading an English translation of Schopenhauer. Tom had just served six months for shooting the crow in a Greenock pub: shooting the crow was ordering and drinking whisky with no intention of paying. MacGill read Victor Hugo in tunnels by the light of a naphtha lamp, and wept over *Les Misérables*. He read *Sartor Resartus*, and Montaigne, and his books got covered with rust, and sleeper-tar, and grease. A ganger called Horse told him he read so much he would end his days in a madhouse or the House of Commons. He detested mission-aries, and said the church allowed a criminal commercial system to continue and then wasted its time trying to save the souls of the victims of that system, 'A missionary,' he wrote, 'canvasses the working classes for their souls just in the same manner as a town councillor canvasses them for their votes.'

MacGill earned his first money as a writer when a newspaper sent him two guineas for his description of the death of a navvy on the works. He worked briefly as a reporter in London, and there his autobiography ends. The war came. He wrote a war book, and then comic novels of Irish life. MacGill married Margaret Gibbons, a novelist who wrote for the same publisher; she was to write twenty-two works, some of which appeared as Red Letter Novels.

MacGill, of course, was writing late in the day, after the navvy age proper. He did work as an excavator, but mostly as a surfaceman in a maintenance gang. But his writings record many of the earlier navvy traditions. In his autobio-graphy there is a song called 'The Bold Navvy Man'. He may have written it himself: on the other hand, it is attributed in the book to a navvy named Two-shift Mulholland, and may have been traditional. Here it is:

I've navvied here in Scotland, I've navvied in the south,
Without a drink to cheer me or a crust to cross me mouth,
I fed when I was workin' and starved when out on tramp,
And the stone has been me pillow and the moon above me lamp.

I have drunk me share and over when I was flush with tin,
For the drouth without was nothin' to the drouth that burned
  within,
And whene'er I've filled me billy and whene'er I've drained me can,
I've done it like a navvy, a bold navvy man.
  A bold navvy man,
  An old navvy man,
And I've done me graft and stuck it like a bold navvy man.

I've met a lot of women and I liked them all a spell –
They can drive some men to drinkin' and also some to hell,
But I never met her yet, the woman cute who can
Learn a trick to old Nick or the bold navvy man.

I do not care for ladies grand who are of high degree,
A winsome wench and willin', she is just the one for me,
Drink and love are classed as sins, as mortal sins by some,
I'll drink and drink whene'er I can, the drouth is sure to come –
And I will love till lusty life runs out its mortal span,
The end of which is in the ditch for many a navvy man.
  The bold navvy man,
  The old navvy man,
Safe in a ditch with heels cocked up, so dies the navvy man.

10

Sin and Sanctity

THE navvies were great sinners. They spoke of God, it was said, only to wonder why he had made them so poor and others so rich; and when they heard, from the lips of an evangelizing clergyman, of the coming state, it was only to hope that there they might cease to be railway labourers. The general view was that they were a godless lot. Yet, on the other hand, Wordsworth celebrated their piety in his 'Sonnet at Furness Abbey'.

> Well have yon railway labourers to this ground
> Withdrawn for noontide rest. They sit, they walk
> Among the ruins, but no idle talk
> Is heard; to grave demeanour all are bound;
> And from one voice, a hymn with tuneful sound
> Hallows once more the long-deserted quire,
> And thrills the old sepulchral earth, around.
> Others look up, and with fix'd eyes admire
> That wide-spanned arch, wondering how it was raised,
> To keep, so high in air, its strength and grace;
> All seem to feel the spirit of the place,
> And by the general reverence God is praised.
> Profane despoilers, stand ye not reproved,
> While thus these simple-hearted men are moved?

Wordsworth, of course, was no railway-lover either, and he had opposed the building of the Lake District lines. Yet here he is praising as delicate amateurs of art and reverent worshippers of the spiritual, navvies whom others, and most others, condemned as herds of infidels. Probably he was lucky in finding them at a quiet moment: he might not have felt the same if he had seen them on a randy. But the common view of navvies as hell-bent savages was equally overwrought. It was perhaps a little harsh to condemn men for working on Sundays when if they did not they would very likely be dismissed.

Behind the condemnation of the navvies was the Church's instinctive dislike of the railway. As men of God the clergymen could always be relied upon to scrape up a few reasons to show that the railway was against the natural order of things: as men of property they could often be relied upon to extract the last halfpenny from the companies who had to cross their lands. In the early days of the railway, the London and Birmingham Railway passed through one estate in such a way that it was obvious to the company that the clergyman who owned the land really required no bridges at all. But this clergyman not only demanded great compensation (considering, doubtless, that his own temporal advantage was essential to the spiritual good of his parishioners), but also required five bridges to be erected. In the course of the negotiations he came down to four, accepting some slight extra compensation in place of the fifth. It was essential to get the land, because the contractors had already been held up by the haggling, so the company was forced to submit and the agreement was signed, guaranteeing to the proprietor bridges at A, B, C, and D. Soon after the owner received the purchase money he wrote to say that he could do without the bridge at A, if the company would give him half the value of it; this was to the company's benefit and so it was agreed, bridge A was done away with, and half what it would have cost was paid to the clergyman. Encouraged by this further payment, he then discovered that he could do without bridge B and offered to commute that with the company on the same terms as bridge A. This being agreed and paid for, he then in succession found that he could dispense with bridges C and D on exactly the same terms and so in the end he made do with no bridges at all.

The Church and the railways also clashed at times when a company wished to carry a line through a graveyard. In Manchester, about 1842, one line was driven through a burial ground opposite the Old Town. The partially decayed bodies were heaped up just as they were exhumed, and piles were driven into new graves, so that the water oozed out of the swampy ground pregnant with putrefying matter and filled

the district with the stench. Later the Church became more
careful of its dead, and when the Midland Railway took a
deep cutting through the old St Pancras churchyard in 1865
the work was supervised on behalf of the Bishop of London
by a firm of architects. At a previous, smaller, excavation a
year or so before, supervised by the same firm, something had
gone wrong; the bodies were supposed to have been reburied
but there were stories of mysterious sacks full of something
that rattled being carted off to the bone-mills, so at St Pancras
the architects took no chances and employed a clerk of works
to oversee the railway workmen. To make doubly sure, a
young architect's assistant called Thomas Hardy, later to
become the novelist and poet, was ordered to visit the works
at odd hours to check that everything was conducted decor-
ously. After nightfall, within a high hoarding that passers-by
could not see over, the exhumation went on by the light of
flares. New coffins were provided in place of those that came
apart in the lifting, and for loose skeletons: those bones that
held together were carried to the new burial place on a board.
It was at this works that the incident of the celebrated Roman
Catholic divine took place. Orders had been given for the
bones of this high French dignitary to be shipped to France,
but when the navvies opened the grave they found the remains of three men. The shrewdest of the diggers suggested
that since the man was a foreigner the darkest coloured bones
would be his, so the blackest bones were sorted out and put
together until they had the right number of lefts and rights,
and the selected skeleton was screwed into a new coffin and
sent across the Channel, to be re-interred with all due
ceremony.

The navvies who did this were not without a rough sort of
tact, which is more than can be said of the many members of
the Church who preached the word of God to the labourers
with the very apparent aim of keeping them in their ordained
places. Typical of this kind of man was a Mr Fox, an engineer
and not a clergyman, but a fervent preacher, who spoke at a
tea-party at Chester on Easter Monday, 1890. Addressing
many navvies from the works, and with a bishop in the

audience, Mr Fox told the men that they were all fellow workers, the only difference being that he worked with his brain while they were horny-handed sons of toil. He mentioned, among other things, the nobility of labour, and supported his argument by declaring that Jesus Christ had been a carpenter.

Altogether the Anglican Church did not cover itself in glory in its dealings with the navvies. In the early years the country clergy seem carefully to avoid having anything to do with them. The men were not members of the parish in which they were working for the time being, and the extent of many a country vicar's interest in the men was to send his curate along to bury a few of them every now and again. Of course the drinking and loose living of the men were fit subjects for sermons, and the navvy way of life was frequently condemned. The clergy would have done the same for any sinners. In the mid forties, however, concern began to grow for the men's spiritual welfare, and some railway chaplains were appointed. The minutes of the Chester and Holyhead Railway Company for 26 February 1845 say that the directors, knowing from experience the damage inflicted on property near the line, the annoyance to the resident gentry, the delay in the progress of the works, and the loss sustained by the contractors from the loose and unsettled character of railway labourers, felt it their duty to hold out some inducement to constant and steady industry and to promote among them the growth of moral habits. They had, therefore, stipulated in the contracts for the building of the line that the contractors should put up huts for the men where there was no room for the navvies to stay in the village along the line, and also that the men should be paid on stated days and in money, that is, with no part paid in truck goods. After stating this the minutes go on:

In addition to these precautions your directors believe that very many and great benefits would arise to the company, no less than to the men themselves, if some suitable means were adopted, under due authority and supervision, for enabling or inducing the men to attend Divine worship on Sundays.

The minutes add that the local churches could not hold the number of navvies expected to be at work on the line, but that other buildings could be used for the time being, if some minister could be found to officiate. The directors then agreed to pay up to £300 to promote the men's spiritual welfare, if a similar sum could be raised locally from other sources. It was. Altogether £380 was subscribed, and to this the company then added its £300. The Chester and Holyhead was unusual in its solicitude for the men, but then it was altogether an exceptionally saintly undertaking. Captain Constantine Moorsom, the resident director, said he had never heard any complaints about truck. He had 'seen paragraphs' in the papers, but had never seen it himself and never asked the men. 'It is my business,' he said, 'to attend to grievances, but not to hunt for them.'

Generally the initiative in appointing chaplains was not the railway companies', or the Church's, but that of groups of gentlemen, who not only feared for the men's souls but also felt that a course of religious instruction might induce them to conduct themselves less ferociously along the line, and instil into them a sense that it was wrong to poach the neighbouring landowner's game. Thus in 1846 the Rev. James Gillies and the Rev. William St George Sargent were both ministering to the men on the Lancaster and Carlisle line. Mr Gillies, whose stipend was paid by a committee of gentlemen in Kendal and by the Church Pastoral Aid Society, looked after a thousand men on ten miles of the line. Every Sunday, he conducted three services, each in a different spot, and his average congregation at first was about ninety. But after a while the work got behind and the contractors started to work Sundays as well, robbing Mr Gillies of his congregation. He was indignant. The men lost all distinction, he said, between the Sabbath and any other day, taking out horses and wagons. At the farm-house where he stayed some of the navvies lodged too, and he had often seen them deliberately leaving for work, stripping off, and working all day, and returning in the evening after a full day's work. 'In my humble opinion,' said Mr Gillies,

Sabbath working wants to be put a stop to; without that, every other effort will be almost in vain, whilst the men are allowed to go in bands to work on the Sabbath.

Mr Sargent agreed. 'Without some stop is suddenly put to the public national sin of Sabbath desecration it is sure,' he said, 'to bring down public judgements.' Like his colleague, he was paid half by a benevolent family pitying the moral destitution of the men, who subscribed £75, and half by the Pastoral Aid Society, who found a similar sum. He distributed lots of bibles, and was not altogether without success. He converted one man in particular. This was a navvy who, when Mr Sargent first came to the works, went round, supposing that the men would have a voice in the matter, and got up a petition to put an end to the chapel. 'That person,' said Mr Sargent,

came for the purposes of opposition to my first service, but the first sermon I preached there induced him not only to give up his opposition, but produced some better impressions: and from being a drunken, ill-conditioned man, he is now respectably dressed and quite a credit to the railway labourers, and has given his wife a very happy life since.

The Rev. John Thompson, who worked on the South Devon Railway, considered himself perfectly acquainted with the nature and character of the men. They were, he said, in perfect darkness; when he had lent them money they had not repaid him; when he gave the men bibles they sold them for drink; and there was, to sum up, not an atom's worth of honesty in them. But though he was able to do little for their souls, he did help to end a strike. The navvies were paid monthly, as was usual, but wanted to be paid fortnightly instead. The contractors refused, and the men struck. Mr Thompson agreed to act as referee, and spent the whole of one Sunday riding backwards and forwards from the contractors to the men, until the employers conceded that the complaint was fair and agreed to pay every two weeks. Mr Thompson had his reward – 'After I had been the means of reconciling that strike my chapel was full the following Sunday.'

But clergymen were not, on the whole, the best people to spread the word of God. Peto, who was himself very much concerned with religious instruction of his navvies, put it like this. It was difficult, he said, to get a man who had received a university education and moved in a higher class of society to come down to the level of the men. Some could, but they were the exceptions. Generally clergymen could not get through to the men as well as a lay reader who lived among them. It was, Peto thought, not the preaching that did good, but the being among them, sitting down together and talking matters over in a more familiar way.

One such lay reader was Thomas Jenour, who worked among the 400 men on the Croydon and Epsom Railway. He started a school in the winter evenings, where he taught reading, writing, and arithmetic, and where the men read the Bible, sang hymns and prayed. Not more than twenty of the men could read at first, but he found that in two months he could teach the others to read a little. One man who had left the line wrote from Leeds to thank him. The men he taught could not read with facility, but they could get through a passage from the Bible. When the long summer evenings came the school broke up because the men stayed later at work, but then Mr Jenour used to meet the men at dinner, twenty or thirty at a time, and talk with them. He also wrote letters for them, and thought his presence among them acted as a sort of social restraint. In this he was like William Breakey, who was sent by the Town Missionary Society to work among 800 navvies on the Chester and Holyhead line. His influence among them seems to have been considerable. They were generally a peaceable lot, but one Sunday morning some Englishmen got drunk and started a riot in a lodging house. Mr Breakey heard the noise and immediately went off to see if he could help. Several of the men who were standing by advised him to keep his distance but he insisted and pushed his way into the house. When the rioters saw it was him they stopped straight away.

'Is it you making use of this shocking language?' he said. 'I am quite grieved.' One of those who had been fighting looked abashed, and let the missionary see him off to bed.

Most of the missionaries and scripture readers were sent by the nonconformists. At Woodhead, for instance, the Methodists and Moravians were the only people who took the trouble to travel from Manchester to do what they could for the men, and these attentions angered the contractors, who did all they could to denigrate them. Occasionally a Roman Catholic priest appeared on a line where many Irishmen were working. These Irish navvies, as naturally devout as they were drunken, welcomed the padre among them, and had the reputation of subscribing liberally for his upkeep. The Irishmen on the Caledonian line at one time presented their priest with a gold watch and purse.

It is easy to criticize the average Anglican clergyman for taking no notice of the gangs of navvies who happened to pass through his parish, but the Anglican Church at the time was not evangelical, and if the parish priests were not to go out and seek to convert the railway sinners they might just as well leave them alone altogether. As it was, it must sometimes have been difficult, when the occasional navvy or his woman came to church, for a conscientious priest to reconcile his duty to the laws of the Church with his humane instincts towards people in need. At Woodhead, for instance, where more than a thousand men worked for years on end throughout the forties, most of the children born were illegitimate, and few were baptized. But the baptism register of St James, Woodhead, shows two who were. The first child (226 in the register) was Sarah, daughter of Thomas and Margaret Nicholson: this ceremony was conducted on 27 February 1842 by George Bamford, curate. Thomas Nicholson, who was at that time employed by the company as superintendent of the works, is described as head engineer. He is the man who was later to become such a scathing critic of those missionaries and dissenting ministers who went preaching to the men on his works. It was a straightforward enough christening. But the very next entry in the same register was not. The ceremony was a month later, on 27 March, and this time the child was illegitimate. Mr Bamford did what he could to help, and entered the child in the register as George, son of Henry Wilkinson and Martha Charlesworth: the parents' surname he wrote down as Charlesworth, their abode Woodhead, and the father's quality, trade, or profession as labourer. Anyone who examined the entry would learn that the parents were not married, though this would not be apparent at a glance. But this compassionate tact was too much for the Church, and later the entry was altered, perhaps by Bamford, perhaps by the vicar when he saw what his curate had done. By the child's name the abbreviation 'Ill.' was added, the father's name was struck out altogether, his occupation of labourer was also struck out, and the words 'single woman' written in its place.

At about this time, and rather more than a hundred miles away, Peto was building the Eastern Counties line from Ely to Peterborough. Three years before he had married for the second time. His new wife, Sarah Ainsworth, was a staunch Baptist and he became one too, caring very much for the spiritual welfare of his men. In 1846 he was employing ten or eleven scripture readers on his works, and if a navvy asked for a bible his name was put on a list, inquiries were made to find out whether he really wanted it and would use it, and then he was given one. All down the Peterborough line Peto's agents gave the men religious books and distributed school books for their children. The Bishop of Norwich noticed this and said that Peto's attempts showed that education could civilize the mind, reform the habits, and elevate the understanding. The gin shops were left deserted and the schools were full. Mr Peto was a dissenter, said the bishop, but he felt that as a catholic Christian it would be dereliction of his duty if he did not express his respect for the exertions used by the contractor for the moral benefit of the railway labourers. Two men who died on this line are commemorated on a tombstone in the porch of the south door by Ely Cathedral. The inscription records the deaths on 24 December 1845 of William Pickering, aged thirty, and of Richard Edger, aged twenty-four, and continues:

THE SPIRITUAL RAILWAY

The line to heaven by Christ was made
With heavenly truth the rails are laid
From Earth to Heaven the Line extends
To Life Eternal where it ends

Repentance is the Station then
Where Passengers are taken in
No Fee for them is there to pay
For Jesus is himself the way
God's Word is the first Engineer
It points the way to Heaven so clear,
Through tunnels dark and dreary here
It does the way to Glory steer
God's Love the Fire, his Truth the Steam,
Which drives the Engine and the Train.
All you who would to Glory ride,
Must come to Christ, in him abide
In First and Second, and Third Class,
Repentance, Faith and Holiness
You must the way to Glory gain
Or you with Christ will not remain
Come then poor Sinners, now's the time
At any Station on the Line
If you'll repent and turn from Sin
The train will stop and take you in

Later on, the Anglican Church was to follow the example
of the dissenters, but in the middle of the century the missionary work continued to be done mainly by the nonconformists
and by irregular preachers. One such was Thomas Fayers,
who worked among the men in Westmorland in the late
1850s and published a tract called *A Navvy's Dying Words, or
Lessons from the Death-bed of a Railway Worker* (limp cloth,
sixpence), which the *Christian News* favourably reviewed,
recommending it as 'a glorious death-bed narrative'. In 1862
he published a longer work called *Labour Among the Navvies*,
which contains practically nothing about navvies but is
almost wholly given over to an immoderate and incoherent
evangelism. One thing Mr Fayers did, however, notice about
his navvies. Those who smoked short pipes lived, he said, 'all

in a skow', in filth and confusion, whereas those who smoked long ones had tidy homes.

Other preachers were former navvies, like Peter Thompson, known as Happy Peter. He died at his chosen work, one evening in July 1869 when he was addressing a large audience in Chatham. It was intensely hot and he had just finished and said amen, when he staggered and dropped dead. The *Gentleman's Magazine*, in reporting his death, said that he had been very successful and had done much good among many of the depraved classes in Chatham.

In the 1870s – rather late in the day – the forces of good began to organize. A Yorkshire vicar called Lewis Moule Evans worked among navvies at Lindley Wood, had recreation huts built for the men, taught them, and above all was liked by them. He did not so much preach to them as work among them, and he used to say, 'I am a navvy too: I work on public works.' He wrote a pamphlet called *Navvies and their Needs*, founded the Navvy Mission Society, and did not lack helpers, mostly ladies of means and Christian conviction who were able to devote their leisure to evangelism. The best known of these women was Mrs Elizabeth Garnett. She was born in 1839, the daughter of the Rev. Joshua Hart, vicar of Otley, Yorkshire. When she was ten she heard, and long remembered, a sermon he preached at the unveiling of a memorial to twenty-three miners and navvies who lost their lives on the Bramhope Tunnel works on the Leeds and Thirsk line. In early middle age she married a parson, Charles Garnett, who died on their honeymoon. After this she threw herself into missionary work, visited Lindley Wood, and then in 1875 formed, within the aegis of the navvy mission, an organization she called the Christian Excavators' Union. She looked upon the union as 'the salt for Christ on our public works', but she must have been in many ways a disappointed woman, for there was not much salt. Membership of the C.E.U. was open to all navvies and to teachers, whether volunteer helpers or those paid by the Navvy Mission, on public works. It started with thirty-seven members and after ten years had collected only 296, and this out of a navvy population which Mrs Garnett herself estimated at 70,000 men at least, not counting their families. A survey of twenty-one public works made by the society in its first year, showed that the average number of huts at each place was eighty-three, the average number of men 919, that only one of these places had a missionary, and that at only three were regular services taken by the local clergy. These were the larger works, and the society then wrote to the managers of seventy-two more. Only thirty-four replied, but this was enough to convince the society that very little was being done for the men's Christian education. But one or two of the managers who did reply offered some sound advice. 'Working people,' wrote one, 'like the prayers offered up in a clear, distinct, audible and reverential voice, not monotoned.' The society was also told that Moody and Sankey's hymn-book was best liked. As an evangelical movement the C.E.U. itself failed, and so did the Christian Excavators' Temperance Pledge. When she asked men who had taken this pledge to wear a bit of blue ribbon on their shirts Mrs Garnett overstretched herself: even those men who were willing to give up beer were not willing to make themselves so conspicuous. The blue ribbons were rare, and so were the badges of the C.E.U., but Mrs Garnett persisted. She had faith, and was always ready to address herself in heightened style to anyone who would listen, or to anyone who might contribute to the funds of the mission. Out on the windblown moors, she said, by the sea-lashed shore, and in the verdant garden land of our England the Lord Jesus had walked, and shown himself as ever seeking and mighty to save our navvies, who had gone astray and were as lost sheep. Every now and again she was consoled by a sudden inclination to Christianity induced on a particular stretch of line either by a heavy crop of accidents or by an unusually diligent scripture reader. At one time twenty-three men from one works saw the light and were confirmed together by the Bishop of Manchester, and that pleased her much. But the mission was making few converts and would probably have remained practically unknown had it not been for Mrs Garnett's instinct for propaganda.

She had visited navvy encampments and had seen how avid the navvies were for news. At the weekend, sporting papers and *Police News* (in style a forerunner of the *News of the World*) were brought into the huts, and those men who could read recited aloud from them for the benefit of the others. Seeing this, Mrs Garnett thought it a great pity that the religious papers of the day were not made more attractive. If, she argued, there could be such a publication as 'a newspaper up in all the news of the day, with striking illustrations, takingly written, yet with a high moral tone', it might in time oust *Police News* and the rest.

She never produced her takingly written and illustrated newspaper. It would have cost far too much. But in August 1878 she did bring out something less ambitious but none the less effective, the first issue of the *Quarterly Letter to Navvies*, which she was to run for more than thirty years.

The first issues of the *Letter* consisted largely of Mrs Garnett denouncing sinners and calling on them to repent. She was inclined to intolerance and her sermons, which thumped home their moral messages with frequent use of bold type, would probably not have been read for pleasure except by her most ardent converts. It is just as well, in the early days at least, that the *Letter* was given away for nothing, because few would have bought it. Quite soon Mrs Garnett began to realize that if she was to get her own preachings read she must also find space for the kind of news the men were eager for. A list was carried of the railway works in progress, which would help men who were on the tramp looking for work, and reports from local branches of the C.E.U. appeared. In the third issue, in the spring of 1879, the death of the Rev. Lewis Moule Evans was reported. He had died young, of consumption, and navvies walked miles to attend his funeral.

A column of notices was started, giving the names of men killed or injured on the railway works, and later on marriages were reported too. The list of deaths is always a long one, even though it cannot have been anything like complete. At Grafton, Marlborough, on 18 May 1881, Charles Baldwin (Upper Leather Punch) slipped as he was tipping, both legs were taken off and he died – 'he was a steady man, worked under Mr Adams nineteen years'. At Tavistock on 5 July 1888 Lendew Davis, aged twenty-seven, of Bristol, took a lighted candle to a powder box. He lived ten days. And so on. Some killed themselves, like Thomas Dawson of Denshaw, who 'hanged himself, low in mind', and one man, John Hicks (Bible John), was gored to death by a cow at Leeds.

All these things are noted briefly and without comment. After all there was nothing anyone could do about falls of earth. But whenever a man was killed after he had been drinking Mrs Garnett rubbed it in. In January 1882, at East Dereham, James West got drunk and was run over. 'The wages of sin,' she commented, 'is death.' On 28 February 1882 George Williams, aged forty-eight, fell asleep drunk and choked – 'No drunkard shall inherit the kingdom of heaven.' On 12 August of the same year, at Hull, Henry Shirley, a ganger, was 'randying the money among his men at the Sportsman' when he fell down dead in a fit. At Guisborough on 12 June 1883 Thomas French, aged thirty-seven, collapsed from a heart attack brought on by drink. He was said to have died happy, but Mrs Garnett would have none of this – '*If* he did it was a *false* peace, and I cannot believe in it.' At Accrington on 6 March 1887 Dick Wilson got drunk and was frozen to death: his nickname is given as Swillicking Dick. And in the issue of March 1891, the *Letter* reports the death on the previous 15 November, in Bolton Hospital, of Thomas Skinner, ganger – 'from having his finger bitten by Lady-killing Punch, while drunk. Skinner died in great agony. See what drink will do. A warrant is out for Punch.'

But Mrs Garnett was not content merely to condemn. She was always ready to help, and in the *Letter* of December 1885 she wrote:

If any of you dread drink and want to leave it off, the following recipe will soon stop the craving and strengthen you. Gentian 1 oz., Quassia ¼ oz., Lemon ¼ oz., ½ gallon of boiling water to be poured over these things; bottled when cold, half a tea-cupful to be taken twice a day.

This is followed by a recipe for rheumatism embrocation, which had to be rubbed in every night before going to bed for three nights, and then left off for the next two 'for fear of bringing skin off'.

Mrs Garnett frequently reported thefts and swindles among navvies. On one occasion she had great pain in saying that five men, claiming to be sent by her, had visited a clergyman and scrounged money from him to buy tools, as they said, promising to repay the next Saturday. They were never seen again. Mrs Garnett was much offended. She had not, she said, known the men, who were liars and thieves and brought disgrace on the honest name of navvy. And in the *Letter* of June 1883, she published this warning:

Beware Landladies: A dark navvy, 'Soldier', is wanted. Soldier was wounded in the leg in India, has a pension of 1s. a day, drew last quarter on July 4th at Gravesend, drank it, was in Boston streets, without food, money or kit. Joe Chapham took him home and gave him tommy and lodge on August 6th. Soldier got up between four and six and showed how he liked their kindness by stealing in money £3 3. 8d. out of the men's pockets, pilot jacket, moleskin trousers, handkerchief, waistcoat, etc., all good, of Jethro Bird's. Jethro says 'he turned out respectable in my rigs, and he skinned me.' Mates, either send his address or pay him out yourselves. Such a rascal is a disgrace to us all, do not give him a lodge, landladies, or work in the same gang with him, mates; turn him off the works.

A little later the readers of the *Letter* were warned to beware of a certain Sinker, who had sunk his mates' sick-club money in beer, and in the issue of March 1888 George Williams (Ene-eyed Conro) was requested to return the fourteen shillings he got by forging a letter in the name of James Williams, better known as Three-fingered Jack, from J. Gardner, who was laid up with a broken leg at Newhead.

Some of these warnings against rogues came from Mrs Garnett herself, but others were inserted in the form of notices, like 'Wanted' small ads in a newspaper, asking for the return of money stolen or the payment of money owed. Among the most frequent advertisers were sloped landladies demanding the rent their navvy lodgers had left without paying. But Mrs Garnett knew that landladies as often cheated the men as were cheated by them. 'All slopers, men and women, are a shame and a disgrace,' she said.

Reports of accidents and deaths were inserted free, but other notices cost a shilling. These notices were many and various. One asked: 'Will W. Davis Wingey write for his artificial arm that he left at Dinston Bassett with Bradfield Dale Wingey,' and one in 1883 announced that at the Hastings Penny Bank a lot of money put in years before by navvies working there had never been claimed, and that the men could have their money, with interest, if they could prove their right to it. By 1888 so many notices were pouring in for the *Letter* that Mrs Garnett made a rule that communications from 'clergymen, missionaries, ladies, or advertisers', would not be answered, or their inquiries inserted, unless the shilling was sent in advance. She then went on:

When inquiries are made for missing husbands or wives, the inquirer must give proof to the Missionary or the friend who writes that the parties are lawfully married. Persons who live together without being married know they have no claim on one another, and must take the consequences in this world as well as in the next of their sin.

She knew that most of the men and women on navvy works were not married and must have known the distress her new rule would cause. She was a great castigator of sinners, but at times hers was a mingy sanctity.

Mrs Garnett explained the shilling charge by saying that if she did not make it the *Letter* would have been full of notices. She probably knew, to her disappointment, that the *Letter* was read more for the bits of news and notices that it carried than for her hellfire. Requests were made from time to time for the *Letter* to give what Mrs Garnett called more business information, such as descriptions of the progress of the works, whether men were wanted or not, and what money was paid there. To this she replied:

It is impossible in the *Letter* to do this, and the Committee of the Navvy Mission Society would never consent that the *Quarterly*

Letter, whose object is to bring you to Christ, should have religion crowded out by business.

The Navvy Mission's real concern was to campaign for God, and it did this by constantly railing against what it called the three great evils on the works – Sabbath desecration, immorality, and drink. 'Sunday,' said Mrs Garnett, 'is marked only by a better dinner, much beer, dog fighting, and strolling about. And this is in Christian England?' She did not know which was the greatest evil – for Sunday to be an ordinary work day, or for it to be used by the men as a holiday, as haircutting and dog-washing day. As for her attitude to the sin of men and women living together unmarried, Mrs Garnett summed that up in her Christmas message of 1883:

Some of you dear friends have spoiled many a past year by living in sin. Now, can years be bright when they are full of shame? Make things right in 1884. Get married, and be able to look your own children in the face. No sin binds a man or woman with such a heavy chain as this. What right have you to disgrace innocent children thus? Have done with it.*

Whenever one of the society's missioners brought a man to God there was great rejoicing. Mrs Garnett tells one piquant story of a sick man, who had seen the light, asking with much anxiety after a fortnight's feverish delirium:
    'What have I said these last three weeks?'
    'Nothing of any count.'
    'Have I said any bad words?'
    'Not one.'
    'What have I said?'
    'Mostly hymns and texts, and such like.'
And then, says Mrs Garnett, a look of peace stole over the man's face as he murmured earnestly, 'Thank God.'

* After the first edition of this book was published in 1965 Mr Herbert Johnson of Styal, Cheshire, wrote saying that in about 1900, when he was seventeen, he was secretary of a navvy mission hall. Mrs Garnett was a frequent visitor, it was evident how much she was loved, and she was a power for good. Mr Johnson wrote: 'I know that Mrs Garnett was a fanatic on irregular unions, but she used to say, "I hate the sin but I love the sinner." '

The missionaries were very strong against swearing. It was asserted that the horses didn't like foul language either, and knew the evil words quite well, and the good ones too, and preferred the navvies to address them properly.

At times the missionaries were assisted by undergraduates who came in the vacation to preach to the men. Four Cambridge gentlemen went down to Devonport at Easter 1888, and it was hoped that their words might not be forgotten. The universities made another contribution to the railway works, as Mrs Hunter of Hunterstown related. Mrs Hunter worked among the men in the hills near Paisley, and one day she saw a dark, middle-aged navvy whose face showed he was a drunk. But, she said, 'Still there was something left – wreck as he was – which whispered, "gentleman".' So she went up and spoke to him.

'You are doing very heavy work, are you not?'

'Yes, it is rather so.'

'I cannot be mistaken in thinking it is not labour to which you have always been accustomed?'

'Ah, you are right there. I took a double-first at Oxford.'

'Then, how is it you came to be here?'

'I am possessed by the demon of drink. Look, look at this shovel; I am actually fond of it, for by tomorrow night it will have earned me ten shillings, and then I can go and have a drink.'

But though the Navvy Mission's main activity was to preach at the men – and a naïve sort of preaching it seems – it also did much for them in other ways: building huts, lending books, and even organizing entertainments. The mission huts were grim to look at, bare structures with wooden benches to sit on and texts round the walls, but any hut where the men could sit and play dominoes when they had no more money left to go to the pub, was welcome to them. The books, too, were mostly devotional, but they were something. The society employed librarians to go round the works with cases of books to be lent out at a penny a time. One librarian, Walter Symes, said he had been mistaken for a cobbler and a watchmaker, and one navvy had asked him if he was John Bunyan.

As for entertainments, the society encouraged its missionaries to teach the violin and any other instruments they might be able to play. The *Letter* said:

> Music is a great counter attraction to young men to the public houses and theatres. . . . There are now very good mouth organs with metal reeds, price 2/6, to be carried in the waistcoat pocket.

Missionaries helped to establish a cricket club and a printing press at Newhaven in 1881, a newspaper was started at East Grinstead the next year, and magic-lantern lectures were often given in the mission huts. At the Grimstone Tunnel, on the Nottingham and Melton Railway, the navvies, with the help of the missionary and the contractors, Lucas and Aird, put on a Negro entertainment in aid of the sick fund at which the labourers appeared as the Nottingham and Melton Christy minstrels.

The society also did what it could to relieve the distress of the men in winter, when they were often out of work. In the severe winter of 1878–9 there were sixteen weeks of frost. 'Oh,' said Mrs Garnett, 'how my heart has been wrung with aching to see groups standing idly about in the frozen snow, looking up at the dull grey sky, which gave no signs of breaking; gaunt and thin, their faces yellow from pining, so patient, so brave, suffering silently.' Navvies who went through that winter never forgot it, and twenty years later young men new to the works who had been children in 1879 were told the story of the year whose hardships became a navvy legend. Soup kitchens were set up in some towns, and navvies walked miles to get a bowl of soup and half a loaf.

The winter of 1881 was a bad one too. At Whitby and Loftus the Rev. H. Pearson, vicar of Lythe, gave soup to the men during one long storm, and at Long Buckley a soup kitchen was opened by a clergyman and three other gentlemen who gave £5 each towards the cost. A quarter of beef was cooked every day and the broth given to the men, until they could go back to work.

In June 1884, Mrs Garnett was exhorting the men to save something against the winter, but many of them were in distress long before the cold weather came. At Hull and Barnsley the works came to a stop in July for want of money, putting thousands of men out of work. The local clergy and the Navvy Mission gave away free grocery tickets for bread and cheese and bacon, and organized teas at which as many as 940 women, men, and children sat down together. Children's dinners were also given, at one of which more than 1,000 boys and girls ate meat-and-potato pie. Next year at Christchurch in Hampshire the work stopped and the navvies starved until the vicar and missionaries went round begging for them. All this was long before the days of the dole.

The mission not only fed soup to starving navvies; it also tried, without much success, to teach them to help themselves. In March 1889 the Leicester plan was announced. A missionary and a few gangers had formed themselves into a committee and had some tickets printed, which were covered in blue cloth and would fold into a waistcoat pocket. Each ticket showed the name of the owner and the place and date it was issued. Gangers would sell a ticket for twopence to any regular navvy, but not to casuals or to local labourers. The advantage was that a man with a ticket could go to any works, show himself by producing the card to be a thorough navvy, and that way stand a better chance of work than a man without a card. Ticket-holders were to pay twopence a week into a fund held by a committee who would use the money to give supper, bed, and breakfast to any ticket-navvy who came to the works penniless. Perhaps the men did not like to pay their twopences: the plan failed.

Much good was done incidentally – by feeding the men when they were starving, by building huts where they could rest, by telling them where they could buy mouth-organs for half a crown – but the mission probably failed in its main evangelical purpose. It made its converts (like the praying navvy of Maindee who used to go upstairs on the horse-bus and pray aloud, much to the annoyance of the conductor who was, however, eventually converted himself) but they were few. In spite of all her fervour, perhaps because of it, Mrs Garnett was a little lacking in charity. She was at times jealous even of other missionary movements. In March 1888, in the obituary of a navvy called Devon, she said: 'He did not run about to other places of worship, but stuck to the Navvy Mission.'

The *Quarterly Letter to Navvies*, though it changed its name in 1893 to *Quarterly Letter to Men on Public Works*, continued to appear long after the great railway works were completed, until, in 1920, it was merged into another misson paper, *The Torch*. Mrs Garnett remained editor until 1917. She died on 22 March 1921 at the age of eighty-one, and a memorial tablet to her was unveiled in Ripon Cathedral in 1926.

To the end the tone of the *Letter* remained as it was in the beginning, fervid. The Christmas message it carried in 1878 from the Rev. D. W. Barrett, formerly chaplain on the Kettering and Manton line, is typical. He asked:

1. Have you prayed much to God during the year?
2. Have you read your bible very often?
3. Have you been as often as you ought, or at all, to a place of worship?
4. Have you or have you not made yourself like one of the beasts that perish by the sin of drunkenness?
5. Have you been a swearing man?
6. Sisters, what about your lives, have they been the lives of Christian women?

And then, continuing his message of good cheer, he asked the navvies to think of the future:

Perhaps you will be killed suddenly by a fall of earth, by the blasting of a rock, by the crushing blow of an engine, by a bruise which may fester, and mortify, and poison the life blood, by a fall, by the slow torture of disease, or by the burning heat of fever. . . . But however it may be, or where it may happen, let me ask you, are you ready now? Shall you be ready to meet death then?

11

Women not their Wives

BURY – At the petty session, on Friday, Mary Warburton, a female about thirty years of age, was charged by Mr Ramsbottom, relieving officer, under the following circumstances: – Mr Ramsbottom stated that, about seven months ago, the prisoner left her husband and four children and ran away with an excavator, taking with her a new suit of clothes, which she had purchased in her husband's name, and for which her husband was now imprisoned. The children became chargeable on the township of Tottington Lower End. The prisoner, who had been residing with her paramour at Tidsley Banks, near Huddersfield, was committed to the Salford house of correction for six weeks, with hard labour.

Manchester Guardian, 19 September 1846

MARY WARBURTON was only one of many women who ran away with navvies. It was frequently observed, and much deplored, that navvies consorted with women, more often than not with women not their wives – and this in Christian England. Certainly navvies found their women where they could, and behaved in this way very much like so many soldiers, but whereas the soldiers could offer fine red uniforms and a sweet smell of patriotism the navvies had only moleskin breeches and hearty appetites. It was not, in the early years at any rate, the navvy custom to marry. They lived freely, and a myth grew up, that of the extraordinarily potent navvy man. The picture is a splendid one, that of a fine muscled animal, standing with legs braced apart, grasping in one hand a pick by the shaft, and in the other a woman by the waist.

One clergyman even turned this proper fear of the rampaging navvy into cash. When the London and Birmingham Railway was being built, and the landowners near the line were claiming compensation for the damage to their property, Peter Lecount, an engineer, found that one reverend and afflicted proprietor complained bitterly that his privacy was ruined, that his daughter's bedroom was exposed to the unhallowed gaze of the men working on the railway, and that he must remove his family to a watering place, to enable him to do which he must engage a curate. All this was considered in the compensation demanded, and paid; yet no curate was engaged, no lodgings at a watering place taken, and the unhappy family, said Mr Lecount, still dwelt in their desecrated abode and bore with Christian-like resignation all the miseries heaped upon them.

Of course the men were sometimes wild, and it was then that the public read about them in newspaper reports. On the Caledonian line in 1845 a barmaid refused a man another drink and he attacked her and broke her leg. A few months later at Penrith, which was a great place for riots, four navvies accosted two women and raped them, and the magistrate who tried the men said he thought no case so bad had ever been tried in England. On randies, too, the men were apt to behave somewhat freely, and a missionary on the Croydon and Epsom Railway complained that at such times there was 'every sort of abomination, lewdness and bad women'.

Tales of wife-selling were common. In the 1880s, Mrs Garnett said that wives not many years before had been sold openly by navvies, and that one she heard of had fetched a shilling, and another only fourpence. At Woodhead, thirty years before, the going price for a wife was said to be a gallon of beer, but Thomas Nicholson would have none of this. 'Now I dare venture,' he said,

that never such a thing happened on these works as a man selling his wife for a gallon of beer; but I can tell you what happened – I have paid miners and masons from £8 to £16 on a pay; the moment they had got it, they have gone down to the large towns in Yorkshire, Lancashire, and Cheshire, and what do you think they have done with their money? Spent it in the filthy dens of those large towns. Aye, in the back streets amongst the girls. These men have come back again impregnated with a disease which has cost the [sick] club more money than all the sickness besides.

When the North British Railway was being built, Alfred List, the superintendent of the Edinburgh County Police who helped to clear up the riots at Gorebridge, said that in the navvy huts there were sometimes one or two women servants, but generally these were of the worst description, 'in fact from the lowest part of Edinburgh and, in many instances, I had every reason to believe, kept for improper purposes'. At about the same time the deputy clerk to the peace for Dumfriesshire was lamenting the 'going together of navvies and women without marriage'. It was common, he said, for a man, when he came to a works, to pay his addresses to one of the young women and live with her for the time he stayed there, and then leave her on the parish when he moved on. Robert Rawlinson said this sort of thing had happened often to his knowledge. The navvy huts were overcrowded, there was no separation of the sexes, and 'demoralization' was rife –

the females were corrupted, many of them, and went away with the men, and lived amongst them in habits that civilized language will hardly allow a description of.

The missionary of the Croydon and Epsom line had a similar experience. 'Indeed,' he said,

that is one great drawback of doing anything with them; they bring women that are not their wives; but I have been able to do some good in that way, by sending several of them away.

The Rev. James Gillies, of the Lancaster and Carlisle line, said that in the huts there were

generally a man and his wife, or a female that passed for his wife; I think, in nine cases out of ten, they were not married.

There were lodgers, too, he said, sometimes as many as eighteen – 'consequently there were nineteen men and one woman in a hut.'

It was the custom to talk of women on navvy works as fallen women, but most had never known anything else, or had anything from which to fall. It was a hard life. Thomas Fayers knew a navvy's wife called Old Alice. She told him she had known many 'hard doos', and that the story of her life, 'would make the best book as was ever written, bar none'. She didn't write it.

Out on the moors, along the new tracks of railway lines

where the tarred huts sprang up, girls were born, grew up un-taught, and went early – at thirteen or fourteen – to live with the navvy men. Whether or not a girl married the man she lived with made little difference. The life was no less hard. All the year round the work went on, keeping house and bear-ing children in a hovel, and with perhaps a dozen lodgers to look after as well. No wonder, then, that some of the women talked of God, as the missionaries found, only to curse Him for having made them navvy women. Women detested the life, and it was a common ambition to retire to a farm, or a shop, or a public house. But this took money, and how could it be made? Not by merely taking in lodgers, who paid only two and six a week for bed and washing, or six shillings for bed and some meals. This barely covered the cost of the food they ate, and no honest landlady made a fortune. The only way was to sell drink. The profit on the beer and spirits was itself great, but this was not all; a half drunk man was content with half-cooked and poor food and with a dirty, comfortless home which he would not have stood if he was sober. So the house became disreputable, the children were neglected, quarrels arose, the men cursed and fought, and there was no peace in the home. If the men did not drink hard and help increase the profits they were made to feel unwelcome. Money entrusted to the landlady for safe keeping disappeared, and was not produced when a man wanted to leave. The woman, like the tommy shopkeepers before her, made her profit out of beer and bad food. Then, thus depraved, she forgot she wanted the money to leave the railway works. She took her profit and drank most of it herself. One such woman was Mrs J., who was known only by that initial. She was the wife of a sergeant-major in the Guards; one of her sons became a Baptist minister, and one daughter married an architect. Mrs J. took to drink, was found wandering and put into the workhouse where she met a navvy, a widower with a family. She went off with him, became known as his wife, and they set up a shanty on a railway works. Of course she sold drink. When she was sober she was a fine-looking, quiet-mannered woman, but when drunk she was a noisy fury. The older children stood as much as they could and then left home, leaving only the two youngest, both little girls, and one of them deaf and dumb. The clergyman of the parish and a scripture reader on the works arranged for this child to go to a Deaf and Dumb Institution, and the navvies made a collection of more than £8 so that she could go away with a set of new clothes, but Mrs J. spent only part of this on the child and drank the rest. The child, however, went to the Institution and stayed there, until the woman in a fit of drunkenness fell and broke her shoulder-blade, and called the girl back to act as servant. The drink-selling and drunkenness went on, and one night at about ten o'clock, with the rain pouring down, a man at the camp heard a child crying bitterly in the darkness. It was one of the little girls; she had been beaten and turned out. The navvy took her in and next day agreed to adopt her on condition that Mrs J. gave up all claim to the child. This was done, and that left only the deaf and dumb little girl, who continued to live miserably. Once they had to rescue her from her stepmother who was laying into her with a poker. Then, one Christmas Eve, Mrs J. got drunk once too often, with four or five of her lodgers. They became boisterous and for a joke they put her on the fire. She died five weeks later.

When they first began to visit railway works the missionaries and well-meaning ladies immediately condemned the immorality they found there, but even they admitted that there was little outright prostitution. One woman missionary said:

Lost women, who live by their sin and go about in flashy clothes vaunting their shame, are unseen on our public works. Young girls carrying babies, and calling their wickedness, in which even their mothers abet them, a misfortune, I have only once or twice met with.

But though there were few formal prostitutes there were the occasional predators among the women. One such woman, who had lived with a man for a year, sold all his furniture as soon as he left her for a few days to try for better work along the line, and went off with another man. She did not act secretly, but, as the missionary said, with pride and grandeur, the guilty pair hiring a cab, unusual thing on a navvy works, to take them off. Some older women were pests wherever they went, trapping young men: it was not unusual to find such women living with men half their age. One woman drove her man to suicide and then, while he lay still unburied, dressed herself in new clothes and went through a mock marriage with a newcomer.

Many of the marriages on the works were no more than shams, men and women accepting each other and living together without benefit of a church service or civil ceremony. As Mrs Garnett put it, 'The sin is there, and all the harder it is to uproot, because it is covered by the idea, though not the fact of marriage.' Respectable women, she went on, kind neighbours, good nurses, who cooked well and sent well-ordered children off to the mission schools, where there were any, women whose lives were otherwise a credit to them, were not married to the men with whom they were living, and indeed their children might have different fathers. Marriage was just not the custom, but the missionaries were never able to bring themselves to understand that. And where the missionaries and scripture readers and chaplains came and preached a Christian morality in which the wages of sin were hellfire, and thereby persuaded a few of the navvies and their women to enter into Christian marriage as a sort of insurance, it achieved little. A navvy had to roam. The circumstances were all against a settled family life. A young couple, in all honesty, could marry in church, take a hut on the works, live together, moving with the line, for some years and have two or three children. The woman lost all connexion with her own parents, if they were still alive, and had only her husband, her children, and her shanty house. Then one day her husband came back early and told her he had jacked it, or been given the sack. He had to find other work, and she must wait for him. He bundled up some clothes, tied up his kit, slung it on his back, and off he went. A trying time for his wife began. If he was tired of her and of supporting his children he just left her there and then: he did not intend to return and she would never see him again. But suppose he honestly sought work and hoped to come back to them, or to send for them when he found a new job, they might still have parted for good. He might wander for hundreds of miles without finding anything, particularly if it was autumn or winter and work was slack. Before he settled down months might pass, and he might be in Cumberland and his family near London where he left them. For the first two or three weeks of his wandering his wife knew she was safe in the hut where he left her, but she also knew only too well that the navvy law said no one could live in a hut save the family of a man working on the job. Occasionally, if a man was killed doing his work, the contractors made an exception and let his family stay, and the woman could make a living and keep her children by taking in lodgers. But this was unusual. So the wife knew that in two or three weeks at the most she must go. Yet her only means of earning enough to stay alive was to remain in the hut and take lodgers. She never dreamed of going on the parish, because there she and her children would be separated, she would have to dress in workhouse clothes, and would be deprived of her liberty. On navvy works she had at least freedom of a sort; the workhouse was unthinkable. So she went day by day down to the works, inquiring after her man. Sometimes a tramp navvy newly arrived at the works would have some fragment of a rumour about him, but it was all garbled and she did not know what to believe.

If she was a loving woman she fretted and was wretched: if she was not she saved herself a little anguish. But either way she knew perfectly well what she had to do. When the time-keeper called for the rent at the end of the fortnight he said, perhaps indifferently, perhaps not, 'I suppose you're going to enter it this week in so-and-so's name?' So-and-so was one of the lodgers. The wife would say yes. Only a fortnight before she had been living contentedly with her real husband; now she was the wife of another. The children took the new man's name, and the neighbours said nothing.

Mrs Garnett realized why so many women had to live as they did. But she still could not concede that it was acceptable for man and woman to live together without marriage. It was a sin before God. The one remedy she suggested was almost absurd. Divorce, she said, and added that it would cost £30. It was a lot, she agreed, but it would be the price of freedom, of a good conscience, and a happy home. 'The deserted wife,' she said,

has her furniture to help her towards this. A man has his strong hands; two summers of not spending one useless penny and he might do it. The only way into the kingdom of God is through much tribulation; take it we must if we are ever to get there.

Now this was so much rubbish. Thirty pounds? The middle-class Mrs Garnett had no conception how much this was to a navvy's wife. But, above all, her crass error was to consider that Christian marriage was necessary to a good conscience. To the likes of Mrs Garnett it was, but navvy women were not the likes of her. As late as the 1860s it was not the navvy custom to marry, and when the missionaries got organized twenty years later and went round preaching holy matrimony, the chief result was a few consciences made miserable, and a lot of bigamous marriages. A man married, went on to another works and married again, and so on. As for the women, they were arguably better off under the old system of casual living together. Then, when a man left and did not return, a woman could quite properly find another protector, and take herself and her children off to the new man. But if she felt her marriage to be a holy sacrament, what could she do? She could not stay alone in the navvy camp: there was no hut for her there. She could either go to the workhouse or go on tramp after her husband – and that way she would very likely end up in a workhouse anyway. Marriage and the navvy life hardly went together.

The best way to get to know how navvy women lived, and to understand the frequent distress of their lives, is to read the inquiries, warnings, and notices in the *Quarterly Letters*.

Weddings at first were few, and the reports sparse. In March 1880 Henry Pugh (Fisherman Harry) married Sarah Ann Brierley. Pincher Martin also married, but the bride was not named and the editors of the *Letter* asked: 'Will friends kindly in future give dates, and the names of the wives as well as the husbands?' In the same year, on 19 August, J. Walker married Dora Mortimer at Barden Moor, and Mrs Garnett, who was waging a hopeless struggle against the iniquity of drinking at the wedding party, triumphantly commented that this was the first teetotal wedding she had had the pleasure of recording. There were other dry weddings, though not many. One was that of Edwin Osbourne (Teetotal Teddy) to Emma Burr at Boston in 1883.

The warnings were many. In September 1885, navvies were told:

Don't buy your girl finery and sham jewellery, nor let her buy them. Make her understand it is not respectable to be dressed in finery.

It is not clear why such finery is to be avoided, unless Mrs Garnett feared it would make a girl more attractive to such men as Devil-driving George of the Salvation Army, who had disgraced himself earlier that year. The man was twenty-one or twenty-two, pale, with no whiskers, and had left Whitchurch, Hampshire, in January in company with his landlady, a stout woman aged thirty-five. They took the poor husband's watch and clothes, besides about £7, leaving him without a penny and with a quarter's rent due.

Women were also advised from time to time to lock up their daughters. In June 1888, the *Letter* carried a paragraph in big type warning all mothers to beware of Peter (surname not known, called Black Lank), and next year all young women were warned to beware of a married man – 'a make-shift navvy and not fit to walk in navvy's shoes'. He was known as Curly, went around as a single man, and had cruelly wronged a woman at Skipton.

Women advertised for their lost men. Here are three such notices:

June 1882 – Gipsy Tom's wife and child, who he left at East Grinstead, recovering from smallpox, have tramped north. They are at South Cave, on the Hull and Barnsley line, and will be glad to hear where he is. Surely he does not intend to desert them.

June 1884 – S. Gunn (45): your wife wants you.

September 1888 – Mrs Barnes, Anderony, Leatherhead, wishes to know if her husband, Jesse William Barnes, who went to Egypt, is dead. Mates please send word.

Children, too, were deserted. On 18 January 1881 Josiah Smith, a little boy, died in Norwich Union workhouse, one of five children left by their parents six weeks before.

We hope the father and mother will see this; and be ashamed of their conduct and fetch the other poor little ones.

And in December 1884 this notice appeared:

Wanted by the four little children, one a baby in arms, left on August 25 at Tilbury, the mother (is she worth the name?).

It is strange that in a magazine run by a woman the most indignant notices should often have been those addressed not to straying husbands but to wives who had run off. One such notice, in December 1888, had a headline all to itself. It read:

Wicked behaviour of a wife – Thomas Harris, of Bere Alstone, a respectable steady man, writes to me: 'My wife, after being married eleven years, and the mother of eight children, went on tramp on September 18 with a man called Cat-eating Scan and took every penny in the house. She broke open even a box our eldest daughter had, and took her money. She took our youngest one with her; but I should like to have that one and all, because she took against the rest of them, and no doubt but that she will serve it the same as it gets older. But I never want to see *her* again. The seven I have got are getting on well, thank God.'

A woman's life on navvy works, as wife or mistress, mother and shanty-keeper, was hard enough, and on British lines women did not take part in the actual excavating work – though at Glasgow, in March 1846, a woman disguised as a labourer applied to the recruiting sergeant to enlist, and when her sex was discovered and she was rejected she left very disappointed, declaring she would turn navvy. Women did, however, labour on railways overseas, for instance on a line near Pisa in 1862. The digging was done lightly with a sort of adze, and the loosened dirt was lifted slowly in a long-shanked scoop and carried away in small baskets on the heads of women and girls. A British engineer on a visit said it was a sorrowful spectacle to see bands of barefooted women tipping their little loads on to a slowly accumulating heap. In Britain the only way a woman could labour on railway works was to live with the navvies or preach to them.

Mrs Garnett, the most vigorous of the evangelizers, was solid middle-class, but some of the women who worked among the navvies for years were ladies of rank. Among them were the Hon. Emily and Gertrude Kinnaird, daughters of Lord Kinnaird; and Diana, Lady Harewood. They provided occasional soup kitchens and frequent bible classes, and their purpose was to preach the good word, but they must have seen that their evangelism was not all that successful. Few navvies went to any sort of church service except when their mates were buried, and navvy life went on much as it ever had. At times these good women despaired, but perhaps they were, indirectly, more of a civilizing influence than they knew – white parasols and little shoes among the black moleskins and big navvy boots. Their mere presence meant something at a time when most people shunned navvies as they did gipsies. The odd chat between a navvy and the Hon. Mrs This-or-that did more than all her hellfire preaching, and even Mrs Garnett, who mostly wrote in a sustained religious rant, must have been capable occasionally of mere conversation with a navvy's wife. Such little acts of kindness meant much in an age of very clear class distinctions. Mrs Garnett tells one story of a navvy and a servant girl. A very nice young fellow, she says, good-looking and well dressed, once amused a lady teacher when they were quietly walking together by saying, 'There is something I wish you would do for me.'

'Yes, what is it?'

'Find me a nice wife.'

'Ah, but you must do that for yourself. The sort of wife for you is a nice, tidy, good servant girl.'

The man replied there was no chance of this, but Mrs Garnett provided a happy ending, of course, and he found 'a very nice wife for himself'.

Now there was no condescension in that woman's advice to the navvy. In those days a servant girl was definitely a cut above a navvy – several cuts – and the man would be bettering himself, and the girl marrying rather beneath her. So the advice was kind, and the story shows how there could, now and again, be some sort of rapport between labourer and lady missionary. It must have been at times a pleasantly ambiguous relationship, that between low-born navvies and high-born ladies (in 1884, navvies were carrying around photographs of Lady Harewood, which she had given to members of her bible class at Eccup), but no story has come down with such a title as 'The Navvy and the Lady'.

What seems to be the only navvy novel was published in 1847. It was called *The Navvies*, was written by Henrietta Louisa Farrer, although the book was published anonymously, and was in two parts. The first, 'Harry Johnson, a tale', tells the story of Agnes, who travels in search of her husband Harry – 'such a good husband,' she says, 'till those cruel railroads taught him to love drink and seek high wages, and then he left me, and, oh, this is what it is come to'. She finds him at last, crippled for life at the age of twenty-eight; they live happily ever after, and the novelette ends with the words:

There is no reason why the navigators should not be as respectable a set as any other labourers, if they each try to do his duty in his own station, and beware of the beershop.

The second tale, called 'Frank Meade', starts in a churchyard where Martha and her children are paying their respects to the grave of her husband, a navvy who had led a bad life. One of these children is the Frank Meade of the title, and, of course, Martha does all she can to prevent him, when he grows up, from going to be a navvy like his poor father. But alas, young Frank, meeting a friend who already works on the railway, is seduced by the sight of the 'velveteen jacket, the yellow handkerchief tied loosely round his sun-burnt neck, the knowing-looking cap and tassel, on one side of the head', and off he goes. He too is slipping into the ways of unrighteousness when he does an heroic act, rescuing the notorious bully Bob Cradock from a fall of earth, is rewarded by the directors, comes to a proper understanding of himself, marries, lives happily ever after, and achieves final respectability when one of his sons becomes a schoolteacher.

This is poor stuff, surprisingly so from an author whose works fill three whole pages of the British Museum catalogue, and who produced, among many other things, a life of one of the saints and a translation of Pascal's *Thoughts*.

But by far the gentlest portrait of navvy life was written by a woman, and also by a Henrietta. She was Henrietta Cresswell, a doctor's daughter at Winchmore Hill, who wrote her memories of the village which was slowly becoming, in mid-Victorian days, just another North London suburb. In 1869 the railway came, the Great Northern line through Enfield. That summer, rather to the astonishment of the villagers, there arrived loads of barrows, shovels, and tip-trucks, and the line was begun by the turning of a few sods in a large field in Vicarsmoor Lane, near where the goods station was later to stand. In a few days rows of wooden huts arose, and gangs of navvies were soon in full possession. Work on the line was also begun at the Wood Green and Enfield ends. There were few houses between Winchmore Hill and Wood Green, except the old cottages on or near the high road, and some gentlemen's houses standing in their own grounds, and no part of West Enfield was built up with the exception of a few large villas. The great business was the spanning of the valley between the village and the hills to the north. The summer was one of heat and drought, the stream was nearly dry, and the engineers did not realize the strength of the watershed from the hills on either side. When the villagers talked of lakes of flood water, of bridges washed away and piled one on top of the other, they were listened to with bare politeness. Later the engineers were to regret their disbelief. The soil was dug from a cutting in Bratt's Field and tipped to form an embankment towards Filcap's Farm, and soon an imposing earthwork was made.

The pretty rows of cottages where Miss Cresswell's grand-father had lived were pulled down, the great ash arbour was relentlessly destroyed, and the garden devastated. The holly hedge, dense as a wall, was grubbed up, scarcely anything re-maining but the tall yew and a golden-knob apple tree, which for years after blossomed and fruited on the top of the cutting by Vicarsmoor Bridge. The lane was closed to traffic, and a notice board proclaimed, 'This road is stopped time the Bridge is being built.'

Often the doctor's daughter watched the navvies at work. 'The excavations were beautiful in colour,' she said,

the London clay being a bright cobalt blue when first cut through, and changing with exposure to orange. There were strata of black and white flints and yellow gravels; the men's white slops and the red heaps of burning ballast made vivid effects of light and shade and colour against the cloudless sky of the excessively hot summer. There were also dark wooden planks and shorings to add neutral tints, and when the engine came the glitter of brass and clouds of steam were added to the landscape. On Sundays and holidays the men were, many of them, resplendent in scarlet or yellow or blue plush waistcoats and knee breeches.

It was not until 1 January 1870 that Dr Cresswell's house, which had to come down to make way for the line, was given over to the railwaymen, and he had to move. It was then deep snow, and the cutting was so close to the side of the house that the garden shrubs were constantly slipping over the edge and having to be brought back and replanted. The garden became a thoroughfare for the navvies at their work.

'There had been much fear in the village,' said Miss Cress-well,

of annoyance from the horde of Yorkshire and Lincolnshire railway men brought in by Firbank, the contractor; but on the whole their conduct was very orderly, and they can hardly be sufficiently commended for their behaviour. . . . A noticeable figure was 'Dandy Ganger', a big north countryman, decorated with many large mother of pearl buttons and a big silver watch chain. He instantly checked all bad language in the neighbourhood of the doctor's garden. Many of the navvies brought their food or their tea cans to be heated on the great kitchen range, and never once made themselves objectionable.

There were delays, caused by the unexpected wetness of the clay in the valley, and also by the thoughtless action of one gentleman who moved the guide posts planted by the engineers in his kitchen garden, which marked the limits of the proposed railway, and by doing this caused the centre line, as originally surveyed, to become incorrect. One of the biggest pieces of building was a skew bridge, which ran over a cutting on the site of the doctor's old garden. For two summers afterwards, that cutting was a forest of rose and carnation poppies, three feet high. They revelled in the new soil and made gigantic blossoms in every shade of crimson, scarlet, white, purple, and grey.

As usual there were accidents. 'Five men,' says Miss Cresswell,

were killed in making the five miles of railway. A man who sleeps on a ballast heap on a cold night never wakes, the fumes are poisonous as those of a charcoal brazier, and this fatality occurred more than once, besides other mischances.

All through 1870 the navvies worked. Clay and gravel were excavated, and tip-trucks filled the valley at Bowes and the much deeper one below the Enfield hills. A viaduct was built over Dog Kennel Lane and the roadway itself raised twenty feet, the streams were imprisoned in culverts and bridge after bridge was built, either to carry rail over road or road over rail. Station platforms were built, sections joined, and the temporary metals became continuous for the whole length of the branch. Miss Cresswell was now and again given an unofficial ride on 'The Fox', one of the engines used on the workings. She thought these trips a wild delight; one lurid night ride home from Palmer's Green seemed to her faster than the Flying Dutchman itself, as the little engine bucketed along the roughly laid tracks with no weight of trucks behind to steady it.

More ballast was laid to settle the permanent way, and heavy rail and cast-iron chairs were put down. Another winter passed, and it was said the railway would be opened early in the year. Then a definite date was given, 1 April, but the villagers had waited so long they only laughed at the day named. But at last the line was completed.

It was the night of the 31st March, 1871, the permanent way was completed, the station was finished and smelled strongly of fresh paint, everything was ready. It was late in the evening, all was very quiet, the familiar sound of the working engine and attendant trucks attracted no attention, but suddenly the village was startled by a loud explosion, a perfect volley of explosions! Many people ran down to the bridge expecting to find some unlooked-for accident had occurred. It was the navvies celebrating their departure with their last train of trucks by a fusillade of fog signals under the bridge. . . .

It was a small work, only five miles, but the navvies who built it were remembered by the doctor's daughter. No one wrote more sympathetically of the coming of the railway, or of the navvies, than Henrietta Cresswell.

12

King of Labourers

BRITISH navvies built more than British railways. At one time or another they worked all over Europe and in America, Africa, Russia, and even in Australia. The English contractors boasted about their English, Irish, and Scots navvies, who were themselves quite conscious of their self-evident superiority. Supervising what he derisively called 'native labour', the British navvy would point to the earth to be moved and the wagon to be filled, say 'damn' with some emphasis, and stamp his foot. The foreigners generally understood.

The first foreign railway on which British navvies worked in any numbers was the Paris and Rouen, which was started in 1841. In the early days France lagged behind in railway-building, lacking both capital and engineering know-how. Britain supplied both; two-thirds of the money to construct the Paris and Rouen line came from Britain, and the railway was built by a British engineer (Locke) and by British contractors (Brassey and William Mackenzie). Most of the navvies, too, had to be British. Brassey needed about 10,000 men to complete the eighty-two miles of line on time. He was not sure he could find that many Frenchmen, and even if he could they would be raw and unused to heavy railway navvying. So in the spring of 1841 he and Mackenzie recruited 5,000 British navvies, assembled them at Southampton, and shipped them across to the villages along the Seine valley where they would be billeted. Five thousand was not enough, but Brassey did not want to send over to France men whom he needed on his other contracts back in England, so he had to take on Frenchmen and anyone else he could get. It was a mixed crew, and on that one line thirteen languages were spoken. The English spoke English, the Irish Erse, the Highlanders Gaelic, the Welshmen Welsh, and then there were Germans, Frenchmen, Belgians, Dutchmen, Piedmontese,

Spaniards, Poles, Savoyards, and one Portuguese. When shouting 'damn' and stamping feet was no longer enough, a lingua franca grew up – one-third French, one-third English, and the rest made up of bits and pieces from half a dozen other tongues. This lingo, with its own forms and a sort of grammar, was spoken on railway works throughout Europe. Some of the Savoyards became so skilled in it that they were engaged as cheap interpreters between the English engineers and the polyglot navvies.

The British navvies remained resolutely British. They persisted in dressing as they always had, wearing, as a defiant sort of uniform, a bit of string tied round the leg below the knee, and in drinking as they always had, except that they now found French brandy cheaper than spirits. They were, as one English director of the line said, not inclined to abstinence, he could not boast of that; but though they were, as ever, inclined to rioting, they found the French gendarmes better organized and better able to keep order than the scrappy English police.

The British navvies, said Locke, spread all over Normandy, where they entertained the curious Frenchmen by their dress, their uncouth size, habits, and manners. They were generally used on the most difficult and dangerous work. They scorned the wooden shovels and basket-sized barrows which the French peasants brought to the work, and used picks and shovels which only the most robust could wield. To watch them work became a new entertainment. 'Often,' said Locke, 'have I heard the exclamation of French loungers around a group of navvies – "*Mon Dieu, ces Anglais, comme ils travaillent*." ' At first the French were suspicious, but the abundance of five-franc pieces after the weekly pay soon made the navvies popular. The reputation of the British increased, so that in tunnelling and other dangerous work Frenchmen could not be induced to join unless there was an English ganger. Even the gendarmes began to get on with the men, learning that sometimes the best way to control them was to humour them.

The French had one lasting grievance – that they were paid less than the British, two and a half francs a day compared with five or six or seven. This was simply because the French could

not do anything like the same amount of work. They ate
lightly, bread and an apple or pear, compared with the Englishmen's beef and bacon and beer, and they were by nature
prudent, of more civilized and settled habits, and unwilling
to take the risks which the navvy took for granted. The
English navvies, like the English engineers, had an urgency
which the French lacked. They were extravagant in everything, in drinking, in eating, in working. The Piedmontese,
too, were good. One Mr Jones, an agent for Brassey, remarked that

all the people born in the mountains, and on poor lands, have more
virtue than those who are born in the plains, and in luxurious
places.

This is a fine Victorian Calvinist remark, though Mr Jones
himself had a reputation for throwing his half-sovereigns
about and drinking too much. The Germans had less en-
durance than many others, and the Frenchmen, when after
a year or so they were becoming accustomed to the work,
sometimes amused themselves harrying the Germans working
alongside them, setting such a pace that the Germans were
distressed and exhausted. The Belgians did not like tipping,
thinking it too perilous. They were also so frugal that they
asked to be paid monthly instead of fortnightly, so that they
could save the money. They never asked for a sub, and never
bought anything from the truck shops. One English contractor
remarked that they had complete confidence in Englishmen,
whom they trusted to keep their money for the month. Perhaps
some of the sub-contractors were more trustworthy than they
might have been back in England because the French police
kept a closer eye on them, and were anxious to see that the men
should be paid at the proper time. A director of the company
said that whenever it became known that a certain sub-contractor 'did not stand well with the people', a policeman or two
would appear at the pay table, to see that he did not run off with
the money.

Some of the works on the Paris and Rouen were difficult.
There were four bridges across the Seine, and four tunnels,

one of them one and five-eighths miles long, through hard limestone, and of course there were accidents. But the men suffered less on this line than on many English railways. By French law the works were supervised by district surveyors who had to be satisfied, among other things, that the method of working was safe. Apart from this, the contractors also had two real inducements to keep the work safe. First, navvies were difficult to come by and not easy to replace, so the contractors kept an eye on the works and appointed doctors to treat those who were wounded or ill. Second, the company was obliged by French law to compensate all those injured on the works, or the families of those men killed. This compensation was a matter of right. The remedy was certain, and it hardly mattered whether the injured man had been careless or not; the company was still liable. In the contracts for the building of the railway, the company transferred this liability to the contractors, who were, therefore, in their own interests, rather more careful than they might otherwise have been. At first it was thought that only Frenchmen could claim this compensation and the families of those Englishmen who were killed went home with such little gratuities as were offered by the contractors or collected on the spot by the navvies, but later the English learned that they too could claim compensation by law. If the amount of damages was not agreed between the injured man or his family and the contractors the aggrieved party could go before either the *Police Correctionelle* or the *Tribunal du Premier Instance* and demand his remedy. When a boy's foot was crushed one contractor was ordered to pay an annuity of 200 francs during the boy's life, and to invest enough money in French funds to produce this amount. At another time, when two gangs of men were pile-driving, one navvy went over, during a break, to ask a man in the other gang for a light. While he was lighting his pipe this man rested his hand on the top of the pile and the piece of iron called the monkey came down and crushed his thumb. He was awarded £60, even though the injury was not sustained, strictly speaking, in the course of his work.

William Reed, a director of the Paris and Rouen, was

astonished that men were compensated where they had been plainly careless and where the fault was theirs. In one tunnel some miners were using powder to blast a rock. They made a hole, primed it, inserted the powder, and expected it to go off. It did not, and, as Mr Reed put it, 'a foolish Irishman was silly enough positively to go and blow'. Two men were severely hurt. The man who blew had both arms blown off, and both eyes blown out. A claim for damages was brought, and Reed spoke to the company's advocate about it.

'Really, it is too bad,' he said,

that the company is obliged to pay not only for the carelessness of common accidents which arise in the course of conducting public works, but here is a man, by a positive act of folly of his own, does that which creates this awful injury to his person, and then comes and asks us to step in the gap, and prevent the pecuniary results of his own act of folly.

The advocate said, 'It is true, but it is so.'

Reed asked, 'What can the man say for himself when he goes before the tribunal?'

'He will say nothing,' replied the lawyer. 'He will go and present his sightless eyes and his armless trunk, and he will have a very large damage awarded him.'

The man was given £200 and sent home.

But Reed came to think the law a good one, and to assert that the amount paid as compensation, 'a miserably small percentage upon the whole of the work', had saved a great many men from extreme misery.

But though conditions were better than on many English lines, the men suffered badly during the long winter of 1842–3. Brassey's son Thomas travelled with him to France, and one of the boy's earliest memories, which he spoke of fifty years later, was of standing by his father's side in the boulevard of Rouen surrounded by hundreds of famishing Englishmen. The works had been held up, there was little work in England for the men to go back to, and so they had nothing. The navvies, he said, were not a provident class, and had not saved enough to support themselves for many weeks without work. Their sufferings, which would have been great in

England, were worse in a foreign country. Soup kitchens were opened, but, said Thomas, 'philanthropy is no adequate substitute for brisk and well-paid employment'. He never forgot 'that dreadful winter'.

Work restarted in the spring, and the line to Rouen was ceremonially opened on 3 May 1843. Though the railway had been made by Protestant sinews, out of Protestant capital, and with Protestant implements, the Roman Catholic French priests came forth in their chasubles, and with their books and candles, to bless the great new marvel. At Pont de Maisons, near Rouen, the navvies sat down to an open-air feast, which the Paris magazine *L'Illustration* called:

un repas en harmonie avec les mœurs Anglaises, et qui rappelle les festins des héros d'Homère. Un bœuf entier a été servi rôti à six cent ouvriers.

The national guard stood by while the men ate. An article in the magazine asked:

Quelle plus douce recompense peuvent désirer ces rudes travailleurs, qui, en deux ans, ont attaché leur nom à une œuvre immortelle?

By this time most of the English navvies had returned home, but about a thousand remained. Some of these went up to Paris and tried to contract with the government engineer for some of the earthworks then being thrown up for the defence of the city. They took some of the work, at the current French prices, and then organized themselves into butty gangs. There was a fosse all round the works, and the stuff from this ditch was taken out and put behind the masonry of the new forts. The Frenchmen there were taking the muck out of the ditch in barrows, which they wheeled up a zig-zag arrangement of planks until they got to the top of the wall. To the eyes of the Englishmen it was all indescribably slow. They immediately put a pulley on top of the wall, and made a swing run. Horses on top of the wall were attached to ropes slung over this pulley, and pulled the loaded barrows up vertically. The empty barrows then descended of their own weight. The navvies worked this way for six weeks, and earned fifteen francs a day each. Then the French engineers began to see that the Englishmen were making them pay an enormous sum for the work, and reduced the price. The navvies, having no other work to go to, had to take it. When the next pay day came round there was another reduction, this time to five francs a day. Then the Englishmen muttered that they were being cheated. If they were going to be paid only five francs they would do no more than five francs' worth of work, and they thereupon slackened off and took things easy.

Though most went home, some navvies stayed on. They could hardly be said to settle in France – they never settled anywhere while they still worked as navvies – but some married French wives and travelled from one of Brassey's French contracts to another, from the Rouen and Le Havre line in 1843, to the Amiens and Boulogne the next year, and to the Rouen and Dieppe in 1847.

The extension of the Paris and Rouen line fifty-eight miles north to Le Havre began in 1843, over more difficult country than the first part of the railway. The works included ten tunnels, many bridges, and, at Barentin, twelve miles from Rouen, a great viaduct 100 feet high, of twenty-seven arches, each fifty feet in span. Many Englishmen worked there, and special omnibuses were run from Barentin to Rouen on the Sunday after the pay, which was monthly on this part of the line. One of these omnibuses, which the navvies called the Great Western, could carry sixty men. In Rouen they crowded the streets and spent their money in the cafés and cabarets, and got so drunk that the work horses back at the viaduct had a monthly rest of three days until the men were rounded up, brought back from Rouen, and given time to recover. After a pay work never started again until the following Wednesday.

But between these outings the work at Barentin pressed on fast through the winter of 1845, until on 10 January 1846, when the viaduct was almost finished, it collapsed, just as the Ashton viaduct had done the year before. Locke was engineer on both lines. No one was hurt this time, but it was a great blow to Brassey. He came from Rouen, inspected the wreckage of the viaduct which had been put up too quickly, in wet weather, and with poor lime, and decided to rebuild straight away. It took six months, cost him £40,000, and occupied nearly all the masons he had in France, but, as he said in his report to the company:

I have contracted to make and maintain the road, and nothing shall prevent Thomas Brassey from being as good as his word.

This greatly enhanced his reputation, though he was still, like all English contractors in France, suspected and denigrated at every opportunity. When the viaduct fell the French Press set up a howl of triumph, charging the English with blundering stupidity, and abusing the French directors for employing foreigners who swallowed up the money of the country in return for scamped-up works. But by 1848 Brassey and his partners had built, mostly with British capital, three-quarters of the railways of France that then existed.

And the coming of Brassey and his navvies had, said Locke, considerably improved the condition of the French working classes. Though the French labourers had at first been capable of much less work, and received much less pay, they soon learned the use of new tools, gained strength, and after a few years were nearly, but never quite, as good as the Englishmen. By the late forties most of the railway work was being done by Frenchmen, who were earning much greater wages than they ever could have in the fields, sometimes double or treble what they had earned before. One sub-contractor who employed Belgian labourers near Charleroi said that when he began to pay them up to two and a half francs a day, about three times their usual wage, they thought he was an angel from heaven. In the fifties, on the Caen and Cherbourg line, English navvies were still doing the most dangerous work, like blasting, and being paid more for it, five francs against the Frenchmen's three and a half, but the local labourers were very competently doing the muck-shifting that they had previously been incapable of.

After the English railway boom had died down, railway building became a service which Britain could dump abroad when there was for the moment no use for it at home. In the early fifties Brassey was at work in Italy, France, Norway, and Austria, taking his English agents, engineers, and gangers with him, but relying now mainly on local labourers except where he had to complete a line rapidly. Some of these native workmen were slower even than the Norman peasants Brassey had found when he first came to France. On one line the Neapolitans came in large troops under their chieftains. Each chief, with a thousand men, would take perhaps ten miles of earthworks and cuttings, but would refuse the heavy work. They left their women behind, but brought their old men and boys, and built huts of wood, which they left in charge of the old men, who also cooked the food. At Maremma these men worked six hours a day for one franc, sometimes staying at work for as long as fifteen hours at a time for two francs. Those who came to work on the line south of Naples near the Abruzzi ate only bread and vegetables and drank water and goat's milk. After six months they would take their money and return to the mountains.

The Danes also had strange ways of working. They began at four in the morning and did not finish until eight at night, but they took five half-hour intervals of rest during the day. The Swedes drank more than the Danes, and had the reputation of being energetic, polite, but troublesome.

But when in 1852 Brassey undertook to build the Grand Trunk of Canada, 539 miles from Quebec to Lake Huron, there was no local labour worth speaking of, and he had to ship out 3,000 navvies from England. Some French Canadians were used, but they were useless except for light work. The only way they could be used was to let them fill the wagons and then ride on the train to the tip, to give them a rest. They could work fast for ten minutes and then they were done. They were not idle, just weak, small, and ill-fed, living on vegetables and scarcely ever eating meat. Even where Canadians could be used they had to be led by Englishmen, who built most of the line themselves. Frequently it was as cold as fifty degrees below freezing. If there was any wind the men's faces and hands immediately froze. They had to work in thick gloves, heavy coats, fur caps which covered their

ears, and with heavy handkerchiefs over their faces. When the
wind blew upstream the men working near the St Lawrence
became covered with icicles and had to stop. In 1854 a third
of Brassey's men were in hospital at one time, with frostbite
and cholera. They were well paid, 7s. 6d. a day, compared
with 5s. at most in England, but even this could not induce
them to stay. They began to return home, and labour became
so scarce that, probably for the first time, an English contractor used that American device the steam excavator. The
work was at last finished in 1859, at a loss to Brassey of nearly
a million pounds. But before then the Crimean War had
broken out, a war from which a few hundred British navvies
were to emerge with considerably more credit than Her
Majesty's Government.

By September 1854, 30,000 British soldiers, together with a
larger French army, were laying siege to the Crimean strong-
hold of Sevastopol, which they could already have taken with
little trouble if the generals Raglan and St Arnaud, surpassing
each other in incompetence, had not dithered about until new
Russian armies arrived to reinforce the defenders. By the late
autumn the British Army was dug in. Two months later it was
in rags and disorder and nearly freezing to death, the generals
having forgotten the Crimean winter. There was nothing to
eat, nothing to drink, no roads, no commissariat, no medicine,
no clothes, no organization; the only thing in abundance was
cholera. Raglan's army was disposed along a ridge outside
Sevastopol, about seven miles from the port of Balaclava,
where a British fleet lay. From the ships to the army there was
one bad road which, after the storms of mid-November, became no road at all. Not even a cart could get through, and
supplies were carried up on horseback or on the backs of
men. There were also a few camels. It was hardly war at all –
just an army starving and catching cholera. If the generals
had been railway contractors they would long before have
gone broke; and, as it was, it was railway contractors who
saved them.

As the news and the casualty lists got back to London, and
as it became quite plain that the British Army was about to be

defeated if not by the Russians then by the winter, Peto had the idea of a railway to connect the port and the camp. He was by then a Member of Parliament, so he spoke to Palmerston, who sent him to the Duke of Newcastle (the Secretary of State for War), who in turn spoke to Aberdeen, the Prime Minister. Peto, his partner and brother-in-law Betts, and Brassey offered to build a Crimean railway at cost, expecting no profit. They proposed to ship all their men and materials, to engineer the line, and then run it. The government accepted. On 30 November Edward Betts, who was organizing the transport of men and materials, wrote to Newcastle saying they proposed to send 200–250 platelayers, navvies, and miners, ten gangers, twenty rough masons or bricklayers, eighty carpenters with three foremen, twenty blacksmiths and foremen, ten enginemen and fitters, four timekeepers, one chief clerk, one draftsman, two practical assistant engineers, and one chief engineer. He also stipulated that this force must come under the direct superintendence of the contractors' engineer. The men were civilians; they were not to be subject to military law, and were to be known as the Civil Engineer Corps. Peto, Betts, and Brassey advertised for men, and on Saturday, 2 December, and on the following Monday, their office in Waterloo Road, on the Surrey side of the bridge, was besieged by navvies, masons, carpenters, blacksmiths, and gangers. They came in crowds, and the contractors could pick and choose. The outer room of the office was filled, and those out in the street tried to elbow their way in. It was like a theatre crush. Many of the men seemed to want to fight rather than shift muck.

'Hope we shall get out quick,' said one. 'Hope they'll hold out till we come.'

'We'll give it to them with the pick and crowbar, them Roosians, instead of the rifle,' said another.

On the second day the door was closed and a notice put up saying: NO MORE MEN WANTED. But some still lingered about, hoping to be taken on after all.

Many of those engaged had already served for a while in Canada, on the Grand Trunk, as had Beattie, who was to be chief engineer of the Crimea Railway. They knew what sort of winter to expect, and how to live through it. The pay was good, from 5s. to 8s. a day, and the men's food and clothes and passages out and back were to be found by the contractors. The engagement was for six months. Beattie's plan was for a double line of rails from Balaclava to the encampment near Sevastopol. From a point near the English positions single lines would then radiate to all the batteries. The line would be worked by stationary engines, four or five of them, pulling the trucks along by wire ropes.

For their generous offer the contractors were lionized. Peto, Betts, and Brassey, it was said, would go about things in a businesslike manner; they were not likely to land their men, as the Army had, without tents or tools, or to fill the hold of a vessel with medical stores and put tons of shot and shell over them, or send out an entire cargo of right-footed boots, any more than they would lay the rails of a line and then tip an embankment on top. The navvies too – the big, bad, demoralized, infidel navvies – were suddenly heroes. The *Illustrated London News* said:

The men employed in our engineering works have been long known as the very élite of England, as to physical power; – broad, muscular, massive fellows, who are scarcely to be matched in Europe. Animated, too, by as ardent a British spirit as beats under any uniform, if ever these men come to hand-to-hand fighting with the enemy, they will fell them like ninepins. Disciplined and enough of them, they could walk from end to end of the continent.

The same week that the navvies were scrambling to volunteer, the survivors of Inkerman were arriving at Southampton. When the *Indus* docked at Southampton the remnants from the Crimea walked ashore on crutches, or were led, or carried. A lane of spectators formed. The pale and maimed appearance of the soldiers prevented anything like cheering. The labourers on the docks stopped work and looked on in silence.

By the end of December several hundred navvies had sailed or were ready to sail. The first body, of fifty-four men, sailed from Birkenhead in the *Wildfire* on Thursday the 21st. They had been delayed by one thing and another, and had started from London on the Wednesday of the previous week, when they gathered at the North-Western Railway terminal at Euston, en route for Liverpool. Many of the men's wives came along to see them off, and before they left the navvies were invited to sign allotment papers directing the contractors to pay part of their wages to their wives at home. The idea caught on, one of the waiting-rooms was requisitioned, and the men queued to sign the papers. Most of them made £1 a week over to their wives. They were due to catch the nine o'clock train, but as all the papers were not signed by then, they refused to leave until ten. They eventually got away to loud cheers.

Their ship was to have sailed from Liverpool on the Friday, but because of the gales there was another delay of nearly a week. The *Wildfire* was a clipper of 457 tons, which the contractors had bought and fitted out between decks with cabins and berths for the men. She was one of the twenty-three vessels which took the navvies to the Crimea, and one of four (the other three were screw steamers) which the contractors were obliged to buy because they could not easily charter enough ships for such a hazardous venture. Other ships were borrowed from Peto's North of Europe Steam Navigation Company.

With the men and the materials and the horses sailed five doctors, four nurses, and three scripture readers – one of them Thomas Fayers, who was to preach in the dark hulk of a navvy ship in Balaclava harbour. Years later, in the Lune valley in Westmorland, he was delighted to be recognized as 'our Crimea parson'. By army standards the force was extravagantly equipped. Each man was issued with:

1 painted bag	1 pr. long water-proof boots
1 painted suit	1 pr. fisherman's boots
3 coloured cotton shirts	1 pr. linsey drawers
1 flannel shirt (red)	1 blue cravat
1 flannel shirt (white)	1 blue worsted cravat
1 flannel belt	1 pr. leggings
1 pr. moleskin trousers	1 pr. boots
1 moleskin vest lined with serge	1 strap and buckle
1 fear nought slop	1 bed and pillow

1 pr. mittens	1 woollen coat
1 rug and blanket	1 pr. grey stockings
1 pr. of blankets	2 lb. tobacco

Then there were the materials – 1,800 tons of rails and fastenings, 6,000 sleepers, 600 tons of timber, and a further 2,000 tons of fixed engines, cranes, pile engines, trucks, wagons, barrows, blocks, chainfalls, wire rope, picks, bars, capstans, crabs, and a variety of other plant and tools, besides forges, carpenters' and smiths' tools, one portable stove for each ten men, and a quantity of Deane and Adam's revolvers. This arming of the navvies was widely criticized, though presumably the guns were to be used only in an emergency, if the Army was overrun and the men had to defend themselves. To issue the revolvers was a mistake, it was said. The navvies were too valuable and expensive to be put in the way of shot if it could be avoided.

Everything was set. At Balaclava, Beattie had found a wharf from which the ships could unload. Raglan admitted that the railway was life and death to many of his soldiers, if not indeed to the Army. Through January, and through storms in the Bay of Biscay, the contractors' fleet sailed out. The navvies rioted in Gibraltar and Malta, demonstrated prizefighting in Valletta, and then, at the beginning of February, began to disembark at Balaclava into the cold of a Russian winter.

They got to work. In ten days they built their own hutted camp and the first five miles of line. Captain Clifford (later to become Major-General Sir Henry Clifford) wrote home that the navvies looked 'unutterable things', and had set to work on the railway 'more because it is their nature to do so than anything else'. He would have preferred a simple road, but later admitted he was astonished at the railway's progress. He said:

The navvies in spite of the absence of beefsteaks and 'Barkley and Perkins Entire' work famously, and as I have before mentioned do more work in a day, than a Regiment of English soldiers do in a week. To be sure the navvies have yet in them the stamina of English living, which has long been worked out of our poor fellows.

William Russell, the correspondent of *The Times* who caused such a furore with his dispatches which revealed the state of the Army in the Crimea, wrote that the railway, where it ran through the main street of Balaclava, had cleared away the crowds of stragglers who used to infest the place. The navvies had pulled down the rackety houses near the post office to clear a way for the terminus of the first bit of what Russell called the Grand Crimean Central Railway. It was, he reported, inexpressibly strange to hear the well-known rumbling sound of the carriages and wagons as they passed to and fro with their loads of navvies, sleepers, and rails. It recalled home more strongly than anything he had heard in the Crimea. He, too, was astonished at the speed of the work. He left one post day, to visit the neighbouring forces, and returned on another, and only with difficulty recognized the place where he had been staying. A railway was running across his courtyard, the walls of which had been demolished; and the navvies gave him a startling welcome by pulling down a poplar right on the roof, which carried away part of the balcony, smashed the roof tiles, and broke two windows.

Russell seems not to have liked the navvies, whom he described in another message as hard at work picking and growling and fighting among themselves. There had, he said, been a regular battle on board one of their ships the night before, and the Provost Marshal would have to 'give them a taste of his quality ere they are brought to a sense of their responsibility in a state of martial law'. Later he reported, in spite of what he had already said about the rapidity of construction, that the only obstructions to be dreaded would arise from the navvies, some of whom had been behaving very badly.

They nearly all struck work a short time back, on the plea that they were not properly rationed or paid, or that, in other words, they were starved and cheated.

There is no other report of any such complaint. The navvies' wages were assured by their written contracts, and it is unlikely that Peto, Betts, and Brassey starved them or that starved men would build a railway so fast. Nor did the navvies complain when they returned home. It looks, then, as though Russell was a bit irritated by the growling and fighting, and would just have liked to flog a few of them, to encourage the others. But Sir Morton Peto had quite distinctly refused to allow his men to be placed under martial law as some of the officers wanted, and maintained that his was a civilian force under his own humane discipline. One navvy was, however, convicted of robbery along with some soldiers, and sentenced to be flogged. He was tough, his courage won him great admiration, and he boasted ever after of his flogging.

Whatever Russell thought of them, General Sir John Burgoyne, the engineer commander, considered the navvies fine, manly fellows, and unsuccessfully asked for some of them to help dig military defences. And the *Illustrated London News* wrote, in March 1855:

It ought to be consolatory to Mr Carlyle and the mourners over the degeneracy of these latter-Days, that there is at least one institution, and that a pre-eminently English one, which, despite climatic drawbacks and all sorts of deteriorating influences, exhibits all its original stamina and pristine healthiness – to wit, the British navvy. Everything we hear and read, from every quarter, testifies to the energetic, skilled, and matured progression of the great undertaking now progressing between Balaclava and the cannon-bristling heights of Sevastopol, and there cannot be a doubt that, when it has reached its terminus, those engaged upon it may safely adopt the motto of their honoured chief, Sir Morton Peto – *Ad Finem Fidelis.*

Though the Army had promised to lend the contractors soldiers to use as temporary navvies, little help was in fact given. At first about 150 men of the 39th Regiment worked for Beattie, and were becoming fair navvies when they were withdrawn. He was then given 200 Croatians who were practically useless, so the entire burden was borne by English navvies.

The railway, which was laid as a double line from its beginning on the quays of Balaclava right up to the hilltop encampments, was worked by horses which walked on planks specially laid between the rails, by stationary engines, and also, as had not at first been intended, by locomotives shipped out from Britain. As a railway it was a bit rough, Brassey having told Beattie not to be too particular about levels and that his principal task was to build a reasonably serviceable track, but it did a lot to save the Army. The engineers had expected to take until the end of April, but by the middle of March things were going much better than they had hoped. A quarter of a mile was being laid every day; the pace was fast. In one instance, a piledriver was landed from the supply ship on one evening, carried in pieces up to the spot where the piles had to be sunk for a wooden bridge across a stream, erected the next morning, and, before that evening, in less than twenty-four hours, the piles were all driven, the machine removed, the bridge finished, and the rails laid down for 100 yards beyond.

By the end of March the line had reached its farthest point and in a week or so more the tributary lines were laid and the railway completed. In all, twenty-nine miles of track were laid. In a letter to his employers Beattie praised his navvies, saying their example had showed the soldiers how to work, and that he was convinced that fifty soldiers would now do more than a hundred would have done before. Soon after it was opened the railway was estimated to have carried 246,600 tons of food and forage (112 tons a day), 1,000 tons of shot and shell, 3,600 tons of commissariat goods. Even then, the idiots of the commissariat refused to make full use of the railway which the navvies had worked night and day to build, incredibly declining to run supplies before eight in the morning or after five-thirty in the evening. But the Army was relieved. Its supplies were assured. Things were never so bad again as in the early winter of 1854, and in September 1855 the fort of Sevastopol fell.

In the Crimea the navvies were perhaps, in the eyes of such an officer as Henry Clifford, unutterable things. They were undisciplined and wore moleskin jackets: the soldiers drilled admirably and wore fine red coats. But the navvies were fit, well fed, well clothed, well paid, experienced in icebound winters, and well led: the soldiers were diseased, starved, tattered, flogged, not expecting it to get cold, and led by a gentleman who is best remembered for lending his name to an overcoat.

The British Army had not fought a war since 1815, but the likes of Peto and Brassey and their men had prospered through many hard campaigns in Britain, Europe, and America. In 1846, for instance, while the Army was suffering occasional defeats in African skirmishes and flogging a man to death at Hounslow for insubordination, the railway contractors had an army of 200,000 navvies at work in Britain alone. It is not, then, strange that the British government was at its wits' end to maintain an army of 30,000 in the Crimea, which was only half the number of Brassey's habitual workforce, or that Brassey, together with Peto and Betts, the two biggest contracting firms in the world, should have found it a simple matter to transport a few hundred navvies to the Crimea and build twenty-nine miles of railway. The contractors came out of the war well. As the *Illustrated London News* said, it was once more proved that the men who had 'made England great by their skill, enterprise, and powers of organization, were of far different calibre from the officials the Government employs'. And the navvies, who returned to a great welcome, were for the time being heroes, having confirmed in the minds of all Englishmen the judgement, which happened to be true at the time but which would have been believed anyway, that the English navvy was the king of labourers.

13

Last Fling

THE last great work executed in Britain by navvies working in the classical way was the Settle and Carlisle line, which was started in 1869 and completed by 1875. This is late in the railway age. George Stephenson died in 1848, Hudson was ruined by 1849, Brunel and Robert Stephenson died in 1859, Locke in 1860, and Brassey in 1870. But the Midland wanted a direct route to Scotland, and so in the late 1860s their engineer, Sharland, walked the seventy miles from Settle to Carlisle in ten days, making a first survey of the line. These works, over moors as bleak and wild as those at Woodhead but much vaster, were among the heaviest of any British railway – a farmer said he bet there wasn't a level piece of ground big enough to build a house on between the two towns – and they were the last of any size to be constructed by navvies and horses, picks and tip-trucks. There was other railway building afterwards. Old lines were widened, new loops were built, but they were small works. One main line, the Great Central, did remain to be built in the 1890s, but that was to be the work not of the navvy alone but also of the mechanical excavator, which was only at this last moment to be used in Britain as extensively as the Americans had used it for forty years and more.

The two horrors of Settle and Carlisle were bog and boulder-clay. To carry supplies the navvies used bog carts, which ran on barrels instead of ordinary narrow-rimmed wheels, which would have sunk hopelessly up to the axles. An engineer said he had often seen these bog carts hauled over the moss by three horses, till they sank up to their middles and had to be drawn out one at a time by their necks to save their lives. Once when four horses were dragging a telegraph pole over such a swamp the exertion became so great that one of the beasts tore a hoof off. In Ribblesdale the clay was normally so hard that it had to be drilled and blasted, yet after rain it turned into a thick, gluey mess, so adhesive and tough that when a navvy stuck his pickaxe into it he could hardly get it out again; and when he did he would not have loosened a small teaspoonful of stuff. Then, when the clay was blasted out as dry rock and put in the tip-wagon, a shower of rain and the jolting of the ride to the tip-head would shake the load into a near-fluid mass of slurry, which settled like glue at the bottom of the wagon, would not be thrown out when the wagon tipped, and so took wagon and all over the embankment. Crossley, one of the Midland engineers, resigned himself to dealing with stuff that was rock one moment and like soup in buckets the next, but the navvies never really became reconciled to it. A man would stick his pick in what had up to then proved to be soft clay, strike a boulder underneath almost as hard as iron, and so shake his arms and body that he would fling down his tools disgusted, ask for his money, and go off. The men trod on wet heather and sinking peat; the little rills, draining the fells and winding and leaping into the valleys, turned to floods and drenched everything; the wind moaned in the brown heather in sympathy with the people. The rain reduced the working days from six a week to three or two, and the men left for other parts of the country where the weather and the work were more settled. One man who had worked in the Rocky Mountains said he had never known such weather as on the moors. At Intake Bank, a thousand feet up, tipping went on for a year without the embankment advancing a yard. The tip-head stayed where it was, while the masses of slurry rolled over one another in mighty convolutions, spreading uselessly out, and going anywhere but the place they were wanted. Swardale viaduct alone took four and a half years. It became impossible to induce the men to remain unless they were allowed to work short time at wages of up to ten shillings a day. As soon as one gang was organized several men left, and works in full swing one day were almost deserted the next. No more than 1,700 or 2,000 men worked on the line at any one time, but more than 33,000 navvies came, stayed for a while, and jacked. 'They are a class of men,' said an engineer, 'very fond of change.'

The rain was torrential – ninety-two inches in 1872 at Dent Head, compared with twenty-five inches in London. Some works just melted in the incessant downpour and had to be started all over again. One gullet, a sort of preliminary cutting, was made big enough to take a few wagons through it, and the rails were laid. But in the night the rain fell, the walls of the gullet slipped, the road was buried several yards deep in slurry and mud, and there it was left. Two years later another and deeper gullet was made, and the men found the remains of the former tram road. 'A splendid discovery for a geological fellow,' said an engineer.

He could prove lots from this. Here is a railway in the glacial period, rails, sleepers and all. Then the world must have been inhabited then; and they had railways then; there is nothing new under the sun.

A few of the navvies came with the contractors and stayed with them throughout, a few miners came specially from Cornwall, and a few were recruited from the men of Yorkshire and Northumberland, counties from which many of the best of the original navvies had come. Most drifted in and drifted out – Irish, Scots, men of all sorts who came on tramp and stayed until the boulder clay got the better of them. In the beginning they invaded the little towns of Settle and Appleby, but out on the moors there were no towns, no villages, not as much as a farmhouse for miles. And so, as at Woodhead thirty years before, they built shanty towns, and called them Sevastopol – the navvies were proud of their part in the Crimea and did not forget it – Salt Lake City, Jericho, and Batty Green. The last was the biggest, and housed at one time nearly 2,000 people, navvies, their women and children. Batty Green was built near Batty Wyf Hole, which had been named after a most navvy-like legend. Batty was a man of the moors who wooed and won a girl who lived in Ingleton Fells. But after a while he fell into evil ways and his wife threw herself to her death into a deep fissure, locally called a hole. There is also another, rather deflating, legend that the place got its name merely because Batty's wife did her washing at the hole.

However it was named, the place was like a gold town in the 1870s. That is to say, it was a great deal nearer to civilization than Woodhead had been. At Batty Green not only were there huts laid out in rows but there was a school with a schoolmaster, a mission house with a missionary, a library, a post office, and a hospital which the contractor built during a smallpox epidemic in May 1871, when eighty died. Bread was baked in Settle and brought up to the camp. Beef-on-the-hoof was driven to Batty Green and there slaughtered to feed the navvies. They ate and drank and fought, but at this camp even the fighting was better organized. Sunday was the big day, when contenders fought bare-knuckled for the title of cock of the camp, the champion later to be matched against a professional fighter brought in for the occasion.

The camps became notorious, and in October 1872 the *Daily News* sent a reporter to see how the men lived. He went to Batty Wyf Hole asking for William Ashwell, the contractor there, but was told he had just left to go up the line. The reporter followed, tramping along the line, a temporary way winding across a hollow already partly spanned by a huge skeleton viaduct. Scrambling along through knee-deep bogs on to piers whose foundations were just level with the surface, past batches of stone-hewers hammering away at blocks of blue stone for more piers, he came to part of the viaduct which had already been erected and looked up at the tangled scaffolding, at the trucks and engines traversing tramroads at great heights, at derricks and blocks and pulleys, and at the silent masons working so far above. From the hollow beneath the viaduct he climbed to the embankment leading to it and picked his way along, using sleepers for stepping-stones but sometimes slipping mid-leg into half-liquid mud. Between the end of the viaduct, and the beginning of a tunnel more than a mile off, was a cutting through the moorland morass, and as the reporter hesitated, wondering whether to go on, he was overtaken by the missionary, an elderly and wiry man with a white beard who was sent by the Manchester City Mission, the same society whose superintendent had visited Woodhead so many years before.

The missionary, who was called 'parson' by the navvies, said that things were rough but not so bad, he hoped, as when he came fifteen months before, and that he had had ninety in his congregation at Batty Wyf Hole the previous Sunday. 'It would do a fashionable curate a world of good,' said the reporter, 'to undertake this worthy man's work for a few months in the winter season.'

The reporter did not find Mr Ashwell, but he did come across Frank Moodie, the contractor's assistant, a Northumbrian who was in charge of the line between Sevastopol and Dent Head, some of the heaviest work in the whole section. He was proud of his navvies: they were the best men, who did the heaviest excavating by piece work and earned great wages. Twenty-five men were clearing out a cutting which had been blocked by a landslip. The heave of their shovels was clockwork, no man stopped for breath, and the reporter thought them the perfection of animal vigour.

Finer men I never saw, and never hope to see. Man for man, they would fling our guardsmen over their shoulders; they have all the height and breadth of the best picked men in a Prussian Grenadier regiment of the Guards Corps, without their clumsiness. For there is no heaviness in the muscular strength of these navvies. The stiff, greasy, blue black clay melts away bit by bit from before their indomitable, energetic onslaught, each man working as if he wrought for his life.

They found another gang of twenty-five, working with a zeal that also spoke of piece work in every stroke. The best men on the working, said Moodie. No ganger was needed over them, and they would not stand one anyway.

'The way the country has come to think now,' he explained, 'good men wonna stand to be ordered about. They wonna have a foreman cursing and bullying about among them.' With piece work there was no need to supervise. All the contractor needed was a man to see that the levels were right, and an engineer to measure the work done every fortnight, to pay for it. The men were all English. As for the Irish, said Moodie, his navvies would take an Irishman by the back of his neck and throw him over the bank into the river.

At the township of Jericho they saw the tommy truck, a peak-roofed affair like a shepherd's cabin and full to the eaves with sides of beef. This was the men's food; mutton they despised and bacon they ate only to fill up the cracks.

A little way off, down in the shaft of the tunnel, twenty-five Cornish and Devonshire miners were working in blue stone rock as hard as millstone. They drilled and then blasted – not a spoonful came out unless they used gunpowder. Tub after tub was wound to the head of the shaft loaded with jagged fragments of the stone. In the tunnel itself, beside the shaft, 500 men were burrowing through Blea Moor. This was the only place where Irish worked alongside the others.

The reporter rode back along the temporary way on one of the contractor's locomotives, down reckless declines and up stiff gradients that would all have to be levelled before the permanent way was put down, past that fashionable part of Sevastopol where a suburb of detached huts was called Belgravia. Then, returning to Batty Wyf Hole, the reporter found a friend:

I encounter a gigantic navvy in a huge moleskin monkey-jacket, with a round bundle on his back, and a great deal more inside him than was good for him. He was about to quit this happy valley. He had begun drinking on Saturday, and had sedulously pursued that walk of life ever since, having drunk all his wages, a Whitney pea-jacket with mother-o'-pearl buttons, six flannel shirts, two white linen ditto, sundry pairs of stockings, a pair of boots, and a silver watch with a gilt chain. Now he was going to try his luck elsewhere, with the meagre remnant of his kit contained in the little bundle on his shoulder. He insisted on treating me, and we tumbled over each other into one of the dogholes which do duty in Batty Wyf Hole for tap-rooms.

About half-way through the second drink the tone of the navvy's conversation suddenly changed. He wanted to fight the reporter, and threatened to kick his head off. But the landlady came and talked to the man gently, and he took this so much to heart that he began to cry, accused the reporter of being his brother, and then went to sleep with his head on his bundle.

The works were heavy. Ashwell said they all worked like Yankees. Many died. In the church of St Leonard at Chapel-le-Dale, near Ribblehead, there is a memorial tablet:

TO THE MEMORY
OF THOSE
WHO THROUGH ACCIDENTS
LOST THEIR LIVES
IN CONSTRUCTING THE
RAILWAY WORKS
BETWEEN SETTLE AND DENT HEAD
THIS TABLET WAS ERECTED
AT THE JOINT EXPENSE
OF THEIR FELLOW WORKMEN
AND THE
MIDLAND RAILWAY COMPANY
1869 TO 1876

The navvies were as lawless as ever, poaching and rioting. 'Threw a Stone Through the Window of The Naked Man Hostelry in Settle,' said one headline. 'Woman Charged with Assaulting another Woman in Hutted Camp,' said another. The police were worried, and the Bench became severe. At Westmorland Sessions in April 1871, John Smith, aged twenty-eight, was given seven years' penal servitude for stealing a half-sovereign, a half-crown, a florin, and a shilling at Kirkby Lonsdale. He had one previous, trivial, conviction.

In 1875 and 1876, as the works came to an end, the men gradually left, but by this time there were few other works they could go to. So throughout the seventies and eighties they had to go farther to look for work. Earl Brassey was once asked why old navvies were so rare. Was it because the work was so exhausting that they all died young? He agreed the work was hard and told on a man, but thought the main reason was that as soon as a man found he could not get constant work at home he went abroad. When an English railway was finished, he had known as many as 350 navvies to sail in one ship from Liverpool on their way to Australia. Some went out to places like the Sudan, built their railway and then returned, as the navvies of the 1840s had returned from their French and Italian contracts, but most were now emigrating for good.

They spread all over the world. J. W. Miles, navvy, writing home from South Africa, said: 'It would make you laugh to see the Black Kaffers come to work with hardly any clothes and no boots on.' Another wrote from Australia to complain that 'a great many colonials got beastly drunk', and another, in Buenos Aires, said he was fine but you should see the gun-fights in the streets. Some went out only to do worse than they had at home – in the late spring of 1888 navvies from London were starving at Toronto – but most prospered. In India they were well paid and greatly privileged. In 1888 Lieutenant Gibbon of the Royal Engineers, an officer of the Military Works Department at Harnai which was building a railway to enable troops to concentrate rapidly on the frontier in case of a Russian invasion of India, said that he found the English navvies at 450 rupees a month cheaper than the natives at only twenty-five rupees: 450 rupees a month at that time was worth something like £400 a year, an enormous wage for a navvy. The Englishmen could not pronounce the names of the natives who worked under them and so chris-tened them Tommy, Charlie, and so on, which much amused Mr Gibbon. Many of the natives, he said, were skilled work-men, but the English were paid so much more because of their character. The gangs of natives were from many different tribes – tall, handsome Afridis from near the Khyber Pass, thin, wiry Punjabis and short, thick tribesmen from near Karachi. Now, said Mr Gibbon, if it were not for the strong English rule, these men would be stalking about loaded with arms instead of 'peaceably working side by side, with pick-axe and shovel, helping forward the great cause of civilization'.

Not all went out to boss the Afridis or to disapprove of Argentinian gunfights. Many stayed at home to help forward the great cause of civilization here, by building docks, reser-voirs, and gas-works, and in the nineties there were still enough of them to build the last few railways of any conse-quence.

In 1892 there were still seventy-nine railway works in progress in Britain. Most were small, and the only one of any size was the West Highland line from Helensburgh to Fort William. In the seventy years since the beginning of the Stockton and Darlington Railway a network of lines had spread to nearly all towns of any size. The great companies – the Great Western, the London and South Western, the London and North Western, the Midland, and the others – were well established, and the railway system seemed complete. But the last main line was yet to be built.

The old Sheffield, Ashton under Lyne, and Manchester Railway, which was created in 1837 and which built the Woodhead Tunnel, had grown since then and was still ambitious. In 1846 it became, by a series of mergers, the Sheffield, Manchester, and Lincolnshire Railway, controlling lines from Manchester to Grimsby and taking a good share of the prosperous mineral traffic of the Midlands. In the 1890s its chairman was Sir Edward Watkin, who was also chairman of the growing Metropolitan Railway which had reached Aylesbury, forty miles from London. It was his idea to build a new trunk line, linking the M.S. & L.R. and the Metropolitan, thus creating a new route from Manchester, through Sheffield, to Nottingham, Leicester, and London. The new line was vigorously opposed: nobody wanted it except Watkin and his colleagues. The older established main-line companies did not want another competitor, and so the Bill for the new London Extension, as it was called, was opposed and obstructed in every possible way in its passage through Parliament. The company asked powers to construct ninety-two miles of new line, beginning in the north at Annesley, nine miles north of Nottingham, the southernmost point of the old M.S. & L.R., then driving through Nottingham and Leicester, through Rugby, and to Quainton Road just north of Aylesbury, where it would join the Metropolitan. The trains would run over Metropolitan rails to Finchley Road, from where a stretch of line would be built to the new London terminus of Marylebone.

The last part of the line was planned to run under Lord's

cricket ground, and this brought great protests. The artists' colony of St John's Wood complained: that didn't matter so much, because public and Parliamentary opinion took little notice of artists. But to offend against cricket was another thing. It was said that Sir Edward deserved to be seized by his own navvies and blown up. In the end the company was generous, because it had to be. It undertook to tunnel under Lord's with great discretion, during the winter so as not to interfere with cricket, and to replace the same turf as if it had never been touched. Furthermore, as an extra consideration, the company bought a parcel of land from an orphanage which stood right next to Lord's, and handed this over to the Marylebone Cricket Club, which thus acquired a much bigger ground than it had before, and did very well out of the deal. The M.C.C. withdrew its objection, the Bill, which had at first failed, eventually ground its way through both Houses at the second attempt and received the royal assent, and on 13 November 1894 Lord Wharncliffe, the first earl and third baron, cut the ceremonial first sod at Alpha Road, near Lord's, just as, fifty-six years before, his ancestor the first baron had turned the first spade of earth at Saltersbrook on the old Sheffield line. The company was still called the M.S. & L.R.; the name was not changed to Great Central until 1897.

The work took four years, and nine thousand men worked on the line at one time or another, but there were also the steam navvies, mechanical excavators. The six contractors between them used thirty-nine of these machines, each of which could do the work of a hundred men. On this last main line the navvies lived more civilly than they used to, in huts made of wood rather than turf, and put up by the contractors, not left to the men to botch up themselves.

To make a way through Nottingham and Leicester the engineers had to demolish whole slum districts. At Nottingham the tunnelling was made more hazardous by the deep cellars of ancient buildings, which had to be shored up while the work was going on. Some of these cellars were so old they were not marked on any map. Under the Guildhall, dungeons were discovered, and the bones of executed criminals. Beneath the Old Cross Keys inn the navvies' tunnel broke into the wine and beer cellars, and they drank what they found. The tunnel also wandered into the cellars of the Dog and Partridge, but there the men found only a kind of herb beer.

In the summer of 1895 Mrs Garnett, who was visiting the works, met an old navvy in a lodging house. He had come to Nottingham looking for work, his feet were skinned, and he was worn out. He was sixty-eight, and this had been his week's tramp:

Llanelly to Llandoyle	29 miles
Llandoyle to Rhayader	32
Rhayader to Newport	28
Newport to Shrewsbury	33
Shrewsbury to Uttoxeter	30
Uttoxeter to Derby	18
Derby to Nottingham	16
	186 miles

Wasn't that hard, she asked. And yet the man was going to try to get set on the morning after he arrived. This, said Mrs Garnett, was a real old navvy. She wished some of the young men would show some of the old spirit of independence and brotherly kindness. Only a fortnight before a ganger had told her:

In the old days never was one of our chaps in trouble but pounds would be given on the works to help him, and now one has more bother to get a penny than formerly a shilling, and as to funerals I had to run about all day before I could get four men to follow a chap who died here.

To which Mrs Garnett added her comment:

You may call yourselves excavators and tradesmen and all kinds of fine names, but the real old navvy was far before you as a man.

The navvy age was near its end and the old navvy was going fast. The missionaries, the contractors, and the men themselves, lamented the passing of the grand old tradition. The golden age was seen as the forties. When an old navvy died it became the custom to say, 'He was an old Crimea navvy,' or, 'He was on the Great Western.' The Balaclava Railway, Brunel's line to Bristol, the Caledonian, the Paris and Rouen, became legendary. So did the London and Birmingham, and when in 1897 the latter-day navvies of the Great Central built a viaduct at Rugby, it was to take their last main line over the old L. & B., one of the first, engineered sixty years before by Robert Stephenson. And when William Falgate (alias Riley) died at Rugby in 1898, at the age of eighty, he had navvied on public works for sixty-two years. The whole of the navvy age is little longer than that. He could have worked for the Stephensons; he was there at the end and almost at the beginning. He saw it nearly all, and he was very likely a walking legend amply rewarded by drink.

A navvy legend *did* grow up, around the known facts that the men shifted twenty tons of earth a day, were apt to be disorderly, and not uncommonly ate fourteen or even eighteen pounds of beef a week. But facts alone were not enough to create the legend, which was as noble as the lives of the saints and about as authentic. According to this legend, a navvy had pride, independence, courage, and freedom.

The pride was such that though, as Thackeray said, every Englishman's hat came off of its own accord when he spoke to a lord, those of a good many navvies stuck on tight. It was such that a wounded man, who had been a proud and practising atheist, could on his death-bed refuse the importunities of those who offered him comfort and Christianity, provided he took them both together. He laughed at them and died with his hands over his ears to keep out their preaching.

The independence was that of Jim on the West Wickham and Beckenham line who broke his foot, refused to go to the workhouse hospital, and stayed under the arch of a railway bridge near a stream. It was summer. Coffee and bread were sent to him twice a day by the ladies who lived near by, and other food and tobacco by his mates. He washed his shirt in the stream and had a fire in a brazier. He got well and went, leaving no trace. Then there was the man who would not beg: he came to the works on the tramp, in double canvas trousers, with a red handkerchief knotted round his head. After only two hours he fell down and was carried to the workhouse where he died in two days. He was starved, but he would not ask for food. 'The hungry look which rested upon his face after death,' said the workhouse secretary, 'was very distressing.' At funerals, too, the navvies wanted things done their own way. Sometimes a few would go to the church-yard in advance, to inspect the grave and, if they did not like it, to improve it to their own ideas.

Then there was the legend of cool, wilful courage. On the Rouen and Paris, so the tale went, a French miner in his blouse and an English navvy in his white smock jacket were buried alive together in a tunnel by the falling in of the earth behind them. In the commotion above, the English engineer, one Mr Meek, quietly measured the distance from the shaft to the sunken ground, satisfied himself that the part of the tunnel where the men had been might not have completely collapsed, and put all his men to driving a new shaft to release them. This shaft of fifty feet was sunk in eleven hours, and the men were brought out alive. The Frenchman, on reaching the top, rushed forward, embraced his friends, sat down on a log, took his head in his hands, and wept aloud and bitterly. The English navvy sat himself down on the same piece of timber, took his cap off his head, slowly wiped the sweat from his hair and face and then, looking intently for some seconds into the shaft from which he had just been pulled, as if calcu-lating the number of cubic yards that had been excavated, said coolly and in broad Lancashire to the men who were staring at him, 'You've been an infernal short time abaaout it.'

The navvies also had their freedom. This was the age of lives spent in factories and sweat shops, but the navvy, with all his hardships, worked mostly in the open, and between contracts he was on the tramp. His life was a strange one, iso-lated and free, quite different from that of his fellow country-men, and unknown to them. Navvies were seldom met in towns. You might find a few at a lodging house, but they did not mix. In prosperous times they were most often seen in third-class railway carriages, because they loved to see what they called the course of the country. When they left a place where they had worked for some time they frequently spent pounds in fares before settling down again. They were nomads. At one time there were 200,000 of them, yet to ordinary people they were practically unknown, and this increased the fear and the legend. In bad times, when there was no money for fares, they walked, and even when they had the money they sometimes preferred to tramp. In the early days they had to go on tramp to find work: later it became such a tradition that a man would tramp from Kent to Westmorland just for the extra fourpence a day he had heard was paid there. A navvy told a parson they were like the Israelites. 'We goes about from place to place, we pitches our tents here and there, and then goes on.'

All this was part of the navvy legend, which, in the late nineties, was dying with the navvy age itself. Only a last fling remained. In 1896, as the London Extension progressed, John Horwood married Ellen Frances Wootton at Leicester; Thomas Walker died at Nottingham of asthma, bronchitis, heart disease, *and* consumption; Alfred Winser, working at Marylebone, had his temple pierced, his intellect in consequence impaired, and was taken to Claybury Asylum; Septimus Creber, missionary, said his open-air services in the Finchley Road were 'well attended, thank God!' and at Loughborough that Christmas 130 children were each given a bun, an orange, sweets, and biscuits.

As the line came near its end Thomas Saltenstall (Virgin Slen) died of pleurisy at Leicester; a missionary called Barnfather was bitten by a dog; Walter Wright (Ginger Suffolk), with an impediment in his speech and 'Love' tattooed on his left arm, left his wife. Booklets called, *A Navvy, a Saint of God*, were offered at 8s. 6d. a hundred. Harrison Hayter, past president of the Institution of Civil Engineers, said in an address to the navvies that he had often thought they were unconsciously preparing the way of the Lord by exalting valleys, lowering mountains and hills, making crooked places straight, and rough places plain (Isaiah xl, 3 and 4). Mr Barnfather recovered of his bite. One W. Shackles went mouching about, begging an idle living, as he had done for years, by pretending he was a disabled navvy, and navvies were warned not to be generous to William Grime, also described as a 'professional moucher'.

Mrs Brown of Stockport, a poor old widow of seventy-one, was sloped by eleven lodgers in nine weeks; at Winterbourne Downs, William Moss, known as William Rice, sloped off with the pay of fifty of his mates; William P. Cox, scripture reader, closing his mission house at Woodford when the works there came to an end, exhorted his men not to neglect the means of grace and God would bless them; and Patsey Brain, last heard of by his wife at Walthamstow, sloped off with a girl of seventeen.

The men finished the last main line and left. Some went overseas. To the South African lines, then building. To Siberia, a few of them, where the third section of the great railway was starting – 'an awful country,' said one, 'the conditions of life are not fit for dogs.' To the Canadian line from Glenora to Teslin Lake, part of a line designed to take emigrants from the ocean to the Klondike in six days. To Gibraltar. A few to the Simplon Tunnel. To Australia, where the Archbishop of Sydney joined the Christian Excavators' Union, and where Pincher King, writing from 55 Fraser Street, Melbourne, said he met Teetotal Devon and Jimmy Dean, two of his old mates from English days.

But in a way this question, 'Where did they go?' is misleading, because it assumes that there was some great and sudden exodus. There was not. From the beginning British navvies had worked abroad, and since the seventies many had gone to settle. Probably no more went in the last years of the century than had gone ten or twenty years before. Most stayed at home and just looked for the next job, though this was harder to come by than it used to be.

But this was the end of the navvy age, and for these reasons:

First, all the great work was done. There were no more main lines.

Second, those contracts that did remain, and there were

seventy railway works in progress in 1900, were mostly patching – making a new diversion here to make the journey a few miles shorter, widening the track there.

Third, what work remained was done more and more by machines. A couple of steam excavators tended by twenty men did work that fifty years before would have taken 200 navvies.

So by 1900, although there were many thousands of labourers (the Navvy Mission Society was still giving away 10,000 copies of each *Quarterly Letter*), they were scattered. As a force they no longer existed. The London and Birmingham and the Settle and Carlisle were many years in the past. Never again would such vast bodies of men be assembled for public works. Never again, after the railways came, would communications be so so bad that a thousand navvies, halfway between Manchester and Sheffield, would be working in a wilderness, cut off from civilization, nine miles from a priest and eight from a surgeon. In an increasingly organized society, the forces of order would never again be so weak that the navvies in their shanty towns could be a law unto themselves and a terror to the countryside. Today perhaps the only proper descendants of the nineteenth-century navvies are those who make the motorways, but the scale of building is different, so much smaller. Lecount, or Brunel – any one of the railway engineers – would have been astonished that such roads should be built in little pieces here and there, and take so long.

In medieval times there was a distinct order of monks called the Bridgebuilders, who kept the roads in repair. To build bridges and clear forests were deeds of salvation for the next world as well as for this, and so to make a highway on earth seemed to them the most likely road to heaven. St Benedict began to earn his canonization with the first stone he laid at the bridge of Avignon, which Pope Nicholas V said was built by the inspiration of the Holy Ghost. A railway is a kind of highway, so perhaps the navvies, in spite of themselves, were closer to salvation than Elizabeth Garnett thought. But whether or not they were saved by their own muck-shifting, the railways they built remain their monument. Of the navvies, Samuel Smiles said that their handiwork would be the wonder and admiration of succeeding generations. Looking at their gigantic traces, the men of some future age might be found ready to say of the engineer and his workmen, that there were giants in those days.

Sources

I. THE NAVVY AGE

Eaton's evidence is from the *Report of the Select Committee on Railway Labourers*, Reports, Committees (9) 1846, 13, hereafter called the 1846 Committee. Details of the Stockton and Darlington Railway are mainly from *The History of the First Public Railway*, ed. M. Heavisides, 1912. Horses on the Liverpool and Manchester from the *Liverpool Mercury* of 18 July 1828. Booth was writing in his *Liverpool and Manchester Railway*, 1830. Lecount describes the navvies as banditti in his *History of the Railway Connecting London and Birmingham*, 1839, and these references also occur in the much inferior book *The London and Birmingham Railway* by Thomas Roscoe, 1839. The Chartist meeting is from the *Manchester Guardian* of 8 August 1846, and the Penmaenmawr riot from the same paper of 27 May 1846. Thomas Carlyle's comments are from a letter of 29 August 1846, to Gavan Duffy, quoted in the *Railway Magazine* of June 1907. Mr Barrett on alligators is from his *Life and Work Among the Navvies*, 1880. Mr Walker on tramp navvies is from the *Quarterly Letter to Navvies* of June 1884, published by the Navvy Mission Society. The two histories referred to are *Our Iron Roads* by Frederick S. Williams, first edition 1852 and another edition of 1883, and *A History of the English Railway* by John Francis, 1851. The comments of the engineer (Robert Rawlinson) and of Peto are from the 1846 Committee.

2. THE WORKS

Lecount on the pyramids comes from his own book (see Chapter 1) and is quoted by Roscoe and F. S. Williams (also Chapter 1). Robert Stephenson at Newcastle is from *Our Iron Roads*, 1852, p. 35. Brassey on a day's work for a navvy is from *Life and Labours of Mr Brassey* by Arthur Helps, 1872. The description of Chat Moss is from *The Struggle for the Liverpool and Manchester Railway* by George S. Veitch, 1930, from the *Story of the Life of George Stephenson* by

Samuel Smiles, 1857, and from the *Liverpool Mercury*. John Mase-field's description of tipping is from his *Grace Before Ploughing, fragments of autobiography* (Heinemann, 1966). The timekeeper's remarks are from Helps on Brassey. The description of blasting, with twanging of horns, is from *The Life of Joseph Locke* by Joseph Devey, 1862. Round Down Cliff is from *Our Iron Roads*. The description of the tunnel under Liverpool is from *The Liverpool and Manchester Railway* by Henry Booth, 1830, from *An Accurate Description of the Liverpool and Manchester Railway* by James Scott Walker, 1830, and from the *Liverpool Mercury*. The Samaritan Society of England is from the *Manchester Guardian* of 10 March 1849. Visit to the Belsize Tunnel from the *Life and Work of Joseph Firbank* by Frederick McDermott, 1887.

3. NAVVY AND CONTRACTOR

Much information on railway contracts is from *Work and Wages* by Thomas Brassey, M.P. (the son of the contractor and later created an earl), 1872 and later editions up to 1919. Peto's organization on the Peterborough and Ely line is from his evidence to the 1846 Committee. The terms of the typical contract are quoted from *Our Iron Roads* (see above). The story of Sir Edward Banks is from the pamphlet of Thomas Nicholson referred to in detail in Chapter 7. The story of Firbank is from his life by McDermott, and that of Brassey from his life by Helps (both see above). The story of Wythes's estimating is also from McDermott. Rawlinson's account of the difficulties of a contractor is from Chadwick's pamphlet referred to in Chapter 7. Benjamin Bailey gave evidence to the 1846 Committee. Benley and Leech are from the *Manchester Guardian* of 19 September 1846. The table of wages is from *Work and Wages* (above). Hawkshaw's remarks are from Helps on Brassey. Peto's Commons speech and other details of Peto, from *Sir Morton Peto, a memorial sketch* by Sir Henry Peto, his son, printed for private circulation, 1893.

4. DEATH AND DISASTER

Anecdotes of courage and recklessness from *Our Iron Roads* (above). Navvy describing danger of work, from *Our Navvies* by Elizabeth Garnett, 1885. Death of Huskisson from the *Manchester Guardian* of 18 September 1830 (a better report than that of *The Times* which is often quoted). The list of accidents at Bath shown to Brunel, and

also the lists from Manchester and Salisbury hospitals, are from the
1846 Committee. Peto on small compensation, from the 1846
Committee. Aged Navvies Fund, from the jubilee edition of the
Railway News, 1914. Ashton viaduct disaster, from the *Manchester
Guardian* of 23 April 1846, and following issues. The story of the
navvy killed on a fine evening, and other Shedlock anecdotes, from
Our Iron Roads, 1883. Body of navvy raffled, from *Life and Work
Among the Navvies*, p. 80 (above). The death of Clerrett, from the
Poole and Dorsetshire Herald.

5. SHANTIES AND TRUCK

The article in *Household Words* is quoted at length in *Life and Work
Among the Navvies* (above). The description of early huts and camps
is largely from the evidence of Speirs, Ramsay, Beggs, Thompson,
List, Baird, and Jenour to the 1846 Committee, and so is Pearce on
landladies. Many details of the Kettering and Manton line are from
Life and Work Among the Navvies. The tale of the navvy and the gin
is first told in Lecount (above, Chapter 1) and by many others later.
Much material on truck is from Chadwick's pamphlet (see Chapter
7). The truck ticket was presented in evidence to the 1846 Committee, who also heard the remarks of Bailey, Deacon, Brunel, and
Peto. Quidhampton strike, from the *Poole and Dorsetshire Herald* of
29 April 1847.

6. RIOTS AND RANDIES

Reports of the Penrith riots are from the *Carlisle Patriot*, the *Scottish
Herald*, and the 1846 Committee. The 1845 riots from the *Scottish
Herald* and the 1846 Committee. The Kinghorn threatening letters
from the *Railway Times* of 28 May 1846, the Kendal riot from the
Manchester Guardian, the Gorebridge murder from the *Manchester
Guardian*, the *Illustrated London News*, and the *Scottish Herald*, and
the Bathampton trial from *The Times*. The remarks of Sir T. Acland
are from the 1846 Committee, the incidents at Marley and Ridge-
way from the *Poole and Dorsetshire Herald* of 11 June 1846 and 28
January 1847, the Wescoe Hill riot from the *Manchester Guardian*,
the Norwich election riots from the life of Peto by his son (see
notes to Chapter 3), from the *Norfolk Chronicle*, and from *The Times*.
The Battle of Mickleton is from the *History of the Great Western
Railway* by E. T. MacDermot, 1927, from the *Railway Times* of 26
July 1851, and from the *Illustrated London News* of the same date.

7. WOODHEAD

The incidents are too many to make detailed reference possible. The principal sources are the report of the 1846 Committee, in particular the evidence of Robert Rawlinson, Henry Pomfret, Wellington Purdon, Edwin Chadwick, and Thomas Eaton. Chadwick's pamphlet, *Papers Read Before the Statistical Society of Manchester, on the Demoralization and Injuries occasioned by the want of proper regulations of labourers engaged in the construction and working of railways,* presented to the society on 18 January 1846, and containing a letter from Roberton, a statement from Rawlinson, and a commentary by Chadwick. *Strictures on a Pamphlet published at the request of the Manchester Statistical Society* by Thomas Nicholson, being his reply to the Chadwick pamphlet. The burial and baptism records of St James, Woodhead, and of Penistone parish church. Reports from the *Manchester Guardian* and the *Sheffield Iris.* Woodhead is also referred to in the lives of Brassey and Locke (see above), in the *Life of C. B. Vignoles* by O. J. Vignoles, 1889, and in the *History of Penistone* by John Dransfield, 1906.

8. CHADWICK, PARLIAMENT, AND DO-NOTHING

Sources are mostly the same as those for Chapter 7, with these additions: *Hansard* reports of Commons proceedings. Letters of Chadwick (in the library of University College, London). And 'Edwin Chadwick and the Railway Labourers' by R. A. Lewis, *Economic History Review,* 2nd series, Vol. III, No. 1, 1950.

9. WELLINGTON, CAT'S MEAT, AND MARY ANN

The story of Old Blackbird is from Mrs Garnett's *Our Navvies,* and so is the tale of the several Smiths or Joneses. Contrairy York is from Barrett's *Life and Work Among the Navvies.* Many other anecdotes in this chapter are from these two books. The story of Warren, alias Brown, is from the *Northampton Herald* of 9 September 1882. The temperance song is from the *Quarterly Letter* of June 1880.

10. SIN AND SANCTITY

Principal sources are the *Quarterly Letter to Navvies* (quoted from throughout this chapter), the annual reports of the Navvy Mission Society, and the two books of Mrs Garnett and Mr Barrett referred to above. The story of the clergyman and his five bridges is from

Lecount's *London and Birmingham* (see notes to Chapter 1). The St
Pancras exhumation from *The Life of Thomas Hardy* by F. E. Hardy,
1962 edition, p. 44, and the incident of the priest's bones from
McDermott's life of Firbank (see above). The minutes of the Chester
and Holyhead Railway are from the archives of the British Railways
Board. Moorsom is quoted from his evidence to the 1846 Committee, and so are Gillies, Sargent, Thompson, Peto, Jenour, and
Breakey. The story of the double-first turned navvy is from *Our
Navvies* (see above). The description of Peto's religious work is from
his son's memorial sketch (see notes for Chapter 3). Fayers is from
his own book *Labour Among the Navvies*, 1862.

11. WOMEN NOT THEIR WIVES

The anecdote of the clergyman's daughters is from Lecount's book
(see Chapter 1). The broken leg, the rape, and the missionary on the
Croydon line (Jenour) are from the 1846 Committee, and so are the
remarks of Alfred List. Nicholson is quoted from his own pamphlet
(see notes to Chapter 7). Mrs J. is from *Our Navvies* (see above). The
British engineer who watched women navvies was William
Chambers, who is quoted in the 1883 edition of *Our Iron Roads* (see
above). Henrietta Cresswell's picture of navvy life was published
in *Winchmore Hill, Memories of a Lost Village*, 1912.

12. KING OF LABOURERS

The 'damn' anecdote is from Helps's life of Brassey (see above),
which also gives an account of the Paris and Rouen line. Much
other information on this line comes from Devey's life of Locke
(see above) and from the several editions of *Work and Wages* by
Thomas (afterwards Lord) Brassey, son of the contractor, and from
the evidence to the 1846 Committee of William Reed, secretary of
the Paris and Rouen. The navvies and the fortifications of Paris,
from Helps on Brassey. Details of the Grand Trunk from *Sir Morton
Peto* by Sir Henry Peto (see notes to Chapter 3), from Helps on
Brassey, and from *The Grand Trunk of Canada* by A. W. Currie, 1957.
Details of the Crimea come from Helps, from *Sir Morton Peto*, from
The War by W. H. Russell, 1855–6, and from *Letters from the Crimea*
by Sir Henry Clifford, 1958. The description of the navvies' recruit-
ment and embarkation, from the *Illustrated London News*.

13. LAST FLING

Details of the Settle and Carlisle line from *The Midland Railway* by F. S. Williams, 1876, from the fifth (1888) edition of the same author's *Our Iron Roads*, from the *Daily News* of 29 October 1872, and from the *Story of the Settle–Carlisle Line* by F. W. Houghton and W. H. Foster, 1948. The letter from Miles is from the *Quarterly Letter* of September 1882, and that from Lieutenant Gibbon in the *Quarterly Letter* for September 1888. Details of the Great Central from *The Last Main Line* edited by R. D. Abbott and published by Leicester Museums, from contemporary issues of the *Nottingham Guardian*, and from the *Quarterly Letters* and annual reports of the Navvy Mission. The stories of the injured navvy and of the man who starved to death are from *Our Navvies* by Mrs Garnett, and that of the French and English navvies buried together from the 1883 edition of *Our Iron Roads*. The detailed personal incidents on the London Extension are mainly from the *Quarterly Letter*. The last quotation, from Samuel Smiles, is from his *Life of George Stephenson*, 1857.

Selected Bibliography

EARLY RAILWAY HISTORIES, MANUALS,
BIOGRAPHIES ETC.

An Account of the Liverpool and Manchester Railway, by Henry Booth,
Wales and Baines, Liverpool, 1830.

An Accurate Description of the Liverpool and Manchester Railway, by
James Scott Walker, Liverpool, 1830.

The History of the Railway Connecting London and Birmingham, by Peter
Lecount, London, 1839.

The London and Birmingham Railway, by Thomas Roscoe, London,
1839. (Based on Lecount, but inferior.)

Drawings of the London and Birmingham Railway, by J. C. Bourne,
Ackermann, London, 1839.

The History and Description of the Great Western Railway, by J. C.
Bourne, David Bogue, London, 1846.

Railway Practice, by S. C. Brees, John Williams, London, in five
volumes 1837–47.

A Practical Treatise on Railways, by Peter Lecount, A. & C. Black,
Edinburgh, 1839.

Ensamples of Railway Making, by John Weale, London, 1843.

A History of the English Railway, by John Francis, London, 1851.

Our Iron Roads, by F. S. Williams, Ingram Cooke, London, 1852,
and other editions of 1883 and 1888.

The Life of George Stephenson, by Samuel Smiles, John Murray,
London, 1857.

The Navvies (a novel), by Henrietta Louisa Farrer, W. J. Cleaver,
London, 1847.

The War, by W. H. Russell, London, 1855.

The Midland Railway, by F. S. Williams, Strahan, London, 1876.

The Life of C. B. Vignoles, by O. J. Vignoles, Longmans, London,
1889.

The Life and Work of Joseph Firbank, by Frederick McDermott,
Longmans, London, 1887.

The Life of Joseph Locke, by Joseph Devey, Richard Bentley, London,
1862.

The Life and Labours of Mr Brassey, by Arthur Helps, London, 1872.

Work and Wages, by Thomas (later Earl) Brassey, Bell and Daldy, London, 1872, and other editions up to 1916.

Sir Morton Peto, a memorial sketch, by Sir Henry Peto, privately printed, 1893.

A Song of Labour and other Poems, by Alexander Anderson, Dundee, 1873.

Songs of the Rail, by Alexander Anderson, Simpkin Marshall, London, 1878.

Gleanings from a Navvy's Scrapbook, by Patrick MacGill, Derry Journal, 1910.

Songs of a Navvy, by Patrick MacGill, published by himself, printed by the Derry Journal, 1912.

Children of the Dead End, the autobiography of a navvy, by Patrick MacGill, Herbert Jenkins, London, 1914.

Winchmore Hill, Memories of a Lost Village, by Henrietta Cresswell, Standard office, Dumfries, 1912.

EVANGELICAL WORKS

Little Rainbow, a Story of Navvy Life, by Elizabeth Garnett, London, 1877.

Our Navvies, by Elizabeth Garnett, Hodder and Stoughton, London, 1885.

Quarterly Letter to Navvies, published by the Navvy Mission Society from 1878.

Labour Among the Navvies, by Thomas Fayers, printed in Kendal, 1862.

Life and Work Among the Navvies, by the Rev. D. W. Barrett, Wells and Gardner, London, 1880.

WORKS ABOUT WOODHEAD

Papers Read Before the Statistical Society of Manchester on the Demoralization and Injuries occasioned by the want of proper regulations of labourers engaged in the construction and working of railways, Manchester, 1846.

Strictures on a Pamphlet published at the request of the Manchester Statistical Society, by Thomas Nicholson, J. Gadsby, Manchester, 1846.

Report from the Select Committee on Railway Labourers, printed by order of the House of Commons of 28 July 1846, Reports, Committees (9) 1846, 13.

The History of Penistone, by John Dransfield, Penistone, 1906.

'Edwin Chadwick and the Railway Labourers', by R. A. Lewis, *Economic History Review*, second series, Vol. III, No. 1, 1950.

MODERN WORKS

The History of the First Public Railway (the Stockton and Darlington) editor M. Heavisides, Stockton-on-Tees, 1912.

The History of the Great Western Railway, by E. T. MacDermot, G.W.R., London, 1927.

The Struggle for the Liverpool and Manchester Railway, by George S. Veitch, Liverpool, 1930.

The Story of the Settle – Carlisle Line, by F. W. Houghton and W. H. Foster, Norman Arch Publications, Bradford, 1948.

Letters from the Crimea, by Sir Henry Clifford, Michael Joseph, London, 1956.

The Last Main Line, editor R. D. Abbott, Leicester Museums, 1960.

The Railway Age, by Michael Robbins, Routledge and Kegan Paul, London, 1962. (Chapter 7, on the impact of railways on the landscape, is most valuable.)

The Making of the English Landscape, by W. G. Hoskins, Hodder and Stoughton, London, 1955. (Chapter 8 is on railways.)

The Master Builders, by R. K. Middlemas, Hutchinson, London, 1963. (The section on Brassey is particularly informative.)

Index